ENGLISH WORKSHOP

INTRODUCTORY COURSE

HOLT, RINEHART AND WINSTON
Harcourt Brace & Company

Austin • New York • Orlando • Atlanta • San Francisco
Boston • Dallas • Toronto • London

T 1 2 3 4 5 6 018 09 08 07

TABLE OF CONTENTS

PREWRITING: JOURNALS AND FREEWRITING

Writing can be easy and fun if you take it one step at a time. The first step in the process of writing is finding a topic to write about. Here are some ways to find good writing topics.

USING A WRITER'S JOURNAL

A *writer's journal* is simply a notebook or folder. In it you write about whatever interests you. Set aside a time to write in your journal every day. Here are some ideas for things to write about in your journal.

- Important people or happenings in your life
- Your dreams, daydreams, and hopes for the future
- Interesting things that you hear or read about
- Songs, poems, stories, or even drawings that you create

FREEWRITING

When you *freewrite,* you write down whatever pops into your head about a subject, without stopping to think too much about those ideas.

- Choose a topic that interests you. This topic might be a memory of a special event, person, or place.
- Begin with a word or phrase. Then write whatever comes to mind. Write for three to five minutes without stopping.
- Let yourself go! Try to keep your pen or pencil moving. Jot down all the ideas that come to you. Don't stop to make changes or corrections.

EXERCISE 1   Using Prewriting Techniques

Think of five activities that you really enjoy. Your ideas might include drawing, ice-skating, riding a bicycle, reading, or going to the movies. Choose one of these activities. Then, on your own paper, write a page about that activity in your writer's journal, or freewrite about it on a separate sheet of paper for three to five minutes.

PREWRITING: BRAINSTORMING AND CLUSTERING

BRAINSTORMING

When you *brainstorm*, you list ideas as quickly as you think of them. Brainstorming can also be done with others. If you do work with others, try to make everyone feel comfortable. Encourage everyone to join in. Listen carefully. Do not stop to judge the ideas that other people suggest. You can judge the ideas later. As you brainstorm, follow these steps.

- Choose a subject and write it on a sheet of paper. Then quickly write down every related idea or word that comes to mind.
- Don't stop until you run out of ideas.

CLUSTERING

Clustering is making a diagram to divide a subject or a topic into smaller parts. When you cluster, follow these guidelines.

- Write the topic in the center of your paper. Draw a circle around it.
- Write related ideas around the topic. Circle each idea, and draw a line from each idea to the topic.
- Continue jotting down related ideas, circling them, and connecting them with lines. Stop when you fill your paper or run out of ideas.

EXERCISE 2   **Brainstorming and Clustering**

Working with a partner, choose one of the writing topics below. After you have picked a topic, work separately to brainstorm about it. Then meet with your partner to compare ideas. Finally, create cluster diagrams with your partner to list details that could be used in the final piece of writing.

cars	video games	shoes
dinosaurs	movie stars	rock stars
basketball	hairstyles	songs

2

PREWRITING: ASKING QUESTIONS

5W-HOW? QUESTIONS

One way to gather ideas for writing is to ask the *5W-How? questions:* questions that begin with *who, what, where, when, why,* and *how.* Here are some *5W-How?* questions about the Indianapolis 500 auto race.

- *Who?* — Who won the first Indianapolis 500 auto race?
- *What?* — What is the fastest speed ever reached in an Indy race?
- *Where?* — Where do the cars used in Indy races come from?
- *When?* — When was the first Indianapolis 500 race held?
- *Why?* — Why is a checkered flag used to start and end the race?
- *How?* — How do drivers train for the Indianapolis 500?

"WHAT IF?" QUESTIONS

To plan a piece of creative writing, try asking **"What if?" questions.** The "What if?" questions below might lead to good ideas for a story or essay.

- *What if I could change one thing in my life?* (What if I were governor of the state?)
- *What if some common thing were uncommon?* (What if it stopped raining for a long, long time?)
- *What if one situation in the world could be changed?* (What if there were no illnesses in the world?)

EXERCISE 3   Using *5W-How?* Questions

You are writing an article for your school newspaper. Your purpose is to give information about a subject. Choose a subject from the list below. On your own paper, make a list of *5W-How?* questions about the subject.

1. a visiting student from a foreign country
2. a new after-school activity
3. tryouts for a school play
4. a new arcade or amusement center in your town
5. a new style of clothing or fashion trend

EXERCISE 4   Working Cooperatively to Use "What if?" Questions

Working with a partner, plan a short story, using one of the story starters given below. With your partner, write five "What if?" questions on the lines below to gather ideas for your story.

1. Animals from a traveling circus are being shipped by train. The train stops in a small town one night, and someone lets the animals out.

2. A child looks into a doll house in a toy store and notices that the tiny people inside are moving around.

3. A family is traveling across the country by car. One night they take a wrong turn and get lost. They drive into a strange town where everything appears exactly as it was fifty years ago.

EX.   1. A student reads a story in a newspaper about a terrible flood in a nearby community.

What if the student decided to organize a drive to supply food and clothing to the flood victims?

What if hundreds of local merchants agreed to donate goods to the student's cause?

What if the people in the town where the flood happened honored the student by giving him or her a key to the city?

PREWRITING: ARRANGING IDEAS

The next step in the writing process is to arrange your ideas in an order that makes sense.

WAYS TO ARRANGE IDEAS	
Type of Order	**Definition**
Chronological	Describes events in the order that they happened
Spatial	Describes objects according to where they are (from near to far, from left to right, and so on)
Importance	Presents details from least to most important or from most to least important
Logical	Places related details together

EXERCISE 5 Arranging Ideas

Read the following descriptions of writing situations. Think about the ideas and details you would use in each situation. Then choose an appropriate order for each. On the line before each sentence, write the type of order you would use.

_____ 1. You are writing a letter to the editor of your local paper. In the letter, you give three reasons why the gymnasium should be open to students after school.

_____ 2. You are writing an essay to describe a town you recently visited.

_____ 3. You are writing an essay about the different breeds of dogs and what they are used for (herders, hunting dogs, watchdogs, and so on).

_____ 4. You are writing a description of how to change a bicycle tire.

_____ 5. You are writing your first letter to a new pen pal describing your friends and family.

WRITING A FIRST DRAFT

First, you find ideas to write about. Then, you arrange the ideas in a sensible order. Finally, you are ready to write your first draft.

- Use the notes that you made during your prewriting.
- If you think of new ideas as you are writing, feel free to include them.
- Get your ideas down on paper as clearly as you can.
- Don't overedit. You can go back and rewrite or edit your work later.

The following paragraph is from a first draft. Notice that the writer has used brackets [ ] to show where she needs more information. Notice, also, that the writer has crossed out one line that is unrelated to the paragraph's main idea. The paragraph contains some errors in spelling and mechanics that will be fixed by the writer later on.

A poison is any substance that causes sickness, injury, or death, especially by chemical means. Insectisides and weedkillers such as [give examples] are poisons often found around homes. other household poisons include bleach, detergents, gasoline, amonia, bleach, furniture polish and some medicines. Such dangerous materials should be kept in a safe place, where children cannot reach them. Special latches can be bought for cabinets and drawers to keep babies and toddlers from accidentally swallowing these dangerous products. [give examples] ~~Small children should also be protected from small objects that they might swallow and from objects that are sharp or easily broken.~~

EXERCISE 6   Writing a First Draft

Using what you have learned so far, draft a short description of a monster for a new Hollywood science fiction film. Use your imagination to come up with something that will thrill audiences. To gather ideas, use one of the prewriting techniques listed on pages 1–3. Write your draft on your own paper. Include concrete details to help the makeup artists and special effects people create your terrifying creature. Share your draft with your classmates.

EVALUATING

When you have finished your first draft, you need to *evaluate* it. When you evaluate a draft, you look at it carefully to see what is good and what needs to be improved. Here are four *standards*, or measures, for judging your writing.

- The writing gets and holds the readers' interest.
- The writing presents a clear main idea.
- The writing presents details to support the main idea.
- The details are arranged in a clear and sensible order.

There are two kinds of evaluation that you can use to judge your own writing and that of your classmates. When you do *self-evaluation*, you study your own work carefully. When you do *peer evaluation*, you look at work by another writer, or you have another writer look at your work. A *peer* is simply another student, like you. Here are some tips for doing self-evaluations and peer evaluations.

| GUIDELINES FOR EVALUATION ||
Self-Evaluation	Peer Evaluation
1. Wait a while before you evaluate your work. You will be able to think about it more clearly if you wait some time and look at your draft with a fresh eye.	1. Tell the writer at least one or two things that are good about the work.
2. Read your draft several times. Each time you read it, think about one of the standards listed above.	2. Pay attention to the content of the paper and the order of the ideas and details. Don't point out errors in spelling and grammar at this point.
3. Read your draft aloud. Listen for awkward or unclear parts that should be replaced or rewritten.	3. Ask helpful questions such as "Can you use an easier word here?" or "Can you make this idea clearer?"
	4. Make specific suggestions for improvement.

EXERCISE 7   Practicing Peer Evaluation

Practice your peer-evaluation skills by evaluating the paragraph below. Use the four standards for good writing listed at the top of the previous page. Write your evaluation on the lines below. Begin with comments on what is good about the paragraph. Then write helpful questions or suggestions about what needs to be improved. (You may make notes in the paragraph if necessary.)

> The first horses lived long, long ago. Scientists call these early horses *Eohippus*. That scientific name means "dawn horse." *Eohippus* was no bigger than a modern-day dog. Unlike modern horses, which have one toe, called a hoof, *Eohippus* had four toes on its front feet and three on its back feet. It was also very small. My favorite modern horses are the famous Tennessee walking horses bred in my home state.

REVISING

When you *revise* a piece of writing, you make changes to improve it. Changes can be made by hand, on a typewriter, or on a word processor. You can make changes by *adding, cutting, replacing,* or *reordering.*

Techniques for Revising	
Add	Add new words, sentences, or paragraphs.
Cut	Take out unnecessary or repeated ideas.
Replace	Replace weak or unclear parts with strong, clear words or details.
Reorder	Move words, sentences, and paragraphs to make their

Example

A constellation is simply a ~~group~~ *pattern* of stars in the sky. In ancient days, people looked at the stars and thought they saw heroes, gods, animals, and objects. People today recognize eighty-eight different constellations in the night sky. *The* ~~Ancient~~ people gave these patterns of stars names such as Orion the Hunter, Hercules, *and* ~~and~~ Cygnus the Swan *and the Big Dipper.* Stars are actually very large objects, like our own sun.

EXERCISE 8   Revising a Piece of Writing

Read and evaluate the description you wrote for Exercise 6. Then use the evaluation standards at the top of page 7 to revise your draft. Next, revise it, using the basic revision techniques. Make your changes by hand directly on your draft. Finally, rewrite your revised paragraph on your own paper.

PROOFREADING

PROOFREADING

When you *proofread,* you check your writing for mistakes in grammar, spelling, capitalization, and punctuation. Finding mistakes will be easier if you wait for a while before you begin proofreading.

One good approach to proofreading is to do it with a friend. Exchange papers with a classmate. Then proofread one another's work. Here are some guidelines to follow when proofreading.

Guidelines for Proofreading

1. Have you avoided sentence fragments and run-ons?

2. Are capitalization and punctuation correct throughout?

3. Do verbs agree with their subjects?

4. Are verb forms and tenses correct throughout?

5. Are adjectives and adverbs used correctly?

6. Are all pronouns used correctly?

7. Is each word spelled correctly?

Symbols for Revising and Proofreading

≡	Capitalize a letter	the statue of Liberty
~	Delete	long, long ago
∼	Change order	a wierd light
¶	Begin new paragraph	¶ In conclusion,
∧	Insert	mispelling

EXERCISE 9   Proofreading a Draft

Proofread the draft that you revised for Exercise 8. Look for errors in grammar, spelling, capitalization, and punctuation. If you need help, you can use a dictionary and the lessons on grammar, usage, and mechanics (pages 81–282) in this book. Use proofreading symbols to mark your errors.

10

PUBLISHING

PUBLISHING

The final step in the writing process is *publishing*. When you publish your work, you share it in some way with other people. Here are some excellent ways to share your writing with an audience.

Ideas for Publishing

- Make a booklet of your writing to share with family, classmates, or friends.
- Send the work to your school newspaper, yearbook, or literary magazine.
- Read the work aloud to your family, classmates, or friends.
- Include the work in a letter to a relative or a friend.
- Put the writing on a bulletin board at school or in a public library.
- Enter writing contests; some winners are published.

Guidelines for the Form of a Paper

1. Use only one side of a sheet of paper.

2. Write in blue or black ink.

3. If you use a typewriter or a word processor, double-space the lines.

4. Leave margins of about one inch at the top, sides, and bottom of each page.

5. Follow your teacher's instructions for placing your name, the date, and the title on the paper.

6. Indent the first line of each paragraph.

7. If your paper is handwritten, do not skip lines.

8. Keep your paper neat and clean.

EXERCISE 10   Working Cooperatively to Find Ideas for Publishing

Working with a partner, read the following descriptions of types of writing. On the lines after each description, list two publishing ideas.

1. a review of a mystery or science fiction story for young people _____

    _____

    _____

2. a letter supporting a candidate for student council president _____

    _____

    _____

3. an original song lyric _____

    _____

    _____

4. a pamphlet asking people to donate old clothing to the drama club _____

    _____

    _____

5. a description of someone you consider to be a local hero _____

    _____

    _____

MAIN IDEAS AND TOPIC SENTENCES

Most paragraphs have one *main idea*. This is the big idea of the paragraph. Sometimes the main idea is stated in a single sentence called the *topic sentence*. When a paragraph has a topic sentence, it is often the first or second sentence. But not always. Sometimes it comes at the end. In the following paragraph, the topic sentence comes at the beginning.

> *Kimchi* is an important part of a person's diet in Korea. In fact, every fall a family prepares enough *kimchi* to last for the winter. This pickled dish combines cabbage and other vegetables with salt and spices. Then during the winter, each family member will eat about fifty heads of cabbage prepared in this way.

A paragraph that tells part of a story or describes something often does not have a topic sentence. The following paragraph has no topic sentence. It does have one main idea—how Ruth started her day.

> Each day, Ruth was the first person to get up. She stepped into her slippers, pulled on a robe, and went downstairs. She turned up the thermostat, preheated the oven, and put water on for herb tea. By the time the bread was baking and the water was boiling, the house was warm. Only then could Ruth bear to change into her work clothes.

EXERCISE 1 Identifying Main Ideas and Topic Sentences

Each of the following paragraphs has a main idea. On the line after each paragraph, write the main idea in your own words. Then look for a topic sentence. If the paragraph has one, underline it.

1. The way we spend our free time shows how different my sister Tru and I are. Tru loves to spend Sunday swimming, skating, exploring the beach, gardening, or doing whatever fits the season. For me the only way to spend Sunday is reading in a hammock, in a stuffed chair, or under a shady tree. I believe we would not be able to survive each other's Sunday.

   Main Idea: _____

2. Before the hurricane arrived, I put tape on the two large windows. I did not want them to shatter in the wind. My sister Eula picked the last tomatoes, ripe or not, and brought them inside. Mom put candles in the holders and filled our lantern with fuel. Jody made a quick trip to the corner store for bread and matches.

    Main Idea: _____

3. In 1968, Kipchoge Keino won the Olympic gold medal in the 1,500-meter race and the silver medal in the 5,000-meter race. His teammate Naftali Temu won the gold in the 10,000-meter race. Another Kenyan, Amos Biwott, won the gold in the 3,000-meter steeplechase. The Kenyan athletes proved to the world that they were great distance runners.

    Main Idea: _____

4. What would you say if someone left a bag of garbage at your front door? What would you say if a strange woman walked through your back yard while you were having a party? Or if a group of people knocked at your door and asked for directions to a candle shop, what would you say? When you live in a tourist area, you never know what people might do or say.

    Main Idea: _____

5. Most people in Nepal are farmers. They often live in villages on the hills above their fields. The villagers' lives are centered around family events. Weddings, harvest and herding celebrations, and religious festivals offer entertainment.

    Main Idea: _____

For Better or For Worse   **by Lynn Johnston**

For Better or For Worse copyright 1982 Lynn Johnston Prod. Reprinted with permission of Universal Press Syndicate. All rights reserved.

UNITY AND COHERENCE

A paragraph is a little like a car. It has to have *unity*—you don't want one blue fender on a red car. And it has to have *coherence*—the back of the car has to be connected to the front.

UNITY

When creating a paragraph, a writer chooses one main idea and includes only those details that are related to that main idea. A paragraph has *unity* when all the sentences tell about the main idea. Read the following paragraph, and notice how the sentences work together.

> Some lakes are remarkably salty. The Great Salt Lake and the Dead Sea are so salty that almost nothing can live in their water. The water that flows into all lakes brings in salt and other minerals. But because these two lakes have no way for water to escape, all the salt and minerals stay in the water. The water just gets more and more salty.

Every sentence tells something about why these two lakes are unusually salty. Suppose one sentence told why the ocean is salty. That sentence would not fit into the paragraph. It would destroy the unity of the paragraph.

EXERCISE 2   Identifying Sentences That Destroy Unity

Each paragraph below has one sentence that does not belong in the paragraph. Find that sentence, and draw a line through it.

1. The Scablands are an unusual landform in Washington State. A flood shaped them about thirteen thousand years ago. The shaping process started when a huge lake formed in Montana and Idaho during the last ice age. There have been several ice ages. One side of the lake was held in place by ice. When the ice thawed, a wall of water from the lake dug out the Scablands. In one week the water created canyons and cliffs that usually need millions of years to form.

2. Some people are allergic to certain plants, such as poison ivy. Poison ivy might grow anywhere, in empty lots or in the woods. After a person touches poison ivy, the skin should be washed right away. Wash any clothes that might also have touched the ivy. I remember the first time I had a rash from poison ivy. Avoid scratching if a rash develops. Scratching can make the rash spread.

COHERENCE

A good paragraph has *coherence.* In other words, all the ideas in a coherent paragraph are connected. One way you can create coherence is to use transitional words and phrases to connect ideas. The following chart lists some common words and phrases used to make transitions.

Showing Likenesses and Differences	also, although, and, another, but, however, instead, similarly, too, yet
Showing Cause and Effect	as a result, because, consequently, for, since, so, so that, that, therefore
Showing Time	after, at last, before, finally, first, next, often, then, until, when
Showing Place	above, around, before, beneath, beside, down, into

The following paragraph has coherence. The transitional words are underlined.

Before Sheila went downtown, she carefully planned her trip. First, she asked her neighbor where the nearest bus stop was. Then she walked to the stop and read the schedules there. None of them had a map, however, so she returned home and looked at the bus map in the phone directory. After that, she wrote down which buses she should take and where to change. Finally, she found all the routes she must follow to get to the museum just as it opened.

EXERCISE 3   Identifying Transitional Words and Phrases

Underline the transitional words and phrases in the following paragraph. Use the chart above as a guide.

[1] I wanted an oak tree, but Dad gave me a rosebush to plant in our yard. [2] Because roses need sun, we found the sunniest place, beside the south wall, to plant the bush. [3] Since the ground was soft, we easily dug a hole for the roots. [4] Next, we put fertilizer into the hole before we put in the root ball. [5] While I scooped the dirt around the roots and pressed it down, Dad filled a bucket with water. [6] After we watered the bush, Dad told me that newly planted roses need lots of water.   [7] Therefore, I have to water the plant often, until its roots take hold.

USING DESCRIPTION AND NARRATION

DESCRIPTION

Have you ever tried to tell someone what your room looks like? To do that, you use *description.* You include *sensory* details to help someone see what you are describing. *Sensory details* are words that appeal to the five senses—sight, hearing, taste, touch, and smell. The following paragraph uses sensory details of sight and hearing to describe a living room.

> The narrow front door opens right into the living room. At first the room seems gloomy. As your eyes adjust, you can pick out the many bright spots. The hooked rug in front of the door has reds and yellows in it. On the left wall is a small, blackened fireplace with a cheerful fire burning. Beyond that, two windows face the door. Their heavy curtains let in narrow columns of daylight. On the far side of the room, a tiny fern grows in the sun that streams in through the third window.

When you write a description, you often use spatial order. *Spatial order* describes details in order of their location. For example, the paragraph above describes the room from near to far. You could also describe a place from top to bottom, from left to right, or from far to near.

EXERCISE 4   Collecting and Arranging Sensory Details

Choose one of the subjects below. On your own paper, make a list of sensory details that describe it. Keep listing details until you run out of ideas. After you have completed your list of details, arrange them in spatial order. Then find a classmate who chose the same subject, and compare your lists. How are they alike or different?

1. your family pet

2. a city street during a parade

3. the schoolyard when school lets out

4. a room in your home

5. a car or truck you particularly like

6. what you think the surface of the planet Venus is like

NARRATION

"What did you do at school today?" You probably would use *narration* to answer that question. *Narration* tells about an event or action that happens over a certain period of time. Narration often uses *chronological,* or time, order. You can use narration to tell a story or to explain a process.

TELLING A STORY

Roy saw that the beavers had been busy the night before. Already a pool of water was growing behind their new dam. The water had come to within fifty yards of Roy's house! Roy squished across the wet ground and started to pull the larger branches from the dam. The mud that held the water back washed away, turning the creek brown. Roy's few minutes of hard work had the water gushing through the opening. He had saved the house from being flooded. Now he had to find a new place for the beavers to build a home.

EXPLAINING A PROCESS

This salad dressing is easy to make. Start by chopping two cloves of garlic into small pieces. In a small bowl, mix together one teaspoon of mustard, one-fourth cup of vinegar, and the chopped garlic. Keep on stirring while slowly pouring in one-third cup of olive oil. Finally, taste the dressing to see if salt and pepper is needed.

EXERCISE 5   Arranging Details in Chronological Order

Choose two of the following topics—one story topic and one process topic. On your own paper, list at least four events for the story and at least four steps for the process. Be sure to arrange each list in chronological order.

1. You begin walking to a friend's house. But the neighborhood seems to have been rearranged since yesterday. (story)
2. You just moved into a new home. In the back of one of the closets is a small, locked trunk. (story)
3. You leave a notebook behind after a softball game. The next day you find it on your desk with a message written in it. (story)
4. Tell your younger brother how to set the timer on the oven. (process)
5. Describe the way you put together your favorite sandwich. (process)
6. Explain how to get from your house to school. (process)

USING COMPARISON/CONTRAST AND EVALUATION

COMPARISON AND CONTRAST

When you show how two things are alike, you *compare* them. When you show how they are different, you *contrast* them. In a paragraph, you may only compare, only contrast, or both compare and contrast things.

When you compare or contrast, *logical order* is a good way to organize your ideas. If something is logical, it makes sense. In the following paragraph, the writer first compares, then contrasts lobsters.

COMPARISON   Some people might think that the American lobster and the spiny lobster are alike. But any lobster fan can tell the two lobsters apart. For one thing, the spiny
CONTRAST   lobster is found in warm seas, such as those off the coast of Florida or southern California. The American lobster lives only in the cold waters of the North Atlantic Ocean. The American lobster has smooth antennae. The spiny lobster has large, spiny antennae that it uses as weapons. The difference that is easiest to see, however, is that the American lobster has large claws and the spiny lobster doesn't.

EXERCISE 6 Comparing and Contrasting Features

Here are some pairs of subjects for comparison and contrast. With a partner, choose one of the subject pairs. On your own paper, write two headings: *Similarities* and *Differences*. Then brainstorm with your partner to list at least three features or details that are alike and at least three that are different.

1. heroes in stories and heroes in real life

2. breakfast foods and lunch foods

3. video games and board games

4. weekend days and vacation days

EVALUATION

You are *evaluating* when you say that you think something is good or bad. For example, you are evaluating when you say that dogs make better pets than cats do. To make your audience believe your evaluation, you need to give reasons that support your thinking.

One way to organize your reasons is *order of importance.* For example, you could start with your most important reason. Then you would give the next most important reason, and so on. Or you could start with your least important reason and end with your most important. The following paragraph uses order of importance.

EVALUATION	Using a push mower is the best way to mow a lawn.
REASON	First, a push mower is quiet. The only sound it makes
REASON	is the whoosh of the blade. Second, pushing a mower
REASON	is good exercise, which most of us need. Third, a push mower does not pollute the environment or use resources that cannot be replaced.

EXERCISE 7   Developing an Evaluation

Choose one of the following subjects to evaluate. On the lines below, write one sentence stating your evaluation of the subject. Then list two reasons to support your thinking.

EX.   Evaluation: The Nightmare Before Christmas is not a scary movie.
         Reason 1: The monsters look funny, not horrible.
         Reason 2: Even the ugliest creatures sing and dance.

1. a rock song
2. a video game
3. a tennis shoe
4. a movie

Evaluation: _____

_____

Reason 1: _____

Reason 2: _____

A THANK-YOU LETTER

Whenever someone helps you, you say, "Thank you." Sometimes, though, you need to show your feelings with more than those two words. For example, you may feel this way when a person gives you a gift or does you a favor. Then you should write a *thank-you letter*. In this letter, you want the person to know that you appreciate the time, thought, or present given to you. In the following letter, the writer thanks her grandfather for a gift.

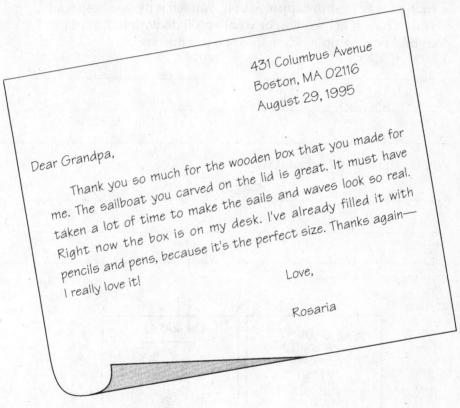

431 Columbus Avenue
Boston, MA 02116
August 29, 1995

Dear Grandpa,

Thank you so much for the wooden box that you made for me. The sailboat you carved on the lid is great. It must have taken a lot of time to make the sails and waves look so real. Right now the box is on my desk. I've already filled it with pencils and pens, because it's the perfect size. Thanks again—I really love it!

Love,

Rosaria

Rosaria's grandpa will feel good when he gets this letter. To think about Rosaria's writing, answer the following questions.

1. Rosaria mentions a specific detail about the wooden box that she likes. What is it?

_____

She wants to compliment her grandfather about this detail. What does she say?

_____

_____

_____

2. In a thank-you letter, a personal comment about the gift or favor is another way to show appreciation. You tell why it was special to you or how it helped you or what you'll do with it. Rosaria does this. For example, where has she put the box?

_____

_____

_____

What is she using it for, and why?

_____

_____

_____

Peanuts reprinted by permission of UFS, Inc.

ASSIGNMENT: WRITING A THANK-YOU LETTER

Write a letter to say thank you for a gift or favor you have received. Tell something specific about the gift or favor to show you appreciate it. That way, you will be expressing personal feelings to the reader.

 **Prewriting**

For this assignment, write about a real gift or favor. If the gift or favor was in the past, you don't have to mail the letter. If it's very recent, though, you can. Either way, you'll be writing about a real experience. You'll get practice for other thank-you letters in the future.

Step 1:   Think of a present you've received or a favor that has helped you. What about birthday and holiday gifts? Or what about thoughtfulness others have shown you?

- Maybe your older sister sent you a special T-shirt for your birthday.
- Maybe your uncle took you and your best friend on a fishing trip.
- Maybe your neighbor let you borrow a suit for a costume.
- Maybe your coach took the whole baseball team out for a team party.

Brainstorm gifts or favors below. Then choose one to write about, and circle it.

Gifts: _____

_____

Favors or help: _____

_____

Step 2:   Think of specific details you can mention about the gift or favor. You can:

- **describe a detail or part you liked** (the pretty color of the T-shirt, learning how to cast a fishing rod)
- **tell how you will use it** (you'll wear the T-shirt to a party)

- **tell why it was special to you or how it helped you** (the suit was the best costume, the team party was a great end to the season)

- **pay a compliment to show your appreciation** (note the person's generosity, skill, or good taste)

On the lines below, write two or three specific details you could include in your letter.

_____

_____

_____

_____

_____

_____

Writing

Now write a draft of your thank-you letter. Write it on the blank letter form on page 25. Follow these steps:

Step 1:   Write the **body** of the letter first. The body is your message to the person. A good plan is to:

- Begin by thanking the person. Name the gift or favor in your sentence.

- Mention *at least one* specific detail about the gift or favor. Use a detail you listed in your prewriting notes.

- End by thanking the person again or by paying a compliment.

Step 2:   After you draft the body of the letter, fill in the other blanks in the letter form. The chart on page 25 explains each part. You can also use Rosaria's letter on page 21 as a model.

[the heading]

[your street] _____

[your city, state, and ZIP Code] _____ , _____

[date] _____ , _____

Dear_____ , [the salutation]

[the body]

_____

_____

_____

_____

_____

_____

_____

_____

_____

_____

[closing] _____ ,

[signature (your name)] _____

Evaluating and Revising

This letter is important. It expresses your feelings to someone. Now you should take time to *evaluate,* or judge, what you've written. If a part could be better, you should change or *revise* it. The following **Questions for Evaluation** will help you and a classmate to improve your thank-you letters.

Questions For Evaluation

1. Does the beginning of the letter thank the person and name the gift or favor? If not, what words or phrases could be added?

    _____

    _____

2. Does the letter mention at least one specific detail about the gift or favor? If not, what information could be added to tell why the writer liked or appreciated it?

    _____

    _____

3. Does the letter end by thanking the person again or by paying a compliment? If not, what could be added to make a good closing?

    _____

    _____

Peer Evaluation

Exchange rough drafts with a classmate. Then follow these steps.

Step 1:   Read the letter carefully. Imagine that you are the person receiving the thank-you letter. Would you feel pleased? Don't worry about mistakes in spelling or sentences. Just pay attention to content.

Step 2:   Answer the **Questions for Evaluation** in writing. When you suggest a change, help the writer by being specific. For example, if the letter needs details about a new tennis racket, suggest possibilities. Or ask the writer a question: "What exactly do you like about this racket?" Also, remember to tell the writer what is good in the letter.

Self-Evaluation

Follow these steps to evaluate your own letter.

Step 1: Read your classmate's peer review of your letter. Make check marks or notes beside comments you want to use or think about.

Step 2: Now read your draft letter again. Keep what your classmate said in mind. Then read your draft once more, and answer the **Questions for Evaluation** for yourself. You can write out your answers or make notes on your draft.

Now revise your thank-you letter. Use your classmate's comments, your own ideas, or both. You can make small changes in the letter—like adding words to make your feelings stronger. You can also make big changes—like adding a completely new detail about a gift. You can revise on the draft or recopy it. Revise until you've written a letter you would like to receive.

 ## Proofreading and Publishing

A thank-you letter goes to someone who wanted to please or help you. You don't want to send that person a sloppy letter. You want to be careful with its appearance by proofreading carefully. To proofread, put your letter aside for a while. You've been reading it a lot during revision. You will probably not notice every word and comma. Distance can make mistakes jump out clearly. Also, it is helpful to use a sheet of paper to cover all the lines below the one you are proofreading. Follow these steps.

Step 1: Use the **Guidelines for Proofreading** on page 10 to find and correct any errors in your letter. Look for mistakes in capitalization, punctuation, and grammar.

Step 2: Check your spelling. Use a dictionary if you're unsure about a word.

Step 3: Be sure to follow the correct form for a thank-you letter. Use the chart on page 25 to check the heading and other parts.

Hint: Try proofreading from the bottom of your letter upward, one line at a time. This makes each word (and mistake) stand out.

Step 4:   Make a clean copy of your revised and proofread letter.

Step 5:   Publish your letter. If you've written a letter for a recent gift or favor, give or mail the letter to the person. If you are not mailing your letter, take it home for your family to read. They will be interested in how you've thanked someone who was kind to you. The form for addressing an envelope is shown below:

Rosaria Reyes
431 Columbus Avenue [your name and address]
Boston, MA 02116

PLACE
STAMP
HERE

[the person's name and address]   Mr. D. J. Reyes
1361 Key Biscayne Circle, # 7
Miami, FL 32844

The Parts of a Thank-you Letter	
Heading	Imagine a line dividing the letter in half from top to bottom. Begin the heading to the right of the imaginary line. The heading has three lines: 1. your street address 2. your city, state, and ZIP Code (Put a comma after the city.) 3. the date (Put a comma after the day of the month.)
Salutation (greeting)	The salutation is your greeting to the person you're writing to: *Dear Grandpa.* Make a margin of about one inch at the left of the paper. Then write the salutation. Use the name you call the person: *Dear Aunt Kiki, Dear Mr. Smith, Dear Coach Tyler.* Capitalize the name and any title. Put a comma after the name.
Body	The body is the message of the letter. The body, like the salutation, begins at the left margin. You indent the first line of each paragraph from the margin.
Closing and Signature	The closing is your polite "goodbye" before you sign the letter. Line it up with the heading. In a thank-you letter, you may use an informal or personal closing: *Love, Your friend, Best wishes.* You may also use *Sincerely* or *Yours truly.* Put a comma after the closing. Then skip a space and sign your name. Sign your first name or nickname if that is appropriate. Sign your full name if the thank-you letter is more formal.

FOR YOUR PORTFOLIO

Respond to the items below, and include your responses with your thank-you letter in your portfolio.

1. Do you usually write thank-you letters for gifts or favors? Be honest! If you don't, why not? Now that you've written a thank-you letter, will it become a habit? Write what you think.

2. You're probably grateful to people for things besides personal gifts and favors. Would you like to thank your favorite basketball player for making games so exciting? an author for a book you loved? a teacher for being kind, fair, and funny? Express your feelings about someone special in a thank-you letter for your portfolio. (You may decide to mail the letter.)

A HAIKU

Do you have a favorite snapshot? What if you put that snapshot into words, so that someone could "see" it just by reading? You would be making a word-picture. One special kind of word-picture is a type of poem called a *haiku* (pronounced HY koo). Haiku is a Japanese form of poetry. A haiku has just three lines and does not rhyme. The first and third lines have five syllables each. The second line has seven syllables. Read these two haiku that students wrote.

Falling Leaves

In the fall the bright

Orange leaves crinkle and pop

Wherever I walk.

Dale Berger

The Winner

A tall skinny boy

Grabs the ball and dribbles fast.

He leaps up, up—swish!

Robin Lamb

Thinking About the Models

These two haiku create very different word-pictures. Yet they are alike, too. Both paint sharp pictures. Both follow the haiku form. Answer these questions to see how the student writers created their word pictures. Your answers will help you create your own special picture.

1. A haiku focuses on a single moment, scene, or object. In your own words, what is the moment or scene in "Falling Leaves"?

_____

What is the scene in "The Winner"?

_____

2. If you divide the first haiku into syllables, it looks like this:

    In / the / fall / the / bright

    Or / ange / leaves / crin / kle / and / pop

    Wher / ev / er / I / walk.

    On the following lines, copy Robin Lamb's haiku, and put a slanted line between the syllables. Read aloud to yourself to sound out the syllables.

    _____

    _____

    _____

    How many syllables are in the first line of Robin's haiku? _____
    How many are in the second line? _____ How many are in the third line? _____

3. Poems use *exact words* to create good descriptions. Exact words are sharp details that help readers see, hear, feel, taste, or smell. In the first model haiku, the words *bright, orange, crinkle,* and *pop* make you see and hear the leaves. In the second haiku, what two exact words describe how the boy looks?

    _____

    What three exact words describe his movements?

    _____

    What exact word describes the sound of the ball in the basket?

    _____

ASSIGNMENT: WRITING A HAIKU

Write your own haiku, or word-picture. Here is the special form you'll use: three lines, with a total of seventeen syllables. The first line has five syllables. The second line has seven syllables. The third line has five syllables. Your haiku should create a clear, vivid picture in the reader's mind.

 ## Prewriting

Remember the idea of a snapshot in words? Keep that in mind as you look for a writing topic. Flash! What do you want to capture with your camera?

Step 1:   Brainstorm topics for your haiku. You have many choices. Japanese haiku often describe **scenes in nature**, especially the changing seasons. They may focus on **one object**, such as a cherry blossom. They may show **people or animals in action**. They may create a **happy or sad picture**. You have all those choices, too—and more. Look at the ideas listed below. Then write your own ideas on the blank lines.

Things and Animals	Scenes and Places
a melting snowman	a graveyard
your dog chasing its tail	a carnival ride
your favorite tennis shoes	someone water-skiing
a tiger running	sunrise on a desert
_____	_____
_____	_____

Step 2:   Choose the topic you most want to describe. (You may choose one of the sample ideas in Step 1, if you like.) Write it in the center circle of the word web on the next page. In the other circles, write exact words that describe your topic. Write words and phrases that tell how the thing or scene **looks, feels, sounds, tastes, or smells.** Think of very sharp, definite details. For example, you could say a desert is *hot*, but the word *blistering* will make readers sweat! Add more circles to the diagram if you need them.

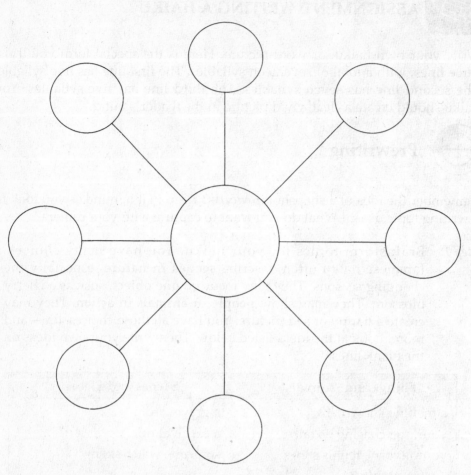

Step 3: On the lines below, *freewrite* a description of your topic. Just put your pen or pencil to the paper, and write whatever comes to you. Use your word-web ideas from Step 2, but add anything else you think of. Don't stop to worry about spelling, punctuation, or grammar.

_____

_____

_____

_____

_____

Step 4:   Now it's time to think about the length of your word-picture. Remember that your haiku will have just seventeen syllables. Your freewriting in Step 3 may have *lots* of syllables or not enough, and that's okay. Take a look to see. Reread your freewriting, and

- circle words and phrases you like
- count the syllables in these words and phrases
- write the number next to the freewriting

Did you circle more or fewer than seventeen syllables? Think about whether you'll have to *cut* or *add* when you write.

 Writing

On your own paper, write a draft of your haiku. Use your circled freewriting words and phrases. Write the poem in three lines, like the models on page 31. Try to write about seventeen syllables, but don't worry about being exact. Just come as close as you can.

Now copy your draft into the boxes below. Put one syllable in each box. If you need help dividing the words into syllables, use a dictionary. Draw more boxes if you have extra syllables. Leave boxes blank if your lines are too short. This is a rough draft.

   REFERENCE NOTE: For information on how words are divided into syllables in a dictionary entry, see page 271.

Title: _____

Line One:

1	2	3	4	5

Line Two:

1	2	3	4	5	6	7

Line Three:

1	2	3	4	5

Finally, think of a title for your poem. Write it in the blank above the boxes.

Evaluating and Revising

When you *evaluate* your writing, you judge it. You decide what is good and what can be better. Then you *revise,* or change it. You make improvements. Work with a classmate to evaluate and revise your haiku poems. You can use the following **Questions for Evaluation.**

Questions for Evaluation

1. Does the poem present a clear, sharp picture? If not, what dull words could be replaced or cut? What exact words could be added to describe sounds, sights, tastes, smells, or textures?

   _____

   _____

2. Does the poem have five syllables in the first line, seven in the second line, and five in the third line? If not, what words can you add, cut, change, or move to get the correct number in each line?

   _____

   _____

Peer Evaluation

Step 1: Exchange rough drafts with a classmate. Read the draft poem carefully. Read it silently, and then read it aloud.

Step 2: Answer the **Questions for Evaluation.** If possible, give your answers to your classmate in person—have a "writer's conference." If you can't, write down your answers. Help the writer by making specific suggestions for changes. Also, remember to give positive criticism. Tell what you liked in the poem.

Self-Evaluation

Step 1: Read or listen to your classmate's evaluation of your haiku. Make notes of comments and ideas you want to use when you revise.

Step 2: Reread your poem silently, and then read it aloud. On your own paper, answer the **Questions for Evaluation** for your own poem.

Now revise your haiku. Use your classmate's suggestions and your own ideas to make your poem better. You may revise more than once. For example, you may change words to make your description sharper. Then you may have to change other words to come out with seventeen syllables. For your revisions, you can draw box diagrams like the one on page 35.

Proofreading and Publishing

Step 1:   Correct any spelling errors in your poem. If you are not sure of a word, look it up in a dictionary.

Step 2:   Be sure each line begins with a capital letter. In the title, capitalize the first and last words and all important words. (See pages 235–237 for help with capitalization.) Correct any other capitalization errors in the poem.

Step 3:   Make a clean copy of your revised and proofread poem.

Step 4:   Publish your poem by sharing it with an audience. Use these ideas, or think of others.

A.   Hold a poetry reading in class. You could read your own poem, or the teacher could collect the poems and let each student "draw" one to read. Either way, practice reciting the poem out loud. Make your voice match what the poem is about.

B.   Play "Guess the Title." Read your poem aloud without giving the title. Ask classmates to suggest titles, and write the titles on the chalkboard. Then write your title on the chalkboard. Students could vote on their favorite. You may want to choose a new title from the list!

C.   With your classmates, put together a booklet of haiku. You could illustrate the poems with drawings or pictures cut from magazines. Also, if you know someone who can write in Japanese, ask that person to write one or more of the poems, using Japanese word-characters. The figures are very beautiful.

FOR YOUR PORTFOLIO

Write down your responses to these items on your own paper. Then put them with your haiku in your portfolio.

1. Did you like writing a poem with exactly seventeen syllables? Or did it drive you crazy? Describe your feelings.

2. If you read or heard your classmates' haiku, name your favorite one. Also name one that surprised you—perhaps one that used a topic you didn't expect. Explain both choices.

3. How did you feel about your haiku when you finished? Will you write any more on your own?

Calvin and Hobbes   by Bill Watterson

Calvin & Hobbes copyright 1990 Watterson. Reprinted with permission of Universal Press Syndicate. All rights reserved.

A "HOW-TO" PAPER

When you write a *"how-to" paper,* you give information that tells readers how to do something. For example, you may want to explain how to teach a parakeet to talk. Or you may want to give directions for baking bread. In the following "how-to", a student tells his classmates how to play a game called *Hold the Rope.*

Hold the Rope
Nathaniel Jourard

Putting your hat on is easy, isn't it? You may not think so if you try a game called Hold the Rope. Children in Israel play it in teams. The whole point is to get the right hat on each team member's head—without using any hands.

To play the game, each team needs a rope long enough for five or six players to hold with both hands. (You could also use long strips of cloth or ribbon.) Every player also needs a hat. Baseball caps work well.

First, choose teams of five or six players each. You need at least two teams, but you can have as many as you want. More people mean more fun.

Next, set up a home base for each team. The base can be a circle in the dirt, a chalk mark on a court, or a piece of cardboard. Then, about twenty feet from their own home base, have the players on each team throw their hats into a pile on the ground.

To start the game, each team gathers at its base. At the count of three, each team picks up its rope and runs toward its pile of hats. Each player must hold the rope with both hands at all times. Now the teamwork and laughs start. All the players must end up with their own hats on their heads.

Except for your hands, you can use any part of your body—arms, legs, feet, teeth—to pick up the hats. Knees and elbows are great for this. If even one person uses hands or lets go of the rope, the whole team is disqualified. The winning team is the first one back to home base with all the hats on the right heads.

Hold the Rope is challenging and really takes teamwork. But best of all it's fun—and also funny—to watch.

Thinking About the Model

Now that you've read the model on page 39, think about how the writer created it. Answer the following questions on the lines provided.

1. The introduction of a "how-to" paper should catch the reader's interest. In the model's first paragraph, how does the writer get you interested in *Hold the Rope*?

   _____

   _____

   _____

2. A "how-to" paper includes needed materials. Sometimes materials will appear in a list, especially if many materials are needed, such as foods in a recipe. Other times, materials will appear within a paragraph. In the model's second paragraph, you learn that you will need hats. What other materials will you need?

   _____

   _____

   _____

3. A "how-to" paper also describes the steps a person will take to complete a process. These steps are presented in the order in which they happen, from first to last. In the model, the first step is "choosing team players." What are the next two steps?

   A. choose teams of five or six players

   B. _____

   _____

   C. _____

   _____

4. Transition words like *before, first,* and *then* help readers follow steps. In the fourth paragraph of the model, what two transition words does the writer use?

   _____

5. In addition to materials and steps, a "how-to" paper gives helpful hints or additional information. In the second paragraph of the model, for example, the writer points out that baseball caps work well. What important or helpful details does the writer give in the following paragraphs?

Paragraph 4: _____

_____

_____

Paragraph 6: _____

_____

_____

6. Like any paper, a "how-to" needs a good conclusion. You can give a final tip, a comment, or a reason for learning the process. What are the final statements that the writer makes about playing *Hold the Rope*?

_____

_____

_____

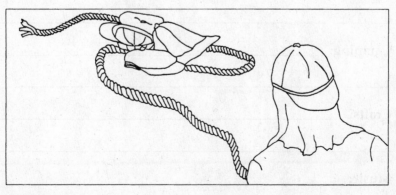

Hoffman Price

ASSIGNMENT: WRITING A "HOW-TO" PAPER

Write a paper that tells someone how to do or make something. Remember that you're writing instructions for others to carry out. They depend on you to be clear and complete.

Prewriting

What do you like to do? What do you do well? To find a topic for a "how-to" paper, start with *yourself*. If you're interested in a process, you can probably make it interesting to your classmates. If you're good at it, you can explain it clearly. Building a birdhouse, paddling a canoe, making popcorn balls, grooming your dog: any activity that you like, and that others may also, is a good topic. These steps will help you find and develop a topic.

Step 1: Use the subjects below to start brainstorming topics. If you wish, work with others to get ideas. Next to a subject, write down any activity or process that you think of. Use the last group of lines for your own subjects and ideas.

Sports: _____

_____

Games: _____

_____

Cooking: _____

_____

Camping: _____

_____

Crafts: _____

_____

Music: _____

_____

Pets: _____

_____

Other Ideas: _____

_____

_____

Step 2:   Now choose the topic you'll write about. Ask yourself
   • **Am I really interested in this topic?**
   • **Do I know it well enough to explain it to others?**
   • **Can I write about it in a few paragraphs?**

   You may need to narrow an idea you wrote in Step 1. For example, if you thought of the sport "fishing," you'll have to focus on one part, such as "how to cast a fly rod." Write your final topic here.

   How to _____

   _____

   _____

Step 3:   What steps will your readers need to take? Listing the steps that you want your reader to follow is a good idea. The steps help you think of materials. Your "how-to" paper will follow the order in which steps happen, from first to last. Write a brief description of each step of the process you will write about. Six steps are shown below. You may not need this many, or you may need to add more steps on your own paper.

   Hint: Close your eyes and picture yourself doing the process.

   Step 1: _____

   _____

   _____

   Step 2: _____

   _____

   _____

Step 3: _____

_____

_____

Step 4: _____

_____

_____

Step 5: _____

_____

_____

Step 6: _____

_____

_____

Step 4:   Reread each step you listed above. Now list the materials needed for the process.

_____

_____

_____

_____

Step 5:   What tips can you give readers about your process? What information will make the process clearer or easier? Go through your steps and materials again, and list important details or helpful hints. You're the expert: What advice can you give?

_____

_____

_____

_____

_____

_____

_____

Writing

Use your prewriting notes to write a draft of your "how-to" paper. You can follow the writing framework below.

Beginning
- Grabs the reader's attention
- Gives a reason to learn the process

Middle
- Tells what materials are needed
- Describes steps in order from first to last
- Gives tips or important details

Ending
- Gives a final helpful hint or benefit of learning the process

Evaluating and Revising

When you *evaluate* writing, you judge it. You decide what is good about it and what you can do to *revise* it, or make it better. You and a classmate will use the following **Questions for Evaluation** to judge and improve your "how-to" papers.

Questions For Evaluation

1. Does the introduction catch the reader's interest? If not, what could be added to tell the reader that the process is challenging, fun, interesting, or useful?

   _____

   _____

2. Are all the materials needed for the process given? If not, what other materials should be added? Are many materials required? If so, would a separate list be clearer?

   _____

   _____

   _____

3. Are all necessary steps given? Are they presented in the order in which they should be done? If not, what are the steps, in the correct order?

   Step 1: _____

   Step 2: _____

   Step 3: _____

   Step 4: _____

   Step 5: _____

   Step 6: _____

4. Are all the details necessary or helpful? If not, which should be cut?

_____

_____

_____

5. Does the paper end with a helpful hint or a reason for learning the process? If not, what hint or reason could be added?

_____

_____

Peer Evaluation

Exchange rough drafts with a classmate, and follow these steps.

Step 1:   Read your classmate's paper. Have a pencil (not a pen) ready. As you read, act out—if only in your mind—the process. If you get confused or stuck, make a small pencil check next to the words you can't follow.

Step 2:   Read the paper again. On a separate sheet of paper, complete the **Questions for Evaluation** on page 46. Encourage your classmate by making clear, helpful suggestions. Don't forget compliments. If you learned something, say so.

Self-Evaluation

Now evaluate your own paper. Follow these steps.

Step 1:   Look over your classmate's evaluation of your rough draft. Circle any of the suggestions that you want to think about or use when you revise.

Step 2:   Answer the **Questions for Evaluation** for your own paper. Write your answers on the lines provided on pages 46–47.

Use your classmate's suggestions and your own answers to the **Questions for Evaluation** to revise your rough draft. If you only have a few changes, you can write on your draft. If you're making big changes in materials, steps, or order, you may want to start your revision on a clean sheet of paper.

Proofreading and Publishing

Step 1:   First, check for errors in spelling. If you are not sure whether a word is spelled correctly, look it up in a dictionary.

Step 2:   Next, check for errors in grammar, usage, and punctuation. Look at the proofreading checklist on page 10. Make sure that every sentence begins with a capital letter. Use the rules for capitalization on pages 227–237 to correct any mistakes in capitalization.

Step 3:   Publish your paper. Here are two ideas.

A.   Work with other students to make a booklet containing all the "how-to" papers. Divide the booklet into parts—such as pets, sports, etc.—and make a table of contents. Also consider adding illustrations or diagrams to your papers. Classmates who draw well could be "artwork advisors."

B.   After the class has read all the "how-to" papers, try some in class, with your teacher's advice and help. A game or a simple recipe might be possible. If your process is chosen, act as director.

FOR YOUR PORTFOLIO

Respond to these items, and put your responses with your paper in your portfolio.

1.   Sometimes people say, "It's easier to do this myself than to tell you how to do it." Now that you have finished this assignment, do you think this statement is true? Explain your answer.

2.   Design a cover for your report. You might draw a sketch of your finished product, show people playing a game, or create any other picture that illustrates your topic.

3.   Find an example of instructions to put in your portfolio. These might be directions that came with a tool or game you have at home. Newspapers and magazines are also good sources. Write your evaluation of the "how-to." Is it complete, clear, interesting? How would you change it?

4.   Draw a diagram to accompany part of your process, if you haven't already done so. Look in magazines or in your science textbook for examples.

AN AWARD NOMINATION

Suppose you want to nominate your mother for a "Great Parent" award. *You* know she deserves the award, but how do you persuade other people? That's your job when you write an *award nomination:* persuading others to agree with your opinion. The following nomination is for a school's "Super Athlete" award. The writer believes her friend should win.

Chantel for Super Athlete

Most people think super athletes are the ones who always win. They score a lot of points or get ribbons and trophies. This year, I think Chantel Tucker should be Monroe Middle School's Super Athlete. She didn't win any races after the middle of the year because she got hurt. Chantel Tucker, though, is a great athlete who really deserves the award.

Chantel has always been the fastest runner on the playground. I've known her since second grade. She can speed down a track like lightning. She has worked hard at it, too. She does exercises and runs laps in the neighborhood. At every track-and-field day for school or at the parks, she has entered races and won.

Then last summer Chantel had an accident on her bike and broke her leg. The doctor said she couldn't run for a long time. Chantel was very sad—for about one week. At home, she spent a lot of time reading books about athletes. She learned about many who had been hurt. Some of these athletes later became stars. Their stories helped her.

Chantel decided to begin doing all the muscle exercises the doctor had shown her. She put in extra hours practicing walking on her crutches, even when it made her tired.

But the most important reason I think Chantel is a great athlete is that she helped other athletes when she couldn't run. I know Chantel wanted to go flying around the track in the warm spring weather, but she couldn't. Instead, she got Mr. Yarbrough to let her help at track-and-field day. She timed practices, brought people water, and helped the young kids line up. She waved one of her crutches and cheered every winner!

Chantel Tucker has worked hard at her sport, even when problems stood in her way. I think that makes Chantel more than an athlete. She is truly a Super Athlete.

Thinking About the Model

You've read the model award nomination. Now think about how the writer persuades others. Answer the following questions.

1. In the first paragraph, the writer of the model quickly gets your attention. What surprising statement does she make about the person she is nominating?

   _____

   _____

2. All persuasive writing starts from an *opinion:* the writer's belief. An opinion is not a fact. An **opinion** is a person's feeling about something or someone. In an award nomination, the writer's opinion is that a certain person should be honored. What sentence in the first paragraph states the writer's opinion?

   _____

   _____

   _____

3. Now the writer has to *support* her opinion. She gives *reasons* and *facts* to convince her readers. For example, the writer says that before the accident, Chantel always practiced hard and won many races. How does the writer show that Chantel deserves the award *after* her accident? List three reasons or facts that she gives.

   _____

   _____

   _____

4. Descriptive words and details are also persuasive. In the model, the words *can speed down a track like lightning* are more convincing than *can run fast.* In the next-to-last paragraph, what descriptive words or details does the writer use? Write two examples on the lines.

   _____

   _____

   _____

5. In persuasion, the writer may give the most important reason first or save it for last. Does the writer of the model put the most important reason at the beginning or end of the nomination?

_____

What is the most important reason, in her opinion?

_____

_____

6. The writer of the model restates her opinion in the nomination's last sentence: "She is truly a Super Athlete." In that final paragraph, she also sums up her support in a strong sentence. Write the sentence.

_____

_____

ASSIGNMENT: WRITING AN AWARD NOMINATION

Nominate someone for a special award of your own choosing. You'll be writing to persuade readers that the person (or even animal) deserves the honor. What support will convince your readers?

Prewriting

Step 1:   What special people or pets do you know? Who deserves a Best Friend Award, a Good Neighbor Prize, a Cool Dad Certificate, a Clever Cat Ribbon, a Dog of the Year Trophy? Brainstorm some people or animals you'd like to honor for their special qualities. Write quickly—list any person or animal you think of.

_____

_____

Now look at your ideas. Which person or pet do you feel most strongly about? Which one would you get excited about nominating? Circle your choice above. This is your **nominee.**

Then make up a title for your personal award, like "Super Athlete." (You can use any title mentioned in this lesson, if it fits your award.) In the chart on page 53, write the name of your nominee and the title of your award.

Step 2:   Next, start gathering your *support.* You'll need *facts* and *reasons* to show *why* your nominee should get the award. Does your dad tell great jokes? Is your best friend a good listener? Can your cat open the screen door? Just focus on the person or pet, and freewrite your ideas on your own paper. Try to fill a page. If you get stuck, write your nominee's name until something comes to you.

Step 3:   In your nomination, you'll need two or three items of support. (You can have more if you like.) Read your freewriting, and choose the details you think are most convincing. List at least three details in the chart on page 53. Finally, list some persuasive words or descriptions that might appeal to your readers' feelings. (Remember the words "flying around the track in the warm spring weather" in the model.)

Name of nominee: _____

Title of award: _____

Supporting details:

Reasons and facts:

- _____

- _____

- _____

- _____

Persuasive words or descriptions:

_____

_____

_____

_____

_____

_____

_____

_____

_____

Step 4:   Some supporting details are more persuasive than others. You want to use the ones that could really change a judge's mind. Look over your details in the chart above and decide which are strongest. Then order the details by their importance. Put a *1* beside the most important, a 2 beside the next most important, and so on.

Writing

Now take up your pencil, and do your best for your nominee! On your own paper, write a draft of your award nomination. You may want to write on every other line. That will leave you room for changes later.

Use your prewriting chart as you write. (Feel free to add any new ideas you think of.) Here's a plan to guide your writing.

Beginning	• Grab your readers' attention. Use a great description, a surprising fact, or an interesting question. • Clearly name your nominee and the name of the award.

Middle	• Present two or three supporting details. Use a convincing order. You can go from most important to least important or from least to most. Put your punch where you want it. • Use a few good persuasive words or descriptions. Get your readers involved!

Ending	• Sum up—quickly, but strongly—why your nominee deserves the award.

Evaluating and Revising

A draft gets your ideas down on paper. Next, you need to judge, or *evaluate,* your draft. Which parts of your writing are strong and which are weak? Then you change, or *revise,* to improve your writing. This step is your chance to make your persuasion convincing to your reader. You can use the following **Questions for Evaluation** to evaluate your paper or a classmate's paper.

Questions for Evaluation

1. Does the beginning grab the readers' attention? If not, what can you change or add? What detail or question might spark your readers' interest?

   _____

   _____

2. Are the person or pet and the award clearly identified? If not, what information should you add?

   _____

   _____

3. Is the support convincing? If not, what reasons or facts can you add? What persuasive words or descriptions can you add?

   _____

   _____

4. Is the support arranged in order of importance—either most important to least or least important to most? If not, how can you rearrange the details?

   _____

   _____

5. Is the ending strong? If not, what phrase or sentence can you change or add? What sums up why the nominee deserves the award?

   _____

   _____

Peer Evaluation

Exchange rough drafts with a classmate. Then follow these steps.

Step 1:   Read your classmate's draft carefully. Pretend you're a judge for the award. Don't worry about spelling or grammar. Just pay attention to what the writer says.

Step 2:   Answer the **Questions for Evaluation** on page 55. Write your answers on a separate piece of paper. Be sure to make specific suggestions.

Step 3:   Ask yourself: Would I vote in favor of this person or animal? Write a final statement about how convincing you think the nomination is. Also write what you liked best in it.

Self-Evaluation

Now use these steps to evaluate your own draft.

Step 1:   If possible, put your paper aside for a while. Be thinking about what you suggested to your classmate. Then reread your draft carefully.

Step 2:   Answer the **Questions for Evaluation** on page 55. Write your answers on a separate piece of paper, or make clear notes on your draft.

Step 3:   Read your classmate's evaluation of your paper. Circle any suggestions you want to use when revising.

Step 4:   Revise your draft. Use your evaluation and your classmate's evaluation to make changes. If you have lots of changes in your first draft, you may want to recopy it. Often, writers revise more than once or twice.

Proofreading and Publishing

Your nomination is about someone special. It's important for your readers to know this the first time they read your paper. You don't want to give them a sloppy paper, filled with errors. Proofreading is just as important as checking your persuasive support.

Step 1: Use the **Guidelines for Proofreading** on page 10 to help you find and correct errors.

    A. Check spelling first. If you think a word might be wrong, look it up in a dictionary.

    B. Find and correct errors in capitalization, punctuation, grammar, and usage.

Step 2: Make a final, clean copy of your paper.

Step 3: Here are some ideas for publishing your award nomination.

    A. Have an awards ceremony for the person or pet you wrote about. This can be a private ceremony—just you and the person. Or it can be with other people, such as your family. You may want to create a trophy or certificate. Then present the award and your nomination letter. You could also read the letter aloud.

    B. Make a nomination speech by reading your letter aloud in class. Pretend that your classmates are judges. Practice gestures and voice tone so that you're as persuasive as possible.

FOR YOUR PORTFOLIO

Write answers to these questions, and keep them in your portfolio with a copy of the nomination.

1. What did you learn about the person or animal by writing your nomination? Did you see something new by putting your opinions into words?

2. What has your nominee done that would help you in your own life? How would this help you?

3. How was persuasive writing different from other writing you've done? Did you enjoy trying to be convincing? Why or why not?

4. Advertisements are a form of persuasive writing. They want to convince you to buy something. Find a magazine ad that you think is good, and put it in your portfolio. Write a few sentences about what makes it good persuasion. Tell which words, ideas, or pictures make the ad convincing.

SENTENCE FRAGMENTS

7a A *sentence* is a group of words that expresses a complete thought.

7b A *sentence fragment* is a group of words that does not express a complete thought. The fragment should not be punctuated as if it were a sentence.

FRAGMENT   Carefully broke the egg into the bowl. [The subject is missing. *Who* broke the egg?]

SENTENCE   The child carefully broke the egg into the bowl.

FRAGMENT   The first frog of the year. [The verb is missing. *What* about the frog?]

SENTENCE   The first frog of the year hopped at the edge of the puddle.

FRAGMENT   Where some birds became the first humans. [This word group has a subject and a verb but doesn't express a complete thought. *What* about the birds?]

SENTENCE   According to Tibetan stories, a mountain in Tibet is the place where some birds became the first humans.

 NOTE   Sometimes a fragment is really a part of the sentence that comes before or after it. You can correct the fragment by attaching it to the sentence it belongs to.

FRAGMENT   Snow never falls in the Bahamas. **Because the islands are so close to the equator.**

SENTENCE   Snow never falls in the Bahamas because the islands are so close to the equator.

EXERCISE 1   Recognizing Fragments

On the line before each of the following groups of words, write *sent.* if the group is a sentence or *frag.* if the group is a sentence fragment.

EX.   *sent.*   1. The bicycle had heavy-duty tires

_____ 1. How did Joey fix the headphones

_____ 2. To make a Christmas pudding

_____ 3. He walked carefully at the edge of the cliff

_____ 4. Nearly lost his balance and fell

_____   5. The salamander under the leaves

_____   6. Where did you hide the presents

_____   7. Dropped the ball but recovered it

_____   8. Don't lean against the garage wall

_____   9. Bought new high-tops with her own money

_____ 10. Whenever I raise my hand in class

_____ 11. Wash your hands

_____ 12. Played with older children

_____ 13. At school, I took apart an old television set

_____ 14. Pedro loves to fly kites

_____ 15. Will be a crossing guard this fall

EXERCISE 2   Revising Fragments

On your own paper, rewrite each sentence fragment below to make it a complete sentence. Add a subject, add a verb, or attach the fragment to a complete sentence.

EX.   1. Left the scooter outside in the rain
      1. Tillie left the scooter outside in the rain.

1. After Tova finished the race
2. In my top desk drawer
3. Because I did not have a key
4. Playing drums in the orchestra
5. Had great seats for the circus
6. On a tour of the fire station
7. Where no human could survive
8. A space mission to Mars
9. Wrestling with his papa
10. A large and hungry dinosaur
11. When the lights went out
12. My cocker spaniel, Rolfe
13. Some paintings by my sister Tia
14. Loves swimming
15. In plain view
16. Two electric guitars
17. Flying above the pines
18. Some cartoons in the Sunday paper
19. Building a set for the school play
20. Sprang up overnight

RUN-ON SENTENCES

7c A *run-on sentence* is actually two or more sentences run together into one sentence.

Like sentence fragments, run-on sentences usually appear in your writing because you are in a hurry to get your thoughts down on paper. You might mistakenly leave out the correct end punctuation (period, question mark, or exclamation point) or use just a comma to separate sentences.

There are two good ways to revise run-on sentences.

(1) Make two sentences.

RUN-ON   Anatole, turn the oven on we will make raisin bread.
CORRECT   Anatole, turn the oven on. **We** will make raisin bread.

(2) Link the two ideas with a comma and a coordinating conjunction (*and, but, or*).

RUN-ON   Separate the red pants from the white T-shirts before you wash them you will have pink shirts.
CORRECT   Separate the red pants from the white T-shirts before you wash them, **or** you will have pink shirts.

A comma alone is not enough to link two complete ideas in a sentence. If you use just a comma between two complete ideas, you create a run-on sentence.

RUN-ON   The electric ray is a fish, it stuns its prey with electricity.
CORRECT   The electric ray is a fish. **It** stuns its prey with electricity.

EXERCISE 3   Identifying and Revising Run-on Sentences

Decide which of the following groups of words are run-on sentences. On your own paper, rewrite each run-on sentence correctly. You can correct it by making two sentences or by using a comma and a coordinating conjunction. If the group of words is already correct, write *C*.

EX.   1. Anton won four athletic trophies last year, Darryl won two.

     1. Anton won four athletic trophies last year. Darryl won two.

1. I like Rosie's new cat, I prefer big dogs.

2. Stella went to Chile she met some of her relatives there.

3. Smoke rose from the campfire, it circled above our heads.

4. Big dogs can be frightening they can be as gentle as small ones.

5. Tony showed me a game on his computer, it was like an arcade game.

6. Lions roared in the distance the tour group ran back to the bus.

7. Jogging is good for you, but you must wear proper running shoes.

8. The Braille alphabet uses raised dots the dots stand for letters and spell out words.

9. Should we go to Houston by airplane should we take a bus?

10. Marc is terrified of spiders, the garage is full of them.

11. My favorite vegetables are corn and tomatoes, my favorite fruits are bananas and oranges.

12. A shooting star blazed through the night sky, everyone stopped and stared at it with amazement.

13. Bill, you can work as an usher, you can stand in the lobby and collect people's tickets.

14. Robots are often used in factories today, for they can do some jobs well.

15. A mighty wind was blowing, the roof of the house was shaking.

16. I love tongue twisters, I always mess up "Peter Piper."

17. My story is about someone as small as an ant, he lives in an acorn under a big oak tree.

18. I love making up rap lyrics I don't like performing.

19. I may become a firefighter one day, perhaps I'll work for the police.

20. The brick wall at the edge of the playground fell down no one was hurt.

21. The sun is many times bigger than the earth, the sun is only a medium-sized star.

22. My older sister is an actor she is an expert on makeup.

23. Ice is water in its solid form, and water vapor is water in its gaseous form.

24. Is that a riddle is it simply a nonsense verse?

25. The story was written long ago in Persia, it is about a flying carpet.

STRINGY SENTENCES

7d   If you string many ideas together with *and*, you create a *stringy sentence*. Stringy sentences don't give the reader a chance to pause between ideas.

STRINGY   We left the store and we walked into the parking lot, and no one could remember exactly where the car was, and we walked everywhere looking for it.

BETTER   We left the store, **and** we walked into the parking lot. **No** one could remember exactly where the car was. **We** walked everywhere looking for it.

In the revised version, only two ideas are linked by *and*. These ideas can be joined in one sentence because they are closely related. However, notice that a comma was added before the *and*. The comma is necessary to show a slight pause between the two complete ideas.

EXERCISE 4   Identifying and Revising Stringy Sentences

On your own paper, revise each of the stringy sentences below by breaking it into two or more sentences. If a sentence is already correct, write C.

EX.   1.   We were practicing the butterfly stroke, and I accidentally inhaled some water, and Julio saw the trouble I was in, and he acted quickly, and he came to my rescue.

    1.   We were practicing the butterfly stroke, and I accidentally inhaled some water. Julio saw the trouble I was in. He acted quickly, and he came to my rescue.

1.   The moon was full, and the sky was full of stars, and I just stared at them for hours, and I felt completely at peace.

2.   Kim was born in Korea, and she wants to go back there someday, and she has heard many wonderful stories about her birthplace.

3.   Help me paint the posters, and we'll get them done quickly, and then we'll hang them in the gym.

4.   Snow had fallen during the night, and we could see tracks in the back yard, and they looked like bear tracks!

5.   Electric cars run on batteries, and the batteries must be recharged, and the owner must plug the car into an electrical outlet.

REVIEW EXERCISE

A. Revising Sentence Fragments and Run-on Sentences

On your own paper, rewrite each of the fragments below to make it a complete sentence. For each run-on sentence, rewrite the sentence correctly.

EX. 1. Came to the top of the stairs and called her kittens.

    1. Friskie came to the top of the stairs and called her kittens.

1. My brother, Juan Carlos, and my uncle, Joaquín.

2. The dance was difficult I finally learned all the steps.

3. Studied the myths of ancient China, India, and Greece.

4. A sudden flash of light.

5. Carlotta called, she will call back tonight.

6. The birds running back and forth by the shoreline.

7. Developed the photographs in the darkroom at school.

8. You can send me a postcard, you can write me a letter.

9. Ms. Mistri is a scientist she collects insects in the rain forest.

10. Threw his cereal bowl off the highchair.

B. Revising Stringy Sentences

On your own paper, revise each of the stringy sentences below.

EX. 1. The auditorium was empty, and no one was around, and I pretended I was an actor, and I did a little song and dance.

    1. The auditorium was empty, and no one was around.
       I pretended I was an actor, and I did a little song and dance.

1. The art class was doing ice sculptures, and Marcie asked me to help her, and we made a dragon, and it won first prize.

2. A coyote howled in the distance, and I felt afraid, and Toshiro said there was nothing to fear, and we settled into our bunks, and we slept.

3. The videotape player was broken, and we couldn't see the movie, and I had burned the popcorn anyway.

4. Light rain fell, and the streets became slippery, and the cars moved slowly, and no accidents occurred.

COMBINING BY INSERTING WORDS

Good writers usually use some short sentences, but they don't use them all the time. An entire paragraph of short sentences makes writing sound choppy. You can often improve choppy sentences by combining them.

7e   One way to combine two sentences is to pull a key word from one sentence and insert it into the other sentence.

Sometimes you can just add the key word to the first sentence and drop the rest of the second sentence.

ORIGINAL   The bush by the door has flowers. They are purple flowers.
COMBINED   The bush by the door has **purple** flowers.

Other times you'll need to change the form of the key word before you can insert it.

ORIGINAL   At the Lexington Library we saw a movie about the Revolutionary War. The movie interested me.
COMBINED   At the Lexington Library we saw an **interesting** movie about the Revolutionary War.

 NOTE   When you change the forms of the key words, you often add endings such as *-ed*, *-ing*, *-ful*, and *-ly* to make adjectives and adverbs.

EXERCISE 5   Combining Sentences by Inserting Words

On your own paper, rewrite each of the following pairs of sentences as one sentence. Insert the italicized key word into the first sentence. The hint in parentheses tells you how to change the form of the key word.

EX.   1.   Paul patched the tire. He was *careful*. (Use *–ly*.)

    1.   Paul carefully patched the tire.

1.   Rita spotted a porcupine. It was a *baby*. (No change)

2.   I saw a golfer in the rain. The rain *poured*. (Use *–ing*.)

3.   Our science teacher showed our class a rock. The rock *amazed* us. (Use *–ing*.)

4.   My canteen is made of plastic. The plastic has been *recycled*. (No change)

5. Sam raced to the door. He was *quick*. (Use *–ly*.)

6. Therese dropped her cleats on the ground. She was *sad*. (Use *–ly*.)

7. I like this whole-grain bread. It has great *flavor*. (Use *–ful*.)

8. I heard Leroy in the music room. I heard him *practice*. (Use *–ing*.)

9. Rajani asked her mother to bake rolls. She asked her to bake them *soon*. (No change)

10. The dog chased the robber. The dog worked for the *police*. (No change)

11. The guitar is safe in its case. The case has a *lining*. (Use *–ed*.)

12. Maura ate the latke. It was the *last* one left. (No change)

13. Helga bought new shoes. The shoes were for *running*. (No change)

14. Rosamunda loaded her things into the van. Her family was using the van to *move*. (Use *–ing*.)

15. In the castle was a fancy carpet. The carpet was very *worn*. (No change)

16. Walking on the sidewalk in front of our house is tricky. The sidewalk has *cracks* in it. (Use *–ed*.)

17. Mr. Proust offered to take us on his boat. He uses it to catch *fish*. (Use *–ing*.)

18. We took Shawn with us. We were *glad* to do it. (Use *–ly*.)

19. The herd of elephants charged. They were *angry*. (No change)

20. Lucinda stared at the bicycle in the store window. She *wished* she could have it. (Use *–fully*.)

21. Li loved her new sweater. It was made of *wool*. (Use *–en*.)

22. Dave liked his father's car. The car was *red*. (No change)

23. Stacy painted a mural in her room. She used many bright *colors* in the mural. (Use *–ful*.)

24. They were bored on the moving train. The train was *slow*. (Use *–ly*.)

25. Dad slipped on the driveway. It was covered with *ice*. (Use *–y*.)

COMBINING BY INSERTING WORD GROUPS

7f   Often you can combine two related sentences by taking an entire group of words from one sentence and adding it to the other sentence.

When the group of words is inserted, it adds detail to the information in the first sentence. Sometimes you'll need to put commas around the group of words you are inserting. Ask yourself whether the group of words renames or explains a noun or pronoun in the sentence. If it does, use a comma or commas to set off the word group from the rest of the sentence.

ORIGINAL   My family is planning a trip to the Boundary Waters. The waters are in Minnesota.

COMBINED   My family is planning a trip to the Boundary Waters **in Minnesota**.

ORIGINAL   I gave Winnie a rubber toy. Winnie is my German shepherd.

COMBINED   I gave Winnie, **my German shepherd,** a rubber toy.

After you combine two sentences, be sure to read your new sentence carefully. Then ask yourself the following questions.

- Is my new sentence clear?
- Does it make sense?
- Does it sound better than the two shorter sentences?

EXERCISE 6   Combining Sentences by Inserting Word Groups

On your own paper, combine each of the following pairs of sentences by inserting the italicized words into the first sentence.

EX.   1.   Yesterday morning we saw a swan. It was *gliding across the lake.*

1.   Yesterday morning we saw a swan gliding across the lake.

1.   Mateo plays in a rock-and-roll band. He plays *the electric guitar.*

2.   The earthquake destroyed many homes. This happened *in southern California.*

3.   Sandra wrote to the mayor. She wrote *about cuts in the school budget.*

4. In the future, will space travel be done all the time? Will such travel be done *by ordinary people?*

5. Arturo's cat has yellow and black stripes. It is *a tabby.*

6. Six howler monkeys played in the trees. They were *making a terrible noise.*

7. I received a beautiful wall hanging. It was *from my grandmother in Vietnam.*

8. Long ago, people made up myths. They told these stories *to explain how things like rivers and volcanoes were created.*

9. The cheetah ran after the the antelope. It ran *with amazing speed.*

10. A package arrived. It was *from Aunt Lucia.*

11. Alice Navarez wrote an essay about crocodiles. She is *a girl in my science class.*

12. The coast guard fired a cannon. The cannon was fired *to warn the boat to stop.*

13. Do you like those mountain bikes? They are the ones *with the big tires.*

14. The special effects were fantastic. They were *in that monster movie.*

15. Opal Whitely was a young girl who believed that she could speak to animals and to little people in the woods. She came *from Oregon.*

16. Artie loves singing. He loves singing *the Motown songs from the 1960s.*

17. The magician made the rabbit disappear. He made it disappear *in a puff of smoke.*

18. Tyrone tutored me in math. He is *my best friend.*

19. The many-colored fish swam in the pond. The pond was *outside the Chinese restaurant.*

20. Six camels rested. They were *beneath the palm tree in the middle of the oasis.*

USING CONNECTING WORDS

7g　**If two sentences have the same subject, you can combine them by making a compound verb. If the sentences have the same verb, you can combine them by making a compound subject.**

ORIGINAL　The moose scratched its head on a small tree. The moose caught its horns in the tree.

COMBINED　The moose **scratched** its head on a small tree and **caught** its horns in the tree.

ORIGINAL　Tran entered a cooking contest. Lita entered a cooking contest.

COMBINED　**Tran** and **Lita** entered a cooking contest.

7h　**Sometimes you may want to combine two related sentences that express equally important ideas. You can connect the two sentences by using a comma and *and, but,* or *or.* The result is a compound sentence.**

ORIGINAL　Today I won the race. Who knows what tomorrow will bring?

COMBINED　Today I won the race, **but** who knows what tomorrow will bring?

7i　**Other times you may want to combine two sentences that are related in a special way. One sentence helps explain the other by telling how, where, why, or when.**

A good way to combine these sentences is to add a connecting word that shows how they are related. In this kind of sentence combining, you create a complex sentence.

ORIGINAL　Navajo Code Talkers invented a secret code. This code helped the United States in World War II.

COMBINED　Navajo Code Talkers invented a secret code **that** helped the United States in World War II.

EXERCISE 7　Combining Sentences by Joining Subjects and Verbs

On your own paper, combine each of the following pairs of sentences by using the conjunction in parentheses. If the sentences have the same verb, combine them by joining the two subjects. If the sentences have the same subject, combine them by joining the two verbs.

EX.   1. The fireworks were pretty. The fireworks were loud. (Use *but*)

      1. The fireworks were pretty but loud.

1. We raise goats on our farm. We grow cotton. (Use *and*.)

2. The Allegheny River runs through Pittsburgh. The Monongahela River runs through Pittsburgh. (Use *and*.)

3. Jamil's mother might drive us to the mall. Jamil's uncle might drive us to the mall. (Use *or*.)

4. Chitsa would like to ski more often. She lives in Florida. (Use *but*.)

5. Sabina's mother makes her own flour tortillas. Sabina's mother lets us eat as many as we want. (Use *and*.)

6. Manuela will play center. Manuela will replace the goalie. (Use *or*.)

7. My friend Leonor is from Honduras. My friend Felix is from Honduras. (Use *and*.)

8. Maska does not enjoy rock-climbing. She is good at the sport. (Use *but*.)

9. Duke Ellington was a pianist. Duke Ellington composed many songs. (Use *and*.)

10. Braids would suit you well. Hair combs would suit you well. (Use *or*.)

EXERCISE 8   Combining Complete Sentences

On your own paper, combine each pair of sentences below by making one sentence. Use the connecting word in parentheses.

EX.   1. I want to visit Maine. I want to see a real moose. (Use *to*.)

      1. I want to visit Maine to see a real moose.

1. Ms. LaFrance came into the room. We began our lesson. (Use *when*.)

2. Sasha wants to be an astronaut. She needs to go to college. (Use *so*.)

3. I wanted to go to Len's birthday party. I have a cold. (Use *but*.)

4. Everybody is singing. We're celebrating Carl's birthday. (Use *because*.)

5. I get hungry. I play in the snow. (Use *whenever*.)

CHAPTER REVIEW

A. Revising Sentence Fragments and Run-on and Stringy Sentences

On your own paper, rewrite the sentences below. Make complete sentences from any fragments. Correct any run-on or stringy sentences.

EX. 1. Going to the movies tomorrow night.

    1. Nina and I are going to the movies tomorrow night.

1. The puzzle was really hard, and I couldn't solve it, and then my little sister tried it, and she solved it in under five minutes.

2. We could visit a Civil War battlefield, we could stay in Washington and see some museums.

3. A gray-and-white sea gull with a large beak.

4. Rode in a virtual reality machine at the mall.

5. A tornado ripped through the town, and it tore down a theater, and no one was hurt, and the theater is being rebuilt.

6. We wanted some new CDs, the music store was closed.

7. A mysterious light over the swamp.

8. A gremlin is an imaginary creature, and it supposedly lives inside computers, airplanes, and other machines, and it does things to the machines, and the machines break down.

9. In the museum we saw some dinosaur eggs they were quite large.

10. Marissa wrote the music, I wrote the lyrics.

11. Grew as big as a house.

12. The speeches were long, and I went to sleep, and an hour later my dad poked me with his elbow, and I woke up to listen.

13. A brown bat, looking like a mouse with wings.

14. My brother is studying audio engineering he works at a local radio station.

15. The temperature dropped, and the pond in the park froze, and the ice was thin, and a sign was posted to warn the skaters of the danger.

B. Combining Sentences by Using Words, Word Groups, and Connecting Words

Revise the sentences below on your own paper. Combine the sentences, using the hints given in parentheses.

EX.   1.   Ms. Rosen lighted a candle. She did this *on the first night of Hanukkah.* (Insert the word group in italics.)

   1.   Ms. Rosen lighted a candle on the first night of Hanukkah.

1.   The children broke the piñata. They were *excited.* (Add the word in italics.)

2.   Paco and I saw many boats in the harbor. The boats *sailed.* (Use *–ing.*)

3.   Ms. Rutkowski bandaged the skier's swollen ankle. She did it like an *expert.* (Use *–ly.*)

4.   The garden was full of flowers. They gave me much *delight.* (Use *–ful.*)

5.   The natives complained that the elephants were pushing down trees. The trees were *on their land.* (Add the word group in italics.)

6.   Would you like to feed Rudolph? Rudolph is *my pet python.* (Add the word group in italics.)

7.   We wanted to lie in the sun. It was too hot. (Use *but.*)

8.   Cleo writes her own music. Cleo plays the piano. (Use *and.*)

9.   The horse stumbled. Its rider fell off. (Use *when.*)

10.   The future will be quite different from today. The world around us is constantly changing. (Use *because.*)

C.   Reconstructing a Message

You have invented a machine that can listen to people talking in the future. However, your "time talk" machine doesn't work very well. It brings back only fragments. Here is part of a conversation that you have recorded. Try to create the complete sentences on your own paper.

going to Mars or to Saturn?

haven't decided   though   is awfully far away for a weekend trip.

not so far, really   the new transporter   in a few hours.

to see the rings   Perhaps I   there.

DIALECTS OF AMERICAN ENGLISH

8a   The form of English a particular group of people speaks is called a *dialect*.

(1) A dialect shared by people from the same area is called a *regional dialect*. Your regional dialect is made up of which words you use, how you pronounce words, and even how you put words together.

EXAMPLES   At noon we came home for **dinner.**
At noon we came home for some **eats.**

We are **going with** Joe to see a movie.
Do you want to **go with?**

(2) A dialect shared by people from the same cultural group is called an *ethnic dialect*.

Because Americans come from many cultures, American English includes many ethnic dialects. One of the largest ethnic dialects is the Black English spoken by many African Americans. Another is the Hispanic English of many people whose families come from Mexico, Central America, Cuba, and Puerto Rico.

NOTE   Not everyone from a particular group speaks that group's dialect. Also, an ethnic or regional dialect may vary depending on the speakers' individual backgrounds and places of origin.

EXAMPLES   Before dinner the guests **noshed** vegetables and dip. ["snacked on, ate"]
Jim, **he be my main man.** ["Jim is my best, or most important, friend."]

NOTE   You can use dialect in short stories to help your reader hear a character's language. When you write dialogue for a character, think about how your character would really talk. Try to capture the sound as well as the meaning of the person's language.

EXERCISE 1   Working Cooperatively to Revise Dialect

The following paragraphs are written in dialect. First, read the passage aloud. Make sure you understand any unfamiliar words. Then, working with a partner, rewrite the italicized portions in your own regional or ethnic dialect. Or, if you prefer, rewrite them as you think a newscaster might say them. Write your answers on your own paper.

EX.   1   *Lan' sakes! Ah's glad ta be home.*
    1. Boy, oh boy! Was I ever glad to be home.

1   Some *a the kinfolk* come over *ta Mamaw's* about dinnertime, and

2   Mamaw she put dinner on the table. *We all et till we could bust.*

3   Afterward, I felt *sick at my stomach* from eating so much, but I

4   *couldn't hep myself.* Mamaw *shore is one mighty fine cook.*

5   Then Tom and I *lit out over the hill* to see about Granny, *who's*

6   *been ailin'. We wuz crossin' over the crick* down by the hog lot when

7   we *seen somethin' spooky a-moving* through the trees on *t'other side.*

8   It looked like some sort of light, but it *wuz a-bumpin' up an down*

9   *kinda regular-like.* We couldn't tell what it was at first, so *me and*

10   *Tom sorta hunkered down* and *squinched up our eyes so's to see what it*

11   *wuz.* Tom said, "Maybe it's aliens." (I think he's been watching too

12   *many a them* television movies.)

13   *Ah says,* "*Naw, it ain't no aliens.* That's Forest Grider, carrying a

14   lantern. He's probably been *over ta Granny's hisself.* Come on."

15   After we had *crost over the crick,* though, we saw it wasn't Forest

16   Grider at all. It *wuz* the sheriff.

17   He said, "Hello, boys. *Y'all hain't been down ta* your Grandma's,

18   have you? She called *down ta the po-leece* station, saying she heard

19   some *sorta ruckus out in her yard.*"

20   "No, sir," we told him. "We *wuz jist a-headin'* over there now."

FORMAL AND INFORMAL ENGLISH

Formal and *informal English* are used for different reasons. For instance, you would probably use informal language when talking to a classmate. You would probably use more formal language when talking to someone to whom you have just been introduced.

8b The most widely used informal expressions are *colloquialisms*. Colloquialisms are the lively words and phrases of everyday speech.

EXAMPLES   Sidney was late again, and the coach **bit his head off.**
How surprising! You could **knock me over with a feather!**

8c *Slang* is made-up words or phrases or old words or phrases used in new ways. Slang is highly informal language.

EXAMPLES   I'd like to get that CD, but I don't have any **dough.**
Cara is **nuts** about video games.

NOTE   Colloquialisms and slang can add interest to language. However, they should be used only in the most informal speaking and writing. Do not use colloquialisms or slang in essays, test answers, or written and oral reports.

EXERCISE 2   Using Formal and Informal English

Each sentence below contains an informal word or phrase in italics. On the line after the sentence, replace the word or phrase with one that is more formal.

EX.   1. Working on the school play was *a real blast.*
Working on the school play was quite enjoyable.

1. Bradley started to get upset, but I told him *to chill out.*

   _____

2. Can you please *pipe down*? You are going to wake the baby.

   _____

3. The new computer game really *blew my mind.*

   _____

4. "Don't *trash* the house while I'm gone," Mom told us as she left.

_____

5. Yolanda got *an awesome* new mountain bike for her birthday.

_____

6. Marcie *is a real couch potato.*

_____

7. We needed some new signs, so I *zipped down* to the art store to buy

   some poster board. _____

   _____

8. What *a wicked* good time we had at that party!

   _____

9. Jake and Al sat in the cafeteria for hours, *yakking* about last Saturday's

   football game. _____

   _____

10. You can't *blow off* this practice. It's our dress rehearsal!

   _____

EXERCISE 3   Using Informal English

On your own paper, rewrite the following overly formal sentences in
informal English that you might use with a friend.

EX. 1. Please extinguish the lights when departing.
     1. Please turn the lights out when you leave.

1. We scanned the crowd to determine José's precise location.

2. Please bring proper writing utensils to the examination.

3. On behalf of my associates, I would like to extend a warm greeting
   to you and your loved ones.

4. One can ordinarily readily recognize when someone has uttered
   an untruth.

5. Please do not hesitate to contact me should you find yourself
   desiring someone with whom you may converse.

DENOTATION AND CONNOTATION

8d **The *denotation* of a word is its actual meaning. Two words can have the same denotation.**

EXAMPLES A **snowstorm** will hit the East Coast tomorrow.
A **blizzard** will hit the East Coast tomorrow.

8e **A word's *connotation* is the meaning that affects people emotionally.**

POSITIVE CONNOTATION We waited **eagerly** for the train.
NEGATIVE CONNOTATION We waited **impatiently** for the train.

POSITIVE CONNOTATION The **fine** cloth fit into a small bag.
NEGATIVE CONNOTATION The **flimsy** cloth fit into a small bag.

NOTE Sometimes you will need to choose between *synonyms*—words that have similar meanings. Think about the connotations of the words, and choose the word that says what you really mean.

EXERCISE 4 Recognizing Denotations

Work with a classmate or in a group to come up with a list of at least five words with the same denotation as each word given below. Write your lists on the lines provided.

EX. 1. talk *gab; gossip; chatter; speak; say*

1. give _____

    _____

2. happy _____

    _____

3. walk _____

    _____

4. destroy _____

    _____

5. like (v.) _____

    _____

EXERCISE 5   Recognizing Connotations

For each sentence below, underline the word in parentheses that seems more positive.

EX.   1. Maria was (*sloppily, <u>casually</u>*) dressed.

1. Mrs. Peabody (*stored, stashed*) her jewelry in a safe-deposit box at the bank.

2. Because we had (*cheap, inexpensive*) tickets for the concert, we had to sit in the back row.

3. The room was filled with the (*scent, odor*) of the perfume that Ms. Bloom was wearing.

4. Ms. Alvira is a (*stubborn, strong-minded*) person.

5. Marc is going through a hard time and is quite (*touchy, sensitive*) these days.

6. Jefferson looked pretty (*grim, serious*) before the math test.

7. Samuel (*asked, begged*) for another chance to try out for the basketball team.

8. My little sister knows better than to tell a (*lie, fib*).

9. Bart and Burt are always (*talking, gossiping*) about their families.

10. Chandra has always been quite a (*bookworm, reader*).

Peanuts reprinted by permission of UFS, Inc.

CHAPTER REVIEW

A.   Revising Sentences Written in Another Dialect

The following sentences contain words and phrases from different American dialects. On your own paper, rewrite the sentences in standard American English.

EX.   1.   We hep my cousin tote his bags.

    1.   We helped my cousin carry his luggage.

1.   They don't know from nothing.

2.   Help me hull these goobers.

3.   I'm a bring home some apples.

4.   He no homeboy, but he be kin.

5.   Enough with the talk!

6.   Pop them yams in that skillet.

7.   Y'all got an extra pen?

8.   She might could do real well this year.

9.   Won't you go down cellar and fetch a barrel?

10.   Our hand will help you carry your goods.

B.   Revising a Paragraph to Make It More Formal

On your own paper, rewrite the following paragraph in formal English.

EX.   [1]   Early people made really neat dolls out of wax, stone, iron, and bronze.

    1.   Early people made very beautiful dolls out of wax, stone, iron, and bronze.

[1] Dolls have been around for lots and lots of years. [2] About five thousand years ago in India, folks made small figures of gods like Brahma and Shiva. [3] Then, in ancient Egypt, things changed like crazy in the world of doll-making. [4] That's because the Egyptians began making dolls that looked like plain old ordinary people. [5] Finally, the ancient Greeks began making dolls in the shape of little

bitty babies, and these led to the dolls used by kids nowadays.

C.   Recognizing Connotations

For each sentence below, underline the word or words in parentheses that seem more positive.

EX.   1.   Ashad brought home a (*scraggly, thin*) kitten.

1.   Mr. Suzuki was (*upset, furious*) when I dropped the glass beaker.

2.   Sheila can be quite (*talkative, chatty*) sometimes.

3.   Marc watches what he spends; he is quite (*stingy, frugal*).

4.   My forehead was covered with (*perspiration, sweat*).

5.   Don't be so (*undecided, wishy-washy*). Try to make up your mind.

6.   The mayor is known for being (*pushy, assertive*).

7.   An interesting (*aroma, odor*) came from the opened refrigerator.

8.   Abel gave Ms. Finch an (*explanation, excuse*) about how he lost his homework assignment.

9.   Jim looked pretty (*relaxed, lazy*) lying there in the hammock.

10.   A (*muscular, hulking*) young man entered the gym.

D.   Creating a Slang Dictionary

Work with two or three classmates to put together a small dictionary of ten modern slang words and phrases. List the slang word or phrase, its part of speech, and its definition in standard English. Include a sentence to show how the word is used. Write your entries on your own paper.

EX.   RAD—adjective—exceptional or wonderful. What a rad bicycle! You are so lucky!

            REALLY CRUISING—phrase—verb—driving very fast. That police car was really cruising after those bad guys.

SENTENCE OR SENTENCE FRAGMENT?

9a   A *sentence* is a group of words that expresses a complete thought.

A sentence begins with a capital letter and ends with a period, a question mark, or an exclamation point.

EXAMPLES   The parrot bit the back of the chair**.**
Wait by the hickory tree**.**
Did you buy the paper**?**
That play was perfect**!**

When a group of words looks like a sentence but does not express a complete thought, it is a **sentence fragment.**

FRAGMENT   The pebbles in Mystery Cove. [This is not a complete thought. What about the pebbles?]

SENTENCE   The pebbles in Mystery Cove are round and multicolored.

FRAGMENT   Relaxes by taking a walk by the ocean. [This is not a complete thought. Who relaxes?]

SENTENCE   Saki relaxes by taking a walk by the ocean.

FRAGMENT   When a sea star loses an arm. [This thought is not complete. What happens when a sea star loses an arm?]

SENTENCE   When a sea star loses an arm, it can grow a new one.

 NOTE   In speech, people frequently use sentence fragments. Such fragments usually aren't confusing, because the speaker's tone of voice and facial expressions help to complete the meaning. Professional writers may also use sentence fragments to create specific effects in their writing. However, in your writing at school, you will find it best to use complete sentences.

EXERCISE 1   Identifying Sentences

On the line before each of the following word groups, write *sent.* if the group is a sentence or *frag.* if the group is a sentence fragment. Add correct punctuation if the group of words is a sentence.

EX. _____*sent.*_____ 1. The lava from the volcano was a boiling red river

_____ 1. The tropical fish were green and blue

_____ 2. Did Frank call you

_____ 3. Spending a night in the woods

_____ 4. Watch out for the wet paint

_____ 5. When the lake is calm

_____ 6. Mushrooms grow in the woods

_____ 7. Look at all the snow

_____ 8. The swimming pool was crowded

_____ 9. Pea pods sizzled in the wok

_____ 10. The hollyhocks by the house

EXERCISE 2   Revising Fragments

On your own paper, revise the fragments below to make complete sentences. Add any words you might need.

EX.   1. The glowing moon
      1. _The glowing moon looked like a pearl._

1. dangling from the ceiling

2. the blue sweater

3. after seeing the falling star

4. at the student art show

5. cooking with vegetables and pasta

6. visit with my grandfather

7. a bowl of oranges

8. on his trip to China

9. singing on stage

10. before breakfast

11. in the lake

12. knitting sweaters

13. the small pond

14. on his desk

15. some yellow flowers

THE SUBJECT

Every sentence has two main parts: a *subject* and a *predicate*.

9b   The *subject* tells whom or what the sentence is about.

EXAMPLE   **The smell of a wood fire** makes me think of camping.

9c   To find the subject, ask yourself *who* or *what* is doing something or *about whom* or *what* something is being said.

EXAMPLE   **My first dog** loved eating turnips. [*What* loved eating turnips? My first dog did.]

9d   The subject does not always come at the beginning of a sentence. It may be in the middle or even at the end.

Sometimes you may have trouble finding the subject of a sentence. In such cases, find the verb first. Then ask yourself *to whom* or *to what* the verb is referring.

EXAMPLES   During the summer, **your brother** could cut grass to earn money. [The verb is *could cut. Who* could cut? The answer is *your brother,* the subject of the sentence.]
Across the busy highway raced **a deer.** [The verb is *raced. What* raced? A deer raced. *A deer* is the subject of the sentence.]

NOTE   The subject is never found in a prepositional phrase.

EXAMPLE   In the drawer was **a pair** of scissors. [*Pair* is the subject of the sentence, not *drawer.*]

EXERCISE 3   Identifying Subjects

Underline the subject in each of the following sentences.

EX.   1.   Behind the tree lurked a <u>tiger</u>.

1.   During the winter, our father enjoys making thick, steaming pots of vegetable stew.

2.   The bulletin board above Alisha's desk is full of photos, banners, and ribbons.

3.   Bobbing in the water was a small sailboat.

4.   In a quiet corner of the library, Sam read a book.

5. On the back porch railing perched a sparrow.

6. The main character wore a tuxedo and slippers.

7. Did Virginia Hamilton write *M.C. Higgins the Great?*

8. As a child, my grandfather sold newspapers.

9. Up the tree ran a squirrel.

10. Harry's cat will jump for a carrot.

11. The zipper on my new winter jacket is stuck.

12. Before winter, we should cover all of the old windows with plastic.

13. When is Jarvis going to visit us?

14. Rena's boots were under the chicken wire in the shed.

15. Across the busy street bounced a football.

EXERCISE 4   Writing Complete Sentences

Add a subject to each of the word groups below. On your own paper, write your sentence with the correct punctuation and capitalization.

EX.   1. danced to the music
      1. Luis danced to the music.

1. worked after school at Brown's Grocery

2. offered us tickets to the game

3. wanted its independence

4. wrote this letter

5. barked at the blowing leaves

6. is the home of the state champions

7. brought dozens of photographs to school

8. hiding behind the curtain was

9. is a snake

10. volunteer their time and skills

11. was helpful

12. gave me a ride

13. opened a bakery

14. stared at the stars

15. climbing the tree was

COMPLETE SUBJECTS AND SIMPLE SUBJECTS

9e The *complete subject* consists of all the words needed to tell *whom* or *what* the sentence is about.

EXAMPLE   The large fender of the bike next to mine is bent.

9f The *simple subject* is the main word in the complete subject.

COMPLETE SUBJECT   The large fender of the bike next to mine
SIMPLE SUBJECT   fender

If you leave out the simple subject, a sentence does not make sense.

EXAMPLE   The large . . . of the bike next to mine is bent.

Sometimes the same word or words make up both the simple subject and the complete subject.

 NOTE   In this book, the term *subject* refers to the simple subject unless otherwise indicated.

EXERCISE 5   Identifying Complete Subjects and Simple Subjects

In each of the following sentences, underline the complete subject once. Underline the simple subject twice.

EX.   1.   The black umbrella by the front door is mine.

1. His white-and-blue cotton sweater shrank two sizes.

2. The screens on the front porch windows are torn.

3. Did the green parrot on your shoulder say something?

4. Across the beach darted long-legged sandpipers.

5. The reporter's long coat looked wrinkled and wet.

6. The thick shells of black walnuts are hard to crack.

7. Do heavy wool mittens keep your hands warm and dry?

8. The Maricopa people of Arizona make unusual pottery.

9. Behind the door purred the happy cat.

10. A tall, thin man with a hat walked down the lane.

11. The conga drum developed from ancient Africa.

12. The best quarterback on the team has a knee injury.

13. The tall bearded man reminded her of Abraham Lincoln.

14. Is this package on the counter for you?

15. The front tire of our new car is flat.

EXERCISE 6   Writing Complete Sentences

Add a complete subject to each of the word groups below. On your own paper, write each of your sentences with the correct punctuation and capitalization. Then underline the simple subject in each of your sentences.

EX.   1. sat on the edge of the roof
     1. A dozen pigeons sat on the edge of the roof.

1. watched the team win

2. are running in our yard

3. tastes good on a hot day

4. is a healthful breakfast

5. belongs to Greta

6. sang at the retirement community

7. were laced too tight

8. had been wonderful

9. wished us good night

10. lit the campfire

11. waved to the ship

12. is sliding into third base

13. enjoyed the music

14. wandered through the museum

15. played with her doll house

16. know the Mitchells

17. bought reflectors for my bike

18. is the new librarian

19. forgot his sleeping bag

20. called a cab

THE PREDICATE

9g The *predicate* of a sentence is the part that says something about the subject.

EXAMPLES   The jellyfish **was trapped on the hot sand.**
Our neighbors **asked us to help with the block party.**

9h The predicate usually comes after the subject. Sometimes, however, part or all of the predicate comes before the subject.

EXAMPLES   **Silently,** the beetle **struggled to climb out of the sink.**
Sitting on the oily dock were a dozen gulls.
On Saturday night will you **stay at your friend's house?**

EXERCISE 7   Identifying Predicates

Underline the predicate in each of the following sentences.

EX.   1. The dogs' leashes <u>were tangled around my ankles.</u>

1. Quietly, we climbed the back stairs.

2. Our foreign exchange student arrived from France.

3. The printer was jammed with legal-size paper.

4. Waiting for the bus was a group of children.

5. Happily, the campers hiked in the woods.

6. My best friend called me on the phone last night.

7. Swiftly, the runners crossed the finish line.

8. Last night, the computer screen flashed on and off.

9. Visiting the Vietnam Veterans Memorial were thousands of tourists.

10. Wearily, the tired shop clerk waited on the last customer.

11. Singing in the shower was my brother Patrick.

12. This winter, Angela is taking a course in t'ai chi ch'uan.

13. Strutting in the muddy garden bed were a dozen large crows.

14. Loudly, the delivery person pounded on our front door.

15. The red shirt looks too big on you.

16. Slowly, the Latin dancers began their warm-up.

17. The three-year-olds seemed too small to reach the piñata.

18. Surprised, the baby stared at herself in the mirror.

19. The boat over there with the sails is a restaurant.

20. Does anyone you know think our team can lose?

EXERCISE 8   Writing Predicates

Add a predicate to each of the word groups below. On your own paper, write each of your sentences with the correct punctuation and capitalization. Then underline the predicate in each of your sentences.

EX.   1. the mongoose
   1. Playfully, the mongoose rolled over on its back.

1. the dark clouds

2. our neighbors across the hall

3. the oak tree

4. a flock of sparrows

5. my younger sister

6. the cold and tired traveler

7. yesterday's snowfall

8. the bold guest

9. a huge whale

10. a group of fans

11. a broken helmet

12. an ancient arrowhead

13. dozens of snowballs

14. my father

15. a good pair of binoculars

16. stir-fried vegetables

17. slush

18. a new CD

19. at least twenty police officers

20. everyone

COMPLETE PREDICATES AND SIMPLE PREDICATES

> **9i** The *complete predicate* consists of all the words that are not part of the complete subject.
>
> **9j** The *simple predicate*, or *verb*, is the main word or word group in the complete predicate.
>
> | | |
> |---:|:---|
> | EXAMPLE | Tulips **bloom in the spring.** |
> | COMPLETE PREDICATE | bloom in the spring |
> | SIMPLE PREDICATE (VERB) | bloom |
>
> NOTE In this book, the simple predicate is usually called the *verb*.

EXERCISE 9   Identifying Complete Predicates and Verbs

In the following sentences, underline the complete predicate once and the simple predicate twice.

EX.   1. Our relatives <u>visit during the holidays.</u>

1. My mother rides the bus to her job.

2. We hang the garlic in the cellar.

3. Racing down the field went the lacrosse team.

4. Uncle Henry called us on the telephone.

5. Cement expands in the heat.

6. The color blue soothes the eye.

7. We hid the gift in the closet.

8. Lara reads a new book every weekend.

9. The clock in the hall chimes on the hour.

10. A gospel music concert opened at the Multicultural Arts Center.

11. She poured hot tea into the cup.

12. The alarm rang early in the morning.

13. The downtown library opens late on Saturday.

14. After the dance program comes a tribute to Dr. Martin Luther King, Jr.

15. Crocuses bloom earlier than tulips in the spring.

EXERCISE 10   Writing Complete Predicates

Add a complete predicate to each of the word groups below. On your own paper, write your sentences with the correct punctuation and capitalization. Then underline the verb in each sentence.

EX.   1. the hungry campers
    1. The hungry campers <u>flipped</u> pancakes on the griddle.

1. a team of scientists

2. pink seashells

3. the heavy downpour

4. the school newspaper

5. ancient pyramids

6. tall pine trees

7. quiet voices

8. my older brother

9. the oranges in the bowl

10. a blue bicycle

11. a pair of skates

12. the bongo drums

13. someone

14. my new sneakers

15. the closet door

16. a school of fish

17. bright lights

18. thick ropes

19. a box of crayons

20. the crowded market

THE VERB PHRASE

9k A verb that is made up of more than one word is called a *verb phrase*.

EXAMPLES   The little girl **was eating** corn on the cob.
The bus driver **should have stopped** two blocks sooner.
Did you **park** at the end of the driveway?

NOTE   The words *not* and *never* and the contraction *–n't* are not verbs.
They are never part of a verb or verb phrase.

EXERCISE 11   Identifying Verb Phrases

In the sentences below, underline the complete predicate. Then put brackets around the verb or verb phrase.

EX.   1. The clam chowder [was simmering] on the stove.

1. We can buy bread at the store.

2. Hank has been painting the fence green.

3. A baseball pitcher is practicing in the bullpen.

4. An old friend was visiting us this afternoon.

5. The weather reporter warned everyone about the storm.

6. A taxi is waiting in front of the house.

7. The young boy had not yet read the letter from his grandfather.

8. The doctor must have seen the patient hours ago.

9. Tulips were blooming before irises this year.

10. Kwok's grandparents are flying from China to the United States.

11. Visitors to the aquarium can watch sharks and stingrays in a tank.

12. At the Japanese restaurant, Alison ordered a sushi plate.

13. Can you play the piano?

14. Nabil must not have seen the stop sign at the intersection.

15. Have you called the theater about the price of tickets?

REVIEW EXERCISE

A. Identifying Subjects, Verbs, and Verb Phrases

In the sentences below, underline the complete subject once and the verb or verb phrase twice.

EX. 1. The small robin was splashing in the birdbath.

1. The alarm clock should have buzzed this morning.

2. A tall glass of ice tea tastes good on a summer afternoon.

3. Every member of the team was practicing the next day.

4. The artist painted the canvas with bright colors.

5. Did you see the bright red cardinal in the tree?

6. Have you tasted the Greek dish made with spinach and feta cheese?

7. Our neighbor's parents are visiting from Norway.

8. Sea urchins look on the ocean floor for food.

9. The beaver colony had built the dam over night.

10. Anyone in the house could have fixed the light bulb.

B. Writing Sentences from Science Notes

In preparing a report for science class, you've gathered the notes below on composting. Use this information to write at least ten sentences on your own paper. Underline the complete subject of each sentence once and the verb or verb phrase twice.

EX. 1. Compost is made from dirt and kitchen scraps.

MAKING COMPOST (also called mulch)
- containers (called composter)
  square bin, needs lid, allow for air
- contents
  only vegetables or plant parts—clippings, leaves, coffee grounds
- process
  packed in 6-inch layers
  forms molds
  add water
  contents break down
  takes from 6-7 months
- uses
  makes rich fertilizer
  put on garden
- results
  enriches earth with nutrients and loosens ground
  tomatoes in our garden twice as big

COMPOUND SUBJECTS AND COMPOUND VERBS

9l A *compound subject* consists of two or more connected subjects that have the same verb. The parts of the compound subject are most often connected by *and* and *or*.

EXAMPLES **Dill** and **chives** grow well in pots. [The two parts of the compound subject have the same verb, *grow.*]
Ms. Chun or **Mr. Shapiro** will teach typing. [The two parts of the compound subject have the same verb, *will teach.*]

Commas are used to separate three or more parts of a compound subject.

EXAMPLE **Ants, moths,** and **beetles** are insects. [The three parts of the compound subject have the same verb, *are.*]

 REFERENCE NOTE: For more about commas, see pages 243–249.

9m A *compound verb* is made up of two or more connected verbs that have the same subject. A connecting word such as *and* or *but* is used to join the verbs.

EXAMPLES Lennie **discussed** the price but **paid** too much anyway. [The two parts of the compound verb have the same subject, *Lennie.*]
Sammy **walks, runs,** or **bicycles** to school. [The three parts of the compound verb have the same subject, *Sammy.*]
The windshield wipers **stopped** once and then **started** again. [The two parts of the compound verb have the same subject, *windshield wipers.*]

EXERCISE 12   Identifying Compound Subjects and Compound Verbs

Underline the subjects once and the verbs twice in the following sentences.

EX.   1. <u>Mr. Rosenberg</u> and <u>his son</u> <u>cook</u> all their own meals.

1. Blue, purple, and green are Suzanna's favorite colors.

2. Andrea enjoyed the soup and asked for another bowl.

3. Ms. Martinez or Mr. Chan will judge the essay contest.

4. Kendra writes or calls her grandmother once a week.

5. Juan or Luis loaded the truck and drove away.

6. Sergio hiked and camped in the foothills of the Himalaya Mountains.

7. Lemons and limes are grown in the South.

8. I washed and ironed all the laundry.

9. Frank and Jeff play soccer after school.

10. Bats, helmets, and mitts are all sports equipment.

EXERCISE 13   Writing Sentences with Compound Subjects

On your own paper, add a compound subject to each of the predicates (verb groups) below. Underline the subject once and the verb twice in your sentences. You may add any other words necessary to make your sentences clear.

EX.   1. will sail around the world
    1. My brother and I will sail around the world someday.

1. eat fish twice a week

2. read the paper each morning

3. like to study in the library

4. will go to a new school

5. shopped at the mall

6. practiced on the basketball court

7. ate dinner at the new restaurant

8. will park our bikes in the garage

9. practice their tubas every morning

10. traveled to Washington, D. C.

EXERCISE 14   Writing Sentences with Compound Verbs

On your own paper, add a compound verb to each of the complete subjects below. Underline the subject once and the verb twice in your sentences. You may add any other words necessary to make your sentences clear.

EX.   1. my oldest brother
    1. My oldest brother Tran plays football and works after school.

1. Mrs. Ramirez

2. the school talent show

3. even my best friend

4. one of the actors

5. Jason, Anna's cousin,

6. music from the radio

7. the art room

8. my first pet

9. the book *Dr. Jekyll and Mr. Hyde*

10. the beautiful sunset

SIMPLE SENTENCES AND COMPOUND SENTENCES

9n A *simple sentence* has one subject and one verb.

Although a compound subject has two or more parts, it is still considered one subject. In the same way, a compound verb or verb phrase is considered one verb.

EXAMPLES   My **grandmother decorates** the prettiest Easter eggs. [single subject and verb]

India and **Pakistan share** a border. [compound subject]

Franco went skating and **enjoyed** it. [compound verb]

Yoruba and **Hausa are** languages and **are spoken** in the Niger-Congo area. [compound subject and compound verb]

9o A *compound sentence* consists of two or more simple sentences, usually joined by a connecting word.

In a compound sentence, the word *and, but, for, nor, or, so,* or *yet* connects the simple sentences. A comma usually comes before the connecting word in a compound sentence.

EXAMPLES   She sings well, **yet** she gets stage fright.
Clicking sounds are part of some languages, **but** English doesn't use them.

Notice in the first example above that a sentence is compound even if the same subject is repeated.

 NOTE   Do not confuse a compound sentence with a simple sentence that has either compound subjects or compound verbs.

EXAMPLES   **We studied** architecture **and went** to the museum.
[simple sentence with a compound verb]
We studied architecture, **and we went** to the museum.
[compound sentence that has two simple sentences joined by *and*]

EXERCISE 15   Identifying Simple Sentences and Compound Sentences

Identify each of the following sentences as simple or compound. On the line before each sentence, write *simp.* for *simple* or *comp.* for *compound.*

EX. _comp._ 1. Anita learned Spanish, and now she speaks it all the time.

_____ 1. Theo walked home and took a nap.

_____ 2. Yolanda loves drama class, yet she sometimes forgets her lines.

_____ 3. Lemons smell sweet and taste sour.

_____ 4. Mikhail and Eric are neighbors and play tag football.

_____ 5. My grandfather plays the harmonica, and we sing along.

_____ 6. We recycle all of our glass, paper, and plastic.

_____ 7. Last night, we listened to a mariachi band on the River Walk.

_____ 8. Our breakfast tasted good, but it cost too much.

_____ 9. The sweater slid from the chair and fell on the floor.

_____ 10. Mandolins and dulcimers are traditional musical instruments.

_____ 11. The grocery clerk carefully placed the eggs on top of the bag.

_____ 12. Her eyes were tired, and her shoulders were sore.

_____ 13. Do you like rock, or do you prefer country music?

_____ 14. Raji and Julia went skating, or they went to the movies.

_____ 15. The Mississippi River rises each spring, but we were not prepared for the flood.

_____ 16. He enjoys laughter, yet he doesn't tell jokes.

_____ 17. Latoya made a cup of almond tea and drank it.

_____ 18. Janice and Fritz are collecting stamps, and they enjoy the hobby.

_____ 19. In 1996, the Summer Olympic Games were held in Atlanta, Georgia.

_____ 20. Have you ever been fishing in salt water?

_____ 21. My cousin Rafael is going hiking, and he invited me.

_____ 22. Abby and Martina built the birdhouse.

_____ 23. The Galapagos Islands in the Pacific Ocean are home to thousands of tortoises.

_____ 24. The room was cold, so I closed the window.

_____ 25. I wanted to ride my bike, but I was too tired.

KINDS OF SENTENCES

9p A *declarative sentence* makes a statement. It is always followed by a period.

EXAMPLE   That can is bulging at one end.

9q An *imperative sentence* gives a command or makes a request. It may be followed by a period or by an exclamation point.

EXAMPLES   Please take the mail when you go.
Stop littering!

The subject of a command or a request is always *you*, even if *you* never appears in the sentence. In such cases, *you* is called the **understood subject.**

EXAMPLES   **(You)** Please take the mail when you go.
(You) Stop littering!

9r An *interrogative sentence* asks a question. It is followed by a question mark.

EXAMPLE   When will you be home?

9s An *exclamatory sentence* shows excitement or expresses strong feeling. It is followed by an exclamation point.

EXAMPLE   What a terrific show we saw!

EXERCISE 16   Classifying Sentences by Purpose

Classify each of the following sentences by writing *dec.* for *declarative, imp.* for *imperative, inter.* for *interrogative,* or *excl.* for *exclamatory* on the line before the sentence. Then add the correct end mark of punctuation. [Note: There may be more than one way to punctuate a sentence correctly.]

EX. ____imp.____ 1. Please call me when you get home

_____ 1. What an exciting movie that was

_____ 2. Did you write a letter to your grandmother

_____ 3. Wait for me

_____ 4. The kitchen smelled of lemons and garlic

_____ 5. Bring your leaf collection to science class

_____ 6. Can you come over this weekend

_____ 7. What delicious spinach pasta

_____ 8. That speech was incredible

_____ 9. Winter seems to last longer every year

_____ 10. Stop talking

_____ 11. What is new, Fred

_____ 12. I have just been on a nature walk

_____ 13. Thea loved the building designed by Louis Sullivan

_____ 14. In my town we say "nonfat milk" instead of "skim"

_____ 15. In Quebec, Canada, many street signs are written in French

_____ 16. Do you know how cheese is made

_____ 17. Our car is very old, but it still runs fine

_____ 18. Lionel, take out the garbage

_____ 19. Before bed, do you prefer a warm glass of milk or a cold
one

_____ 20. The pig is escaping

EXERCISE 17   Writing T-shirt Messages

You work for a company that puts messages on T-shirts. Choose one of the
subjects below, and on your own paper, write four one- or two-sentence T-
shirt slogans about that subject. Use at least one of each kind of sentence.
Label the types of sentences you use.

EX.   1. favorite book
1. I got caught in _Charlotte's Web._ (declarative)

1. favorite movie   5. fishing

2. birthday celebration   6. cooking

3. athletic skill   7. favorite place

4. your pet animal   8. words of advice

CHAPTER REVIEW

A. Identifying Sentences

On the line before each group of words below, write *sent.* if the group is a sentence or *frag.* if the group is a sentence fragment. Add correct punctuation if the group of words is a sentence.

EX. _sent._ 1. The girls in the photograph are laughing

_____ 1. The delightful spring air

_____ 2. The fire crackled in the wood stove

_____ 3. Did you receive a basket of oranges

_____ 4. Please wait for me

_____ 5. Seashells on the beach

_____ 6. The little boy's mittens

_____ 7. Pasta with sauce steamed on our plates

_____ 8. Dark choppy waves

_____ 9. A fox flicked its red tail

_____ 10. Will you visit soon

B. Identifying Simple Subjects and Verbs

Underline the simple subjects once and the verbs twice in each of the sentences below.

EX. 1. On the table sits a cat.

1. After studying, Peter jogged through the park.

2. The ice-cold water took his breath away.

3. In the attic are boxes of photographs.

4. Before school, Tomás ate a bowl of oatmeal.

5. Sally is starting a postcard collection.

C. Identifying Simple Sentences and Compound Sentences

Identify each of the following sentences as simple or compound. On the line before each sentence, write *simp.* for *simple* or *comp.* for *compound.*

EX. _comp._ 1. Tasha and Tanya are twin sisters, and they share many interests.

_____ 1. Both girls enjoy baseball.

_____ 2. Tasha plays first base, and Tanya pitches.

_____ 3. After school, the sisters practice hard, but they laugh on the way home.

_____ 4. At home, Tasha washes their baseball uniforms, and Tanya sets the table.

_____ 5. On the radio one of their favorite songs is playing.

_____ 6. Lani calls and asks them about tomorrow's science test.

_____ 7. Tanya invites Lani over.

_____ 8. In the kitchen is a big table.

_____ 9. After dinner, the three girls can sit and study there.

_____ 10. At the end of the evening, all of the girls are ready for the science test.

D. Writing Sentences

Identify each of the word groups below as a subject or a predicate. Then use each group in a sentence. On your own paper, write your sentences with correct capitalization and punctuation. Use at least one sentence of each type, and label the sentence types. Use *dec.* for *declarative,* *imp.* for *imperative,* *inter.* for *interrogative,* or *excl.* for *exclamatory.*

EX. _pred._ 1. taste good with granola
  1. Do raspberries taste good with granola? (inter.)

_____ 1. a moth-eaten scarf

_____ 2. went to the party

_____ 3. we

_____ 4. the little boy from next door

_____ 5. behind the door was

_____ 6. Moshe

_____ 7. in the gym sat

_____ 8. canoed down the Colorado River

_____ 9. were my closest friends last year

_____ 10. will take the bus from Tennessee to Arkansas

_____ 11. in the mail arrived

_____ 12. published a poem

_____ 13. Dr. Seuss

_____ 14. the keyboard for the computer

_____ 15. saves many lives

NOUNS

10a A *noun* is a word that names a person, place, thing, or idea.

Persons	brother, Tom Ross, jury, sisters
Places	county, Hawaii, house, river
Things	boat, Korean War, dog, pencil
Ideas	courage, freedom, joy, peace

 NOTE Nouns that are made up of more than one word, like *Aki Sakamoto, Bunker Hill Monument, and living room,* are counted as one noun.

10b A *proper noun* names a particular person, place, thing, or idea. It always begins with a capital letter. A *common noun* names any one of a group of persons, places, things, or ideas. It is not capitalized.

Proper Nouns	Common Nouns
Aunt Mary	woman
India	country
Newsweek	magazine
Boston Bruins	team

 REFERENCE NOTE: For more about capitalizing proper nouns, see pages 227–235.

EXERCISE 1 Identifying Common and Proper Nouns

Underline the nouns in the following sentences. On the line before each sentence, write *comm.* for a *common noun* or *prop.* for a *proper noun.* If there is more than one noun in a sentence, separate your answers with a semicolon.

EX _*prop.; comm.*_ 1. Jeremy always takes the early bus.

_____ 1. Janell belongs to a group that studies the environment.

_____ 2. In the myth, Theseus killed the Minotaur.

_____ 3. The ancient Egyptians built pyramids in the desert.

_____ 4. Tariq comes from Bangladesh.

_____ 5. The Cherokee were forced to leave their traditional homelands.

_____ 6. Joseph told me about the African American celebration Kwanzaa.

_____ 7. I would not have wanted to run into that _Tyrannosaurus Rex!_

_____ 8. My family loves to celebrate Thanksgiving every year.

_____ 9. Today's paper printed a review of _Homeward Bound._

_____ 10. Senator Inouye stated his views during the interview.

EXERCISE 2   Substituting Proper Nouns for Common Nouns

On the lines after each sentence below, revise the sentence by substituting a proper noun for the common noun in italics. You may need to change or delete some of the other words in the sentence. You may also make up proper names.

EX. 1. My _grandmother_ teaches people how to use computers.

Clara Riordon teaches people how to use computers.

1. That famous basketball _player_ scored many points in his career. _____
   _____

2. That _river_ is famous in United States history. _____
   _____

3. My best _friend_ knows how to make me feel good about myself. _____
   _____

4. My favorite _author_ writes entertaining stories about young people. _____
   _____

5. We will study that foreign _country_ in social studies next year. _____
   _____

PRONOUNS

10c   A *pronoun* is a word used in place of a noun or more than one noun.

EXAMPLES   Call Palia and Maria, and tell Palia and Maria to go to the gym.
Call Palia and Maria, and tell **them** to go to the gym.

Singular	I, me, my, mine, you, your, yours, he, him, his, she, her, hers, it, its, myself, yourself, himself, herself, itself, this, that, everybody, someone
Plural	we, us, our, ours, you, your, yours, they, them, their, theirs, ourselves, yourselves, themselves, these, those

The word that a pronoun stands for is called its ***antecedent.***

EXAMPLES   Although the salad was two days old, **it** tasted fine. [*Salad* is the antecedent that *it* refers to.]
Javier has planned **his** next report. [*Javier* is the antecedent that *his* refers to.]

 NOTE   Some teachers prefer to call possessive pronouns (such as *my, your,* and *their*) adjectives. Follow your teacher's directions.

EXERCISE 3   Identifying Pronouns

Underline each pronoun in the following sentences. Some sentences contain more than one pronoun.

EX.   1. Ana was glad that she was wearing gloves.

1. The Urus used totora reeds to make those dwellings and boats.

2. Tim told us that this movie was so long that it bored him.

3. Nomads move around to find food for themselves and grazing land for their animals.

4. The coach smiled at her players as she held up their victory banner.

5. Before the actor went on stage, she went over her lines again.

6. We watched the American kangaroo rat hop about on its long hind legs.

7. Nuna's grandfather is teaching her and us how to walk on snowshoes.

8. After George Washington Carver studied the peanut, he knew that it would grow in southern soil.

9. The house is so old that it needs to have bathtubs installed.

10. Our kayakers train steadily for their Olympic white-water runs.

11. "Tennis is my favorite sport," said Terri as she swung at the ball.

12. Sylvia wondered, "Will I last until dinnertime without a snack?"

13. As Craig crossed the finish line, he turned in his wheelchair and waved to the cheering crowd.

14. In their experiment, researchers have found that they can grow plants in Israel's Negev Desert.

15. Chim said, "Paula, do you want to answer that question yourself, or shall I?"

EXERCISE 4   Using Pronouns in Narration

On your own paper, write five sentences about the cartoon below. Write what has happened, what you think will happen next, or what the dog might be saying. In each sentence, use a pronoun. Try to use a variety of pronouns in your sentences. Underline each pronoun, and draw brackets around each pronoun's antecedent.

EX.   [Weederman] is telling <u>his</u> master that <u>he</u> can't get the slippers because <u>he</u> is napping.

Mr. Boffo reprinted by permission: Tribune Media Services.

ADJECTIVES

10d An *adjective* is a word that modifies a noun or a pronoun.

To *modify* a word means to describe the word or to make its meaning more definite. An adjective modifies a noun or a pronoun by telling *what kind*, *which one*, *how much*, or *how many*.

EXAMPLES   Rita went on a **long** journey. [The adjective *long* tells *what kind* of journey.]

I need to wash **my yellow** sweater. [The adjectives *my* and *yellow* tell *which* sweater.]

It rained for **forty** days and nights. [The adjective *forty* tells *how many* days and nights.]

 NOTE   Some teachers prefer to call possessive pronouns (such as *my*, *your*, and *their*) adjectives. Follow your teacher's directions.

Adjectives usually come before the words they modify. Sometimes, however, an adjective comes after the word it modifies.

EXAMPLE   The grass was **brown.** [The adjective *brown* modifies *grass.*]

 NOTE   The adjectives *a*, *an*, and *the* are called **articles**.

EXERCISE 5   Identifying Adjectives

In the following sentences, draw one line under the adjectives and two lines under the noun or pronoun each adjective modifies. Do not include the articles *a*, *an*, and *the*.

EX.   1. The <u>hungry</u> <u>giraffe</u> peered over the <u>leafy</u> <u>treetops</u>.

1. The driest area in the world is a desert in Chile.

2. Put on the red jacket, grab the warmest scarf, and let's go!

3. Would you make a jelly sandwich for my lunch?

4. I have not yet reached the third level of the newest game!

5. Opossums in New Zealand have big eyes, pink noses, and brushy tails.

6. The house was cold and dark when we arrived.

7. In the story, a space traveler crosses a time dimension and lands in a new world.

8. The weather forecaster says that the summer will be long and hot.

9. The strong winds reached fifty miles an hour last night.

10. The bright, frisky cat weighs seven pounds.

11. Sylvia Earle explored deep waters to study sea life.

12. Scott and I are going to make a raisin cake for the class party.

13. Cara made green beans and grilled tomatoes for supper.

14. Steve made a colorful diagram of the taproot system of a carrot plant.

15. Farmers in Mali often work on rugged mountainsides to plant their crops.

EXERCISE 6   Writing Adjectives for a Story

Complete the story below by adding an appropriate adjective for each blank. Do not use the same adjective twice. Write your adjectives on your own paper.

EX.   [1] This is an _(what kind?)_ story about a rabbit and a turtle.
   1. amusing

The Hare and the Tortoise: A Fable Retold

[1] One _(what kind?)_ day in a(n) _(what kind?)_ forest _(how many?)_ years ago, there lived a rabbit and a turtle. [2] The rabbit, quick on its feet, knew that it was _(what kind?)_ than the turtle, who always took its time. [3] Yet, the _(what kind?)_ turtle challenged the rabbit to a race. [4] The _(what kind?)_ rabbit quickly agreed. [5] As soon as the _(what kind?)_ race began, the rabbit took the lead. [6] A _(how much?)_ way ahead of the turtle, the rabbit decided to take a _(what kind?)_ nap. [7] The turtle just kept plodding along the _(which one?)_ path. [8] Eventually the turtle reached the _(what kind?)_ line. [9] When the _(what kind?)_ rabbit woke up, it knew that it was in trouble! [10] The rabbit raced to the finish line, only to find the _(what kind?)_ turtle waiting there.

PROPER AND DEMONSTRATIVE ADJECTIVES

10e **A proper adjective is formed from a proper noun and begins with a capital letter.**

Proper Nouns	Proper Adjectives
Siberia	Siberian husky
Persia	Persian Gulf
a trip to Greece	a Greek island
a street in Chicago	the Chicago skyline

 REFERENCE NOTE: For more about capitalizing proper adjectives, see page 237.

10f *This, that, these,* **and** *those* **can be used both as adjectives and as pronouns. When they modify a noun, they are called** *demonstrative adjectives.* **When they are used alone, they are called** *demonstrative pronouns.*

ADJECTIVE   Take **these** eggs to Mr. Wong.
PRONOUN   Take **these** to Mr. Wong.

EXERCISE 7   Finding Common and Proper Adjectives

In the paragraph below, underline the common adjectives once and the proper adjectives twice. Do not include the articles *a, an,* and *the.*

EX. [1] Bobbi told me that <u>rice</u> cakes are often served at <u><u>Korean</u></u> celebrations.

[1] Many cultures have unique foods that are part of the American menu. [2] Fruit soup, for example, is a Chinese dessert. [3] Several Mexican foods contain black beans and hot spices. [4] Blue cornmeal has long been used in Hopi dishes. [5] Some Japanese recipes use powdered ginger and sticky rice.

EXERCISE 8   Changing Proper Nouns into Proper Adjectives

Change each proper noun below into a proper adjective. Then on your own paper, write ten sentences using each of the proper adjectives. [Note: Some proper nouns do not change spelling when they are used as proper adjectives.]

EX.   1. France
         1. French—I want to visit several French castles on my trip.

1. Britain   5. Spain   9. Congress

2. China   6. England   10. Alps

3. Alaska   7. Oklahoma

4. Germany   8: Jerusalem

EXERCISE 9   Identifying Demonstrative Adjectives and Pronouns

In the sentences below, underline all the demonstrative adjectives once and all the demonstrative pronouns twice.

EX.   1. Give this book to Julie, and give those to Samuel.

1. Those old shoes are Gina's favorites.

2. This is the last class before vacation.

3. Take that sample to the biology lab, and put these in the freezer.

4. Those who already have tickets should stand in this line.

5. Are these clocks really from Switzerland?

6. That cardinal usually comes to this bird feeder.

7. Is this an example of origami, traditional Japanese paper folding?

8. Stack this horseshoe with those in the corner.

9. Is this the Big Dipper, or is that?

10. This jacket looks like those worn in Finland.

11. That satellite will circle the earth for many years.

12. Was that pottery made by the Anasazi?

13. Let's include these patches in the quilt, but not those.

14. If this is the correct answer, what is that?

15. Didn't Wilma Rudolph break that record in the 1960s?

CHAPTER REVIEW

A. Identifying Nouns, Pronouns, and Adjectives

Identify each italicized word in the sentences below. On the line before each sentence, write *comm.* for *common noun*, *prop.* for *proper noun*, *pron.* for *pronoun*, or *adj.* for *adjective*. Separate your answers with a semicolon.

EX. _____comm.; adj._____ 1. Harriet stuffed the *books* in her *school* backpack.

_____ 1. A *great* fire occurred in *Chicago* in October of 1871.

_____ 2. Hans said that *he* would look after the *stray* dog.

_____ 3. Tabouli salad, made with fresh *vegetables*, is a favorite *Lebanese* dish.

_____ 4. As the crowd cheered, John raised *his* arms in *victory*.

_____ 5. Though the *Seminoles* used dugout canoes in the past, today *they* use airboats.

_____ 6. Lien has chosen *these* lanterns for the *festival*.

_____ 7. The guide raised the telescope to *her* eye, then put *it* away.

_____ 8. *Mexican* soldiers captured the *Alamo* in 1836.

_____ 9. Grady is reading an *exciting tale* about a Vietnamese family.

_____ 10. Having completed *her first* draft, Krista is now working on the *final* report.

B. Writing Sentences Using Nouns, Pronouns, and Adjectives

For the following items, write ten sentences, using the parts of speech given. In each sentence, underline the word that is the listed part of speech.

EX. 1. adjective
    Four feet of snow fell in the mountains last night.

1. a proper noun

_____

2. an adjective that tells *which one*

_____

3. a pronoun

_____

4. an adjective that tells *what kind*

_____

5. a common noun

_____

6. a demonstrative pronoun

_____

7. an adjective that tells *how many*

_____

8. a common noun

_____

9. a pronoun

_____

10. an adjective that tells *what kind*

_____

C.   Writing a Postcard

Your pen pal in another country has asked you about the favorite pastimes of young people in your country. Write a postcard to describe some of the things you do that you think your pen pal would like to hear about. On your own paper, write at least five sentences for your postcard. Underline and label at least two nouns, two pronouns, and two adjectives.

EX.

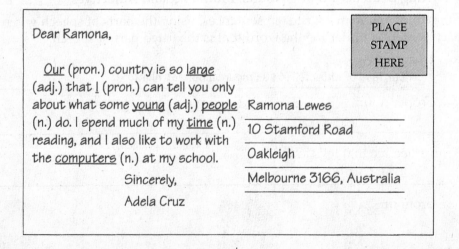

Dear Ramona,

    Our (pron.) country is so large (adj.) that I (pron.) can tell you only about what some young (adj.) people (n.) do. I spend much of my time (n.) reading, and I also like to work with the computers (n.) at my school.

                    Sincerely,

                    Adela Cruz

PLACE
STAMP
HERE

Ramona Lewes

10 Stamford Road

Oakleigh

Melbourne 3166, Australia

THE VERB

11a   A *verb* is a word that expresses an action or a state of being.

Every sentence has a verb. The verb says something about the subject.

EXAMPLES   The parakeet **flew** through the room.[action]
Are the Castros from Puerto Rico?[state of being]

   REFERENCE NOTE: For more about subjects and verbs, see pages 83–93.

11b   An *action verb* is a verb that expresses physical or mental action.

EXAMPLES   I **am washing** the dishes.
Harriet **memorized** most of her lines that weekend.

EXERCISE 1   Identifying Action Verbs

The subject is italicized in each of the following sentences. Underline the action verb that tells what the subject does.

EX.   1. *Jean* <u>swam</u> across the Nile River.

1. The *librarian* showed us the reference section.

2. In other words, *I* like Chinese food.

3. *We* ran on the track during gym class.

4. In December, postal *workers* deliver many packages.

5. My *stomach* ached.

6. On my birthday, *I* go to the bowling alley.

7. *Myra* jumped over the old brown dog.

8. Queen *bees* hibernate in winter.

9. *We* measured the plank four times.

10. *Ms. Merlot* dropped her change purse.

11. *Many* of the continents touch each other.

12. After January, *Jody* was not a member of the CD and tape club.

13. *I* went to my room after supper.

14. The *audience* stood during the encore.

15. *I* painted the living room.

16. *Toby* presented a new book to the library.

17. *She* rode towards the woods.

18. *Chester* brushes his hair often.

19. *Lynn* kicked three goals on Saturday.

20. *Mother* bought a new computer for us.

EXERCISE 2   Writing Sentences with Action Verbs

Choose five verbs from the group below. Use each verb to write a sentence. You may use different tenses of the verb. Underline the verbs in your sentences.

EX.   write
   1. *Grigor wrote a letter to his grandfather in Vladivostok.*

remember	laugh	enjoy
watch	remove	open
carry	construct	sing
sweep	kick	believe

1. _____

   _____

2. _____

   _____

3. _____

   _____

4. _____

   _____

5. _____

   _____

TRANSITIVE AND INTRANSITIVE VERBS

A *transitive verb* is an action verb that expresses an action directed toward a person, place, or thing.

11c **Transitive verbs show an action that passes from the doer—the subject—to the receiver—the *object*.**

EXAMPLES   Trapdoor spiders **dig** burrows. [The action of *dig* is directed toward *burrows*.]
We **saw** the bonfire last Fourth of July. [The action of *saw* is directed toward *bonfire*.]

11d **An *intransitive verb* does not pass action to a receiver or an object. It simply expresses an action or tells something about the subject.**

EXAMPLES   The speaker **coughed.**
The giant **stepped** over the house.

Some verbs may be either transitive or intransitive, depending on how they are used in a sentence.

TRANSITIVE   Last week Justin **ran** a four-minute mile.
INTRANSITIVE   Justin **runs** faster than anyone else on his team.

EXERCISE 3   Identifying Transitive and Intransitive Verbs

In the following sentences, identify each italicized verb. Write *trans.* for *transitive* or *intr.* for *intransitive* on the line before the sentence.

EX. _trans._ 1. Giraffes *eat* leafy greens.

_____ 1. I *saw* Jill's little sister on the way to school.

_____ 2. The circus *comes* to town next month.

_____ 3. I just *saw* a frog catch a bug!

_____ 4. The runners *jumped* over the largest puddles.

_____ 5. Phil *let* us use his telescope.

_____ 6. The person sitting on the park bench *knitted* slippers.

_____ 7. Jackie *sang* for us.

_____ 8. Reggie *mailed* the package last Tuesday.

_____ 9. I *walked* with a tour group this afternoon.

_____ 10. Sammie *collects* seashells by the dozen.

_____ 11. Will Grandpa *give* us each gloves again?

_____ 12. Sheila *sent* a thank-you note to Atu.

_____ 13. Please *buy* some milk on your way home.

_____ 14. The sea gulls *soared* across the sky.

_____ 15. Bill *will sing* with Harry at tomorrow's concert.

EXERCISE 4   Writing Sentences with Transitive and Intransitive Verbs

It is a beautiful, sunny day at the beach. Some children are playing in the sand and swimming. Others are flying kites and playing ball.

Write ten sentences describing these children and their activities. In your sentences, use five of the following verbs in two sentences each, once as a transitive verb and once as an intransitive verb. You may use different tenses of the verbs.

play	stop	run
throw	splash	move
win	fly	practice
call	learn	watch

EX. 1. Three girls played kickball.

       Two boys played with some seaweed.

1. _____

   _____

2. _____

   _____

3. _____

   _____

4. _____

   _____

5. _____

   _____

LINKING VERBS

11e A *linking verb* links, or connects, the subject with a noun, a pronoun, or an adjective in the predicate. In some cases, the verb *be* is not followed by a noun, a pronoun, or an adjective. *Be* can express a state of being without having a complement.

EXAMPLES   Fiji **is** an island nation. [The verb *is* connects the noun *nation* with the subject *Fiji*.]

Vergie **will be** better after she has rested. [The verb *will be* connects the adjective *better* with the subject *Vergie*.]

Lemuel **seems** tired today. [The verb *seems* connects the adjective *tired* with the subject *Lemuel*.]

This **can**not **be**! [The verb *can be* has no complement; it expresses a state of being about the subject *This*.]

Linking Verbs Formed from the Verb *Be*		
am	has been	may be
is	have been	might be
are	had been	can be
was	will be	should be
were	shall be	would have been

Other Linking Verbs					
appear	become	feel	grow	look	remain
seem	smell	sound	stay	taste	turn

Some verbs may be either action verbs or linking verbs, depending on how they are used.

ACTION   We carefully **tasted** the steaming chili.
LINKING   The milk **tasted** fresh. [The verb *tasted* links *fresh* with the subject *milk*.]
ACTION   Dad **turned** to the grocery clerk.
LINKING   Inez just **turned** thirteen. [The verb *turned* links *thirteen* with the subject *Inez*.]

EXERCISE 5   Identifying Linking Verbs

Underline the linking verb in each of the sentences below.

EX.   1.   We <u>have been</u> tired before, but never this tired.

1.   Lani felt fine after the race.

2.   We stayed warm by the fire.

3.   With these crystals in the solution, the liquid turned green.

4.   Clementine looks much better now.

5.   This sushi tastes wonderful.

6.   Those apples are yours, Bobby.

7.   You may be right about the time.

8.   My horse may be a palomino.

9.   Margo, your painting looks great!

10.   The road repair crew seemed exhausted.

11.   After a big breakfast I feel excitement about the new day.

12.   Please remain in your seats during the test.

13.   The smell of Jane's new perfume was a surprise to most of us.

14.   That may be my parents in the car in front of your house.

15.   You can be Red Riding Hood in our skit.

EXERCISE 6   Identifying Linking Verbs and Action Verbs

Underline the verb in each of the sentences below. On the line before each sentence, write *l.v.* if the verb is a linking verb or *a.v.* if it is an action verb.

EX.   _l.v._   1.   Sarah, a poet, <u>was</u> a romantic.

_____   1.   The monsters in the movie seemed real.

_____   2.   I felt the soft cloth.

_____   3.   Do you feel tired yet?

_____   4.   Tamisha smelled smoke in the hall.

_____   5.   You look beautiful in that dress.

HELPING VERBS

11f A *helping verb (auxiliary verb)* **helps the main verb to express an action or a state of being.**

EXAMPLES **can** help   **will** climb   **should have been** swept

Together the main verb and its helping verb or verbs are called a *verb phrase.*

EXAMPLES **Can** everyone **help** decorate the hall?
Matt and Sarah **will climb** that mountain tomorrow.
The front steps **should have been swept** by now.

Helping Verbs					
am	were	have	did	can	will
is	be	had	may	could	would
are	been	do	might	shall	
was	has	does	must	should	

Sometimes a verb phrase is interrupted by another part of speech.

EXAMPLES You **would** never **speak** so rudely. [The verb phrase *would speak* is interrupted by the adverb *never.*]
We **must**n't **wait** another day. [The verb phrase *must wait* is interrupted by the adverb *not* in the form of the contraction *–n't.*]
Have you **practiced** that new dance? [The verb phrase *Have practiced* is interrupted by the subject *you.*]

 The adverb *not* is never part of a verb phrase.

EXERCISE 7   Identifying Verb Phrases and Helping Verbs

Underline each verb phrase in the following paragraph. Draw a second line under all helping verbs.

EX. [1] Kwanzaa <u>was created</u> as an American holiday in 1966.

[1] Kwanzaa is based on African traditions. [2] During Kwanzaa,

African Americans will celebrate their African heritage, their
families, and their communities. [3] The holiday will begin on
December 26 and will last for seven days. [4] Each of the seven days
is given a special meaning. [5] I am spending the first day, *Umoja*, or
unity day, at Sylvan's house. [6] I am bringing slides and pictures of
my family. [7] At Sylvan's house we will light one of the seven
candles on the *kinara*, or candleholder. [8] Each day we may give a
small gift to someone. [9] However, we may not open the gifts until
the last day of Kwanzaa. [10] On the last day, January 1, we will feast
on African American foods.

EXERCISE 8   Using Helping Verbs in Sentences

On your own paper, write complete sentences using helping verbs. Use each
of the word groups below as the subject of your sentence. Make some of the
sentences questions. Then underline the verb phrase in each sentence.

EX.   my friends
   1. Soon my friends <u>will take</u> me home.

1. the student council
2. Celine and her father
3. Jones & Jones Co.
4. the five of them
5. the principal
6. you and I
7. Bill and Sung
8. the clowns in the circus
9. the rest of the family
10. Zelda, Scott, and Gerald

11. the city
12. the entrance to the park
13. several teams
14. my English paper
15. the heavy rain
16. the aerobics class
17. some people
18. the good news
19. seat belts
20. an important issue

THE ADVERB

11g   An *adverb* is a word that modifies a verb, an adjective, or another adverb.

An adverb answers the following questions.

Where?	How often?	To what extent?
When?	*or*	*or*
How?	How long?	How much?

EXAMPLES   The snake **swiftly** slithered away. [*Swiftly* is an adverb modifying the verb *slithered*; it tells *how.*]

We were playing the music **quite loudly.** [*Quite* is an adverb modifying the adverb *loudly*; it tells *to what extent. Loudly* is an adverb modifying the verb *were playing*; it tells *how.*]

My suitcase is **rather** heavy. [*Rather* is an adverb modifying the adjective *heavy*; it tells *to what extent.*]

Now we can see **outside.** [*Now* is an adverb modifying the verb *can see*; it tells *when. Outside* is an adverb modifying the verb *can see*; it tells *where.*]

The word *not* is an adverb. When *not* is part of a contraction like *hadn't*, the *–n't* is an adverb.

EXAMPLES   Have**n't** you studied long enough?
Daniel is**n't** the only one working hard.

11h   Adverbs may appear at various places in a sentence. Adverbs may come before, after, or between the words they modify.

EXAMPLES   **Later** the salmon will swim upstream. [*Later* comes before *will swim*, the verb it modifies.]

The salmon will **later** swim upstream. [*Later* comes between *will* and *swim*, the verb it modifies.]

The salmon will swim upstream **later.** [*Later* comes after *will swim*, the verb it modifies.]

Avoid using *very, too,* and *so* in your writing. These adverbs have lost much of their force because they have been used too much.

EXAMPLES   We were very tired after the track meet.
We were **extremely** tired after the track meet.

EXERCISE 9   Identifying Adverbs and the Words They Modify

Underline the adverbs in the sentences below. Draw an arrow to the word or words that each adverb modifies. [Note: A sentence may contain more than one adverb.]

EX.   1. The breeze was blowing gently.

1. Do you act badly when you are angry?

2. The biscuits were almost ready when Sven got home.

3. Our conversation went surprisingly well.

4. Millie made change quickly and always said, "Thank you."

5. The surprised and amused children grinned broadly.

6. Do you notice her unusually blue eyes?

7. Mike played his trumpet quietly in the evenings.

8. Greedily, the hungry chipmunk grabbed the nut.

9. It was sunny and extremely hot at the beach today.

10. Francie plays hide-and-seek quite well.

EXERCISE 10   Writing Appropriate Adverbs

For each blank in the sentences below, write an adverb that answers the question in parentheses. Do not use *very, too,* and *so.*

EX.   1. The men laughed ___loudly___ . (how?)

1. Our boat sailed _____ . (when?)

2. The vinegar made the salad taste_____ sour. (to what extent?)

3. I was _____ angry, and then I laughed. (how much?)

4. On Tuesdays, the bakery _____ makes bread. (how often?)

5. I walked _____ across the quiet room. (how?)

6. Where I was born in Mexico, the sun shines_____ . (how often?)

7. Susie ran her fingers_____ across the harp's strings. (how?)

8. When the baby is cranky, she cries _____. (how much?)

9. Will you choose your paintbrush _____? (when?)

10. We found an old key_____ . (where?)

THE PREPOSITION

11i A *preposition* is a word that shows the relationship between a noun or a pronoun and some other word in the sentence.

Commonly Used Prepositions				
aboard	at	down	off	under
about	before	during	on	underneath
above	behind	except	over	until
across	below	for	past	up
after	beneath	from	since	upon
against	beside	in	through	with
along	between	into	throughout	within
among	beyond	like	to	without
around	by	of	toward	

EXAMPLES   Put the needle **through** the cloth. [The preposition *through* shows the relationship of *put* to *cloth*.]

The tiny tree **beside** you is fifty years old. [The preposition *beside* shows the relationship of *you* to *tree*.]

NOTE   Some prepositions are made up of more than one word. These are called *compound prepositions*.

Compound Prepositions		
according to	in addition to	next to
because of	in front of	on account of
aside from	instead of	prior to

EXAMPLES   **In place of** walnuts I used pecans.

Sal was late **because of** the traffic problem.

EXERCISE 11   Identifying Prepositions

For the following sentences, underline each preposition. Some sentences may contain more than one preposition.

EX.   1.   <u>In</u> our house we eat many kinds <u>of</u> cereal.

1.   I ran for the porch through a shower of snowballs.

2.   A large group of children chased after the kite.

3.   The park near Mario's building is his favorite.

4.   After supper we sat around the campfire telling stories.

5.   Lem brought his art supplies with him.

6.   Gina often leaps over the old fence instead of using the gate.

7.   After the storm I thought of a great weather experiment.

8.   The elephant reached with its trunk for the peanuts.

9.   Tammy and Erica usually sit next to each other.

10.   I did some baking for the holiday.

11.   Marshall spoke about the new books.

12.   Because of Tawanda's illness, the math club canceled its meeting.

13.   Do not go off the path!

14.   In front of the exercise gym is a large parking garage.

15.   "Get down from there!" Doug yelled at our Saint Bernard puppy.

EXERCISE 12   Writing Notes with Prepositions

You and your family are planning a trip across your home state. On your own paper, make some notes to help you plan your route. Think about any special historical sights or points of interest you might want to visit on the trip. In your notes, use at least ten different prepositions and underline each preposition you use.

EX.   We will start our trip <u>from</u> Houston <u>on</u> June sixth and drive <u>to</u> San Antonio the first day.

THE PREPOSITIONAL PHRASE

11j A *prepositional phrase* is a group of words consisting of a preposition, a noun or pronoun that serves as the object of the preposition, and any modifiers of that object.

EXAMPLES   Luisa dragged the mattress **across the floor.** [The preposition *across* relates its object, *floor*, to *dragged*. The article *the* modifies *floor*.]

The box **of old photographs** was found this week. [The preposition *of* relates its object, *photographs*, to *box*. The adjective *old* modifies *photographs*.]

A preposition may have more than one object.

EXAMPLE   Derek collected cans **of soups and fruits.** [The preposition *of* relates its objects, *soups* and *fruits*, to *cans*.]

 REFERENCE NOTE: For more about prepositional phrases, see Chapter 12.

EXERCISE 13   Identifying Prepositions and Their Objects

In the sentences below, underline the prepositions and circle their objects.

EX.   1.   She stopped working after (dinner).

1.   Lisa's father made gumbo for the class Valentine's Day party.

2.   A thoughtful gift is welcome among friends.

3.   Did you sit beside Clem or Otto?

4.   The striped beach ball bounced over the wall.

5.   Frightened, the parakeet flew toward the window.

6.   She rode her bicycle to Jean's house and the park.

7.   I like my peanut butter with bananas.

8.   Our teapot was chipped in its box.

9.   Of all the girls, only Rebecca remembered the flan recipe.

10.   Mr. Mendez spoke clearly into the microphone.

Some words may be used as prepositions or as adverbs. Remember that a preposition always has an object. An adverb never does. If you can't tell whether a word is used as an adverb or a preposition, look for an object.

PREPOSITION	The hotel is **below** the falls. [*Falls* is the object of the preposition *below*.]
ADVERB	The hotel is **below**. [no object]
PREPOSITION	We haven't been there **since** Thanksgiving. [*Thanksgiving* is the object of the preposition *since*.]
ADVERB	We haven't been there **since**. [no object]

EXERCISE 14 Writing Sentences with Prepositions and Adverbs

Choose five words from the list below. On the lines provided, write two sentences for each word. In one sentence use the word as an adverb. In another sentence use the word as a preposition.

EX. off

1. Tom pulled his boots off.

   Tom picked up his boots off the floor.

above	under	down
around	on	before
along	in	across

1. _____

   _____

2. _____

   _____

3. _____

   _____

4. _____

   _____

5. _____

   _____

REVIEW EXERCISE

A. Identifying Action Verbs and Linking Verbs

Underline the verb or verb phrase in each of the sentences below. Then on the line before each sentence, identify each verb by writing *l.v.* for *linking verb* or *a.v.* for *action verb*. If the verb is a linking verb, circle the two words that it connects.

EX. ___a.v.___ 1. This recipe <u>calls</u> for honey instead of sugar.

    ___l.v.___ 2. The (animal) under that leaf <u>is</u> a (toad).

_____ 1. Do you like garlic as a seasoning?

_____ 2. Two tiny kittens lay in Connie's lap.

_____ 3. One of the hammers was new.

_____ 4. Some people with long names have nicknames.

_____ 5. Mandy studied Frisian, a language of the Netherlands.

_____ 6. Marge and Irene took turns on the diving board.

_____ 7. Blackberries in breakfast muffins taste very good.

_____ 8. The waves broke on the rocks at high tide.

_____ 9. That church's clock strikes on the hour.

_____ 10. You can be a leader for the group.

B. Identifying Adverbs and Prepositions

Identify the italicized word in each of the following sentences as either an adverb or a preposition. On the line before each sentence, write *adv.* for *adverb*, or *prep.* for *preposition*. Underline the object of each preposition.

EX. ___prep.___ 1. Isaiah stuck his hands *into* the gooey <u>mud</u>.

_____ 1. Two loggers raced *up* two trees.

_____ 2. Throw the ball *up*, and then hit it.

_____ 3. Excuse me. May I get *by*?

_____ 4. Will you get that book *down* for me, please?

_____ 5. I walked *down* the stairs.

_____ 6. *On* the way here we saw Regina.

_____ 7. After lunch Joe and Joanne stayed *around*.

_____ 8. *Above* the door someone had hung a horseshoe.

_____ 9. You are *among* friends.

_____ 10. Look *up*!

C.   Identifying Transitive Verbs and Intransitive Verbs

Underline the verb or verb phrase in each sentence below. Then on the line before the sentence, identify the verb by writing *trans.* for *transitive* or *intr.* for *intransitive*.

EX. _intr._   1. Can you come to my party?

_____ 1. I have invited five other friends of mine.

_____ 2. We will be eating some great things.

_____ 3. I planned some games with my mother.

_____ 4. A magician may perform for us, too.

_____ 5. You will come, won't you?

D.   Writing a Paragraph

Finish the paragraph below by putting a prepositional phrase in each blank. Use the list of prepositions below to create your prepositional phrases.

EX.   below
[1] The sun sank __below the horizon__ .

over	in	behind	next to	out of
on	into	in addition to	around	to
after	of	onto	with	aside from

[1] The sunset _____ was beautiful. [2] Strange

colors reflected _____ . [3] My friends and I shut our

eyes and shouted _____ . [4] Sea gulls squawked and flew

_____ . [5] We found pieces _____ .

[6] We left a million footprints _____. [7] The sand got

_____ . [8] Waves splashed _____ .

[9] Finally the sun went down _____ .

[10] _____ it was time to go back home.

CONJUNCTIONS AND INTERJECTIONS

11k   A *conjunction* is a word that joins words or groups of words.

The most common conjunctions are the *coordinating conjunctions.*

Coordinating Conjunctions
and   but   for   nor   or   so   yet

Conjunctions may join words, phrases, or clauses.

WORDS   rocks **and** pebbles   tapes **or** discs
         sadder **but** wiser   knives, forks, **and** spoons

PHRASES   see the shuttle **or** visit the theme park
          during the concert **and** before the solo
          after lunch **but** before dinner

CLAUSES   We ran for the canoe, **but** it was already afloat.
          Saburo jogged slowly home, **for** he was enjoying the day.

   REFERENCE NOTE: For information on using commas in a
series of words, see page 243. For information on using commas
to join clauses, see page 245.

EXERCISE 15   Identifying Conjunctions

Underline the conjunction in each of the following sentences. [Note: A
sentence may contain more than one conjunction.]

EX.   1. Jenny <u>or</u> I will call you.

1. Tanya's eyes were sparkling, for she was very happy.

2. No one I know but Lu has ever been to that museum.

3. I'll play something by Beethoven or by the Beatles.

4. Guess who saw Lisa and me at the convenience store?

5. It's too late to catch the train, so I will take the next bus.

6. Bill said he would do that job, yet he has not done it.

7. We're getting another car, for our old one has been giving us
   trouble.

8. Do you prefer wool or cotton socks?

9. Jen and Jim are twins, aren't they?

10. Chip had saved a seat, yet Dale was already seated.

11. We put the laundry in the dryer and deposited three quarters.

12. Light shined through the windows and onto the table.

13. Paint it red or pink, and it will match the curtains.

14. Trina didn't know it, but she had earned the highest marks.

15. We looked for the missing glove but could not find it.

---

111   An *interjection* is a word used to express emotion.

An interjection has no grammatical relationship to the rest of the sentence. Usually an interjection is followed by an exclamation point. Sometimes an interjection is set off by a comma. Some common interjections are *oh, hooray, goodness, ouch,* and *aha.*

EXAMPLES   **Wow!** Did you see that car?   **Oh,** did you call me?
            Well, we expected better seats.   **Rats!** I forgot my book.

EXERCISE 16 Writing Interjections

On the lines below, write interjections to complete the sentences.

EX.   1. ___Yipes___ , I have no cash!

1. _____ , I dropped it!

2. _____ , I will do that for you.

3. _____ ! I'm stuck!

4. _____ ! Watch where you're going!

5. _____ ! That's my foot you stepped on.

6. _____ ! Something in the oven is burning!

7. _____ , Marie! Be careful of the icy sidewalk!

8. _____ , we didn't win this time.

9. _____ , you'll love the hayride.

10. _____ ! The water is coming in everywhere!

DETERMINING PARTS OF SPEECH

> **11m** **You can't tell what part of speech a word is until you know how it is used in a particular sentence. A word may be used in different ways.**
>
> | | |
> |---|---|
> | VERB | Did you **exercise** today? |
> | NOUN | Did you finish the **exercise** today? |
> | | |
> | ADVERB | The hare was **behind.** |
> | PREPOSITION | The hare was **behind** the turtle. |
> | | |
> | NOUN | The wishing **well** glittered with pennies. |
> | ADJECTIVE | Fred is not feeling **well.** |
> | INTERJECTION | **Well,** we better get started. |

EXERCISE 17   Identifying Parts of Speech

Identify the part of speech of each italicized word in the following sentences. On the line before each sentence, write *adv.* for *adverb, conj.* for *conjunction, intj.* for *interjection, prep.* for *preposition, v.* for *verb, n.* for *noun, pron.* for *pronoun,* or *adj.* for *adjective.*

EX. _*n.; adv.*_ 1. They both played *football well.*

_____ 1. Tie-dyeing *shirts* can be *quite* fun.

_____ 2. Those tall *rubber* boots *are called* Wellingtons.

_____ 3. The *blue* sky was full *of* autumn birds.

_____ 4. Bill, my best friend, took me *to* the *football* game.

_____ 5. The *ball* was made of *gray* plastic.

_____ 6. Aminée *always* uses *blue* in her paintings.

_____ 7. *Boy,* I'd love a *mango* pie for dessert.

_____ 8. I need another pen, *for* mine is *not* working.

_____ 9. Don't call me, *but* send me a *note.*

_____ 10. Inez *noted* that the *boys* helped with the dishes.

EXERCISE 18   Writing Sentences Using Words
as Different Parts of Speech

Choose ten words from the list below and write two sentences for each word. In each sentence use the word as a different part of speech. Underline the word that you use.

bench	up	dress	paper	watch
over	for	well	plant	record
jump	near	on	drive	note

EX.   help

1.   Parents <u>help</u> children with their homework.
      <u>Help</u>! I need someone!

1.   _____

      _____

2.   _____

      _____

3.   _____

      _____

4.   _____

      _____

5.   _____

      _____

6.   _____

      _____

7.   _____

      _____

8.   _____

      _____

9.   _____

      _____

10. _____

      _____

CHAPTER REVIEW

A. Identifying Verbs, Adverbs, Prepositions, Conjunctions, and Interjections

Identify the part of speech of each italicized word in the sentences below. On the line before each sentence, write *adv.* for *adverb, conj.* for *conjunction, intj.* for *interjection, prep.* for *preposition,* or *v.* for *verb.*

EX. __*prep.*__ 1. We wrote answers *on* the line before each sentence.

_____ 1. The squirrel *ran* away.

_____ 2. After it rains, the sunset is often *beautifully* colored.

_____ 3. Beside me lay a giant stuffed giraffe *and* a striped umbrella.

_____ 4. The flooding had receded *by* Tuesday.

_____ 5. Both he *and* I brought salads.

_____ 6. *Hey!* Change into your costume quickly!

_____ 7. Darby broke the tuba *accidentally.*

_____ 8. Grandmother and Grandfather *waltzed* to the music.

_____ 9. We went to the theater but it was *already* full.

_____ 10. Min sneezed, coughed, *or* sniffled most of the night.

_____ 11. The surprised burglar broke *into* the police station.

_____ 12. "I don't think so, *no,*" she said.

_____ 13. Put the tortillas in the oven *soon!*

_____ 14. All of the children *except* one played instruments.

_____ 15. It was *almost* dark when the show was over.

_____ 16. You could hear the cheering *for* miles.

_____ 17. Cherie *dragged* the enormous log all the way home.

_____ 18. They all worked hard, *for* the teacher inspired them.

_____ 19. Please *examine* the enclosed information.

_____ 20. My cousins *in* New Mexico raise llamas.

B.   Writing Sentences Using Words as Different Parts of Speech

On your own paper, write ten sentences, using the following words as directed. Underline the word and give its part of speech after each sentence.

EX.   1.   Use *quite* as an adverb.

1.   Use *told* as a verb.
2.   Use *on* as a preposition.
3.   Use *and* as a conjunction.
4.   Use *smiled* as a verb.
5.   Use *on* as an adverb.
6.   Use *to* as a preposition.
7.   Use *yes* as an interjection.
8.   Use *or* as a conjunction.
9.   Use *discovered* as a verb.
10. Use *ouch* as an interjection.
11. Use *by* as a preposition.
12. Use *buy* as a verb.
13. Use *completely* as an adverb.
14. Use *over* as an adverb.
15. Use *over* as a preposition.

C.   Writing a Report

Your community youth club went on a field trip to the new Inner Earth Amusement Park. As club secretary, you have been asked to write a short report about the trip for the local newspaper. On your own paper, write at least ten sentences. Use at least one adverb, preposition, conjunction, and interjection. Underline and label each required part of speech.

EX.   Our youth group was <u>extremely</u> interested in caves, <u>so</u> we took a
         trip <u>to</u> the new Inner Earth Amusement Park.

PREPOSITIONAL PHRASES

> **12a** A *phrase* is a group of related words that is used as a single part of speech. A phrase does not contain both a subject and a verb.
>
> Phrases cannot stand alone. They are used with other words to make sentences.
>
> | PHRASES | at the pool | with brown fur |
> |---|---|---|
> | SENTENCES | Dad was still **at the pool.** | I saw a bear **with brown fur.** |
>
> **12b** A *prepositional phrase* is a group of words consisting of a preposition, a noun or pronoun that serves as the object of the preposition, and any modifiers of that object.
>
> A preposition shows the relationship of a noun or pronoun to another word in the sentence. The noun or pronoun that follows a preposition is called the *object of the preposition.*
>
> EXAMPLES   The pigeon **on the roof** was cooing.
> **During the concert** Pete began to applaud.
> Would you like another spoonful **of mashed potatoes?**
>
> A preposition may have more than one object.
>
> EXAMPLES   Felix cut the rope **for Lita** and **Kung.** [two objects]
> Alejandro saved his money **for a cell phone, a guitar,** and **a video game.** [three objects]
>
>   **REFERENCE NOTE:**   For a list of commonly used prepositions, see page 121.

EXERCISE 1   Identifying Prepositional Phrases and Their Objects

Underline the prepositional phrases in the following sentences. Circle the object or objects of each preposition.

EX.   1. We bought popcorn <u>at the (theater)</u>.

1.   The bareback riding at the Calgary Stampede is daring.

2.   They prepared brown rice and a salad for the banquet.

3.   The food served in the airport was unusually tasty.

4.   Before a tennis match, Sara drinks water.

5. The peanuts at the basketball game are the best anywhere.

6. Ivan likes munching on carrots and celery.

7. Stan sold pretzels along the parade route.

8. Our Fourth of July party by the river is always a success.

9. He took a break from work and ate lunch.

10. You can't bring soft drinks into the theater.

11. The restaurant in the museum was closed.

12. What a big basket of fruit and nuts that is!

13. Let's eat after the movie.

14. Mikey likes eating his cereal without any milk.

15. Everyone except Fran and me packed a lunch.

16. Throughout the circus tent, straw covered the ground.

17. Their apartment is above a Chinese restaurant, and the smells are great.

18. Between the fourth and fifth innings, Sam changed uniforms.

19. The trainer threw fish to the otters and seals.

20. How do astronauts fix their meals during space missions?

EXERCISE 2   Writing Appropriate Prepositional Phrases

Use the prepositions given to complete each sentence below with an appropriate prepositional phrase. Do not use the same preposition twice.

at   by   from   beside   for

EX.   1. Here is the book __from the library_____ .

1. The students sat quietly _____ .

2. Antonio forgot his jacket _____ .

3. The letter _____ never arrived.

4. She brought a gift _____ .

5. The chair _____ has a broken leg.

ADJECTIVE PHRASES

A prepositional phrase used as an adjective is called an *adjective phrase.*

12c An *adjective phrase* modifies a noun or a pronoun.

Adjective phrases follow the words they modify and answer the same questions that single-word adjectives answer.

> What kind?   Which one?
> How many?   How much?

EXAMPLES   A huge chunk **of dirt and ice** blocked the road. [The phrase *of dirt and ice* modifies the noun *chunk* and answers the question *What kind?*]

My sister is the one **in the purple jacket.** [The phrase *in the purple jacket* modifies the pronoun *one* and answers the question *Which one?*]

Is the secret door an opening **underneath the house?** [The phrase *underneath the house* modifies the noun *opening* and answers the question *Which one?*]

More than one adjective phrase may modify the same noun or pronoun.

EXAMPLE   Every night the basket **of oranges by the well** disappeared.

EXERCISE 3   Identifying Adjective Phrases

Underline the adjective phrases in the following sentences, and draw an arrow from each phrase to the word it modifies.

EX. 1. She read some facts about animals and insects.

1. The legs of one Mexican tarantula have bright red stripes.

2. Grasshoppers with strong back legs can jump twenty times their body length.

3. There are many types of chameleons.

4. The chameleon's skin changes color to match the color of its surroundings.

5. The wart hog is a strange looking creature with long legs and a short neck.

6. The odd shape of its body means that the wart hog must eat kneeling down.

7. As this article explains, Komodo dragons in Indonesia can climb trees.

8. The large claws on their feet make climbing easy.

9. Koala bears also have strong feet with sharp claws.

10. The secret of a polar bear's good balance is its feet.

11. The bottoms of a polar bear's feet are furry so that they don't slip.

12. Some stink bugs rub their legs together and make a sound like the sound of a grasshopper.

13. An African elephant has feet with soft soles so that it can move its giant body quietly.

14. The long claws of the striped skunk are important.

15. They help the skunk dig up its meals of grubs, worms, and roots.

EXERCISE 4   Writing Adjective Phrases

Complete each sentence below with an appropriate adjective phrase.

EX.   1. The man _____*by the door*_____ is my uncle.

1. The girl _____ showed us her wooden shoes.

2. Jan opened the can _____ and began cooking lunch.

3. His car is the one _____ .

4. Many recipes _____ use rice and vegetables.

5. Mia wore the big red hat _____ .

6. That pile _____ gets bigger every day.

7. Kim mailed us postcards _____ .

8. Mrs. Rosini made enough lasagna _____ .

9. The letter _____ has no stamp.

10. I rode the horse _____ .

ADVERB PHRASES

A prepositional phrase used as an adverb is called an *adverb phrase*.

12d   An *adverb phrase* modifies a verb, an adjective, or another adverb.

Adverb phrases answer the same questions that single-word adverbs answer.

When?	*How?*	*To what extent?*
Where?	*How often?*	*How long?*

EXAMPLES   Herb saw nothing **through the fog.** [The phrase *through the fog* modifes the verb *saw*, telling *where*.]
Carla was most helpful **with her directions.** [The phrase *with her directions* modifies the adjective *helpful*, telling *how*.]
Early **in the day,** Ellis goes jogging. [The phrase *in the day* modifies the adverb *Early*, telling *when*.]

Like adjective phrases, more than one adverb phrase may modify the same word.

EXAMPLE   **Past the school,** we turn left **onto Main Street.** [The phrases *Past the school* and *onto Main Street* modify the verb *turn*.]

An adverb phrase may be followed by an adjective phrase that modifies the object of the preposition in the adverb phrase.

EXAMPLE   The Shapiros went **to the fair in Topsfield.** [The adjective phrase *in Topsfield* modifies *fair*, the object of the preposition in the adverb phrase *to the fair*.]

EXERCISE 5   Identifying Adverb Phrases

Underline the adverb phrase in each of the following sentences, and draw an arrow from the phrase to the word it modifies.

EX.   1. Mom and Dad took us to Blanchard Springs Caverns.

1. The caves are found in Arkansas.

2. The guide led us along the twisting path.

3. Inside the caves, the temperature is less than 60 degrees Fahrenheit.

4. Mark and I brought our jackets with us so that we could stay warm.

5. A sign said, "Do not lean against the rocks."

6. Even touching the rocks with our fingers could damage them.

7. Our guide Jim said that the caves were inhabited by many unusual creatures.

8. We saw a grotto salamander run quicker than a fox.

9. In the cave, Jim showed us bats' nesting places.

10. The bats flew in a wide circle overhead.

11. Crayfish swam in an underground stream.

12. From Jim, we learned that the caves were formed long ago.

13. Dripping water wore through the soft rocks and made interesting shapes.

14. We looked at the unusual stalagmites that grew from the cavern floor.

15. Late in the evening, we were still discussing our adventure.

EXERCISE 6   Writing Sentences with Adverb Phrases

On your own paper, write ten sentences, using ten of the word groups below as adverb phrases. Underline each phrase. Then draw an arrow from the phrase to the word or words it modifies.

EX.   1. by six o'clock

   1. I always awake by six o'clock.

1. by the dentist	11. in the afternoon
2. without a map	12. against the building
3. until tomorrow	13. through the weekend
4. into the sky	14. under an umbrella
5. during the race	15. from behind the wall
6. for two hours	16. with an eraser
7. across the ocean	17. on the hillside
8. after school	18. before next summer
9. behind a giant tree	19. to the corner
10. on a sunny day	20. with Julio

CHAPTER REVIEW

A. Identifying Adjective and Adverb Phrases

Underline the prepositional phrase in each of the sentences below. Decide what kind of phrase it is. On the line before each sentence, write *adj.* for *adjective phrase* or *adv.* for *adverb phrase*. Then circle the word or words the phrase modifies.

EX. ___adv.___ 1. The dog (poked) his nose <u>through the fence.</u>

_____ 1. We carried the groceries into the house.

_____ 2. Gil rides a bike with a bright yellow seat.

_____ 3. The bear ate all the food at our campsite.

_____ 4. Bobby Fischer won his fourth United States chess championship at age seventeen.

_____ 5. My little brother is afraid of bugs.

_____ 6. Junko Tabei from Japan was the first woman who climbed Mount Everest.

_____ 7. My dog was waiting patiently for its dinner.

_____ 8. Jane was always careful with her handwriting.

_____ 9. Ken brought us a huge plate of sliced fruit.

_____ 10. I will wear my new jeans to Anabelle's party.

B. Writing Sentences with Adjective and Adverb Phrases

Use each of the following phrases in two separate sentences. On your own paper, write one sentence that uses the phrase as an adjective. Write a second sentence that uses the phrase as an adverb. Underline the word or words each phrase modifies.

EX. 1. down the hall
   1. The <u>room</u> down the hall is my mother's office.
   1. May <u>followed</u> us down the hall.

1. by the gate
2. in the crowded room
3. between those two countries
4. on that wall
5. under the bridge

6. in the water
7. across the sky
8. over their heads
9. around the yard
10. with rice

C.   Working Cooperatively to Write Safety Rules

You and a friend help the lifeguard at the neighborhood swimming pool.
She has asked you to create a poster that lists the pool's safety rules. With a
classmate, write at least five rules on the lines below. Include at least two
adjective phrases and two adverb phrases. If you like, draw a picture to
illustrate one of the rules.

EX.   1. Do not bring glass bottles into the pool area.

_____

_____

_____

_____

_____

_____

_____

_____

_____

_____

_____

_____

RECOGNIZING COMPLEMENTS

> **13a A *complement* is a word or a group of words that completes the meaning of a verb.**
>
> Every sentence has a subject and a verb. In addition, the verb often needs a complement to complete its meaning.
>
> INCOMPLETE   Vera called [*whom?*]
> COMPLETE   Vera called **Mescal.**
>
> INCOMPLETE   Holden is [*what?*]
> COMPLETE   Holden is **a dancer.**
>
> INCOMPLETE   The crowd seemed [*what?*]
> COMPLETE   The crowd seemed **restless.**

EXERCISE 1   Identifying Complements

Underline the complement in each of the sentences below.

EX.   1. Elaine helped her sister.

1. Simon ate that carrot.
2. Last night, Paulina walked the dog.
3. I know the answer.
4. Lorna earned money yesterday.
5. Carlotta needs your advice.
6. My friend Jamal forgot his gloves.
7. Jason was late for class.
8. My mother is a chemistry teacher.
9. I designed a shirt for myself.
10. The house is cold.
11. The Japanese restaurant serves soybean soup.
12. The bluefish is a beautiful fish.
13. Our cat had kittens.
14. Paul borrowed a rowboat.
15. The snowmobile made tracks.

EXERCISE 2 Writing Sentences with Complements

Complete each of the sentences below by adding a complement. Add any other necessary words also.

EX. 1. Evan is ____a good writer____.

1. Maggie learned _____.

2. My friends saw _____ last night.

3. We invited _____.

4. The athlete threw _____.

5. After school I was _____.

6. Do you believe _____?

7. My good friend had _____.

8. Darnel was _____.

9. At the party, we exchanged _____.

10. I enjoy _____.

11. Did Rudy receive _____ in the mail?

12. My cousin heard _____.

13. My family was _____.

14. We planned a _____.

15. Melvin tossed the _____ into the trash can.

16. Ezra had met _____.

17. At the end of the day, we will call _____.

18. If this works, I will be _____.

19. Please help _____ today.

20. Did you praise _____?

21. Gil pulled _____.

22. Have you heard _____?

23. Hans collects _____.

24. Will you close _____?

25. Molly cooks _____ on the grill.

DIRECT OBJECTS

The *direct object* is one type of complement. It completes the meaning of a transitive verb.

13b A *direct object* is a noun or a pronoun that receives the action of a verb or shows the result of that action. A direct object answers the question *Whom?* or *What?* after a transitive verb.

EXAMPLE   Lyle called **Robin.** [*Robin* receives the action of the verb *called* and tells *whom* Lyle called.]

A direct object may be compound, having two or more objects.

EXAMPLE   I made **necklaces** and **bracelets.** [*Necklaces* and *bracelets* tells *what* I made.]

 REFERENCE NOTE: For more on transitive verbs, see page 113.

A direct object can never follow a linking verb because a linking verb does not express action. Also, a direct object is never included in a prepositional phrase.

LINKING VERB   Tara is a soccer goalie. [The verb *is* does not express action. Therefore, it has no direct object.]

PREPOSITIONAL   He works on a farm. [*Farm* is the object of the
PHRASE   preposition *on*. It is not the direct object of the verb *works.*]

 REFERENCE NOTE: For more about linking verbs, see page 115. For more about prepositional phrases, see page 123.

EXERCISE 3   Identifying Direct Objects

Underline the direct object in each of the following sentences. [Remember: A direct object may be compound.]

EX.   1. Mark stole a <u>glance</u> at Andrea.

1. Luke loves games and puzzles.

2. Did you see the program last night about repairing the space telescope?

3. The scientists discovered the footprints and bones of a dinosaur by the riverbank.

4. The plastic raft released air from a tiny hole in its side.

5. Only Nathaniel heard that strange sound in the middle of the night.

6. Paula broke the glass fruit bowl.

7. For an after-school snack, we ate oranges and walnuts.

8. Mr. Chen teaches Chinese at the community center.

9. After the eruption, lava covered the streets.

10. Libby plays the banjo and the harmonica in a bluegrass band.

EXERCISE 4   Writing Sentences with Direct Objects

Complete each sentence below by adding a direct object. Add any other necessary words also.

EX.   1. Luwanda completed her _____ *test* _____ early.

1. We left _____ early in the morning.

2. Mom had put _____ and _____ in the cooler for a picnic.

3. Dad drove _____ to Murphy Lake.

4. A writer built a little _____ by the lake years ago and lived there for a while.

5. Jerome always wears _____ and

   _____ when swimming.

6. I love _____ but do not swim well.

7. Dad watched _____ from the shore.

8. At the lake we saw many other _____.

9. Like us, they were having _____.

10. We all enjoyed our _____.

11. At the picnic table, I met _____.

12. His family included his _____ and his

   _____.

13. To play touch football, we formed two _____.

14. Our team won _____.

15. I hope we will see _____ again.

INDIRECT OBJECTS

The *indirect object* is another type of complement. Like a direct object, an indirect object helps to complete the meaning of a transitive verb. A sentence with an indirect object always has a direct object.

13c **An *indirect object* is a noun or pronoun that comes between a verb and a direct object. It tells *to whom* or *to what*, or *for whom* or *for what*, the action of the verb is done.**

EXAMPLES Alani sent **me** a letter. [*Me* is the indirect object of the verb *sent*. It tells *to whom* Alani sent a letter. *Letter* is the direct object.]

     Jacob told **Azi** a joke. [*Azi* is the indirect object of the verb *told*. It tells *to whom* Jacob told a joke. *Joke* is the direct object.]

Like a direct object, an indirect object may be compound, having two or more objects.

EXAMPLE Leo gave **Risa** and **Marco** a guitar lesson. [*Risa* and *Marco* are the indirect objects of the verb *gave*. They tell *to whom* Leo gave a guitar lesson. *Lesson* is the direct object.]

Do not mistake the object of a preposition for an indirect object.

OBJECT OF A PREPOSITION Omar prepared a fine meal for **me.**
INDIRECT OBJECT Omar prepared **me** a fine meal.

EXERCISE 5 Identifying Direct Objects and Indirect Objects

In each of the following sentences, underline the direct object once and the indirect object twice. [Remember: Objects may be compound.]

EX. 1. Gabriel gave Lorena his old computer.

1. The beauty salon offered customers a free shampoo.

2. Adrian told no one his secret.

3. The crew sent us an SOS signal.

4. Would you tell me a story, please?

5. The police officer read the supect his rights.

6. I can draw you a picture of the spaceship.

7. Chico taught his parrot six new words.

8. Margaret loaned José and Albert her calculator.

9. The pitcher threw Sandra a curveball.

10. The doctor wrote Elena a note.

11. My uncle showed her and me his rare coins.

12. Will you bring us some chowder?

13. Tom gave Darla and her puppy his water.

14. Carmen owes her brother five dollars.

15. The salesman sold Ann a CD.

**EXERCISE 6   Writing Sentences with Direct Objects and
Indirect Objects**

You have received in the mail an ad for computer games. The ad has
arrived just in time for the end-of-the-year holidays. You have saved
forty dollars to spend on gifts for friends and relatives. On your own
paper, write five sentences telling what you will buy and for whom.
Underline the direct and indirect objects in your sentences.

EX.   1. I will buy my cousin the Checkered Flag Auto Racer.

SUBJECT COMPLEMENTS

> **13d** A *subject complement* **completes the meaning of a linking verb and identifies or describes the subject.**
>
> There are two kinds of subject complements—the *predicate nominative* and the *predicate adjective*.
>
> EXAMPLES   Nigel is a **plumber.** [*Plumber* identifies the subject *Nigel.*]
> The mechanic was **busy.** [*Busy* describes the subject *mechanic.*]
>
> Subject complements always follow linking verbs, not action verbs.
>
> | Common Linking Verbs | | | |
> |---|---|---|---|
> | appear | feel | remain | sound |
> | be | grow | seem | stay |
> | become | look | smell | taste |
>
> **REFERENCE NOTE:** For more about linking verbs, see page 115.

EXERCISE 7   Identifying Linking Verbs and Subject Complements

In each of the following sentences, underline the linking verb once and the subject complement twice.

EX.   1. Paco <u>grew</u> <u><u>taller</u></u> during the summer.

1. The dogcatcher looked unhappy.

2. This milk tastes sour.

3. My mother is a lawyer.

4. The sky became cloudy.

5. Althea is our next president.

6. This glass of orange juice tastes great.

7. Al's story sounded unbelievable.

8. The wool sweater felt scratchy.

9. Dennis seems quiet today.

10. Jerome was my best friend in kindergarten.

EXERCISE 8   Writing Sentences with Subject Complements

Complete each sentence below by adding a subject complement.

EX.   1.   Luanne looked_____*serious*_____ during the fire drill.

1.   Will Patty be our _____ this season?

2.   Before the show, the singer appeared _____.

3.   Ms. Destefano was _____ of the city for four years.

4.   The audience grew _____ as the show began.

5.   These Brussels sprouts taste _____.

6.   Do you feel _____ than before?

7.   This band's new CD sounds _____.

8.   "I will be _____ some day," said Malcolm proudly.

9.   "Everyone was _____ ,"said the police officer.

10.   After winning the game, Misha seemed _____.

11.   It was quite _____ last night.

12.   The roses smell and look _____ .

13.   Dinosaurs grew _____.

14.   Will you be my _____?

15.   Robert appeared quite _____ just now.

16.   That man is the _____ of my science class.

17.   The cat grew _____ during the night.

18.   "Please remain _____ ," the captain ordered.

19.   You sometimes sound _____ when you have a cold.

20.   This fabric feels _____.

21.   Because of the snow, we will stay _____.

22.   Your front tire looks _____.

23.   After law school, Mr. Redfield became _____.

24.   The new computer game seems _____.

25.   The hot-and-sour soup smells _____.

PREDICATE NOMINATIVES

> **13e** A *predicate nominative* is a noun or pronoun that follows a linking verb and explains or identifies the subject of the sentence.
>
> EXAMPLES   Manuel is the **conductor.** [*Conductor,* following the linking verb *is,* identifies the subject *Manuel.*]
> My aunt became a **surgeon.** [*Surgeon,* following the linking verb *became,* describes the subject *aunt.*]
>
> A predicate nominative may be compound.
>
> EXAMPLE   Chad is my **brother** and best **friend.** [Both *brother* and *friend,* following the linking verb *is,* identify the subject *Chad.*]
>
> Be careful not to mistake a direct object or the object of a preposition for a predicate nominative.
>
> DIRECT OBJECT   I saw the **sculpture.**
> OBJECT OF A PREPOSITION   I took a photograph of the **sculpture.**
> PREDICATE NOMINATIVE   That statue is a famous **sculpture.**
>
> NOTE   Expressions such as *It's I* and *That was she* sound awkward even though they are correct. In conversation, many people say *It's me* and *That was her.* Such expressions may one day become acceptable in writing, also. For now, however, it is best to follow the rules of standard English in your writing.

EXERCISE 9   Identifying Predicate Nominatives and Linking Verbs

In each of the following sentences, underline the linking verb once and the predicate nominative twice. [Remember: Predicate nominatives may be compound.]

EX.   1. Reza <u>is</u> the <u>leader</u> of the chorus.

1. Andrew remains my friend to this day.

2. Yesterday, my sister became Mrs. José Martinez.

3. Mr. Olafson is chief of staff at the hospital.

4. Kate will be a teacher or a scientist someday.

5. Birds may be descendants of dinosaurs.

6. Cara was queen of the homecoming parade.

7. That story remained an interesting mystery until the last page.

8. Leonardo da Vinci became an artist and an engineer.

9. The dogs in the newspaper photo are Fido and Red.

10. During my childhood, *Where the Wild Things Are* was my favorite book.

EXERCISE 10   Writing Sentences with Predicate Nominatives

On your own paper, write ten sentences using the words in the columns below. You may use any combination of the words, as long as you use the words as the headings of the chart indicate. Each word should be used once and underlined in each of your sentences. Add any necessary words.

EX.   light   was   spaceship

    1.   The blue light outside was an extremely odd spaceship.

Subjects	Linking Verbs	Predicate Nominatives
party	was	captain
Hector	may become	Marieke
plant	is	reproduction
fossil	was	"Operation Birthday"
name	will be	superstar
singer	has become	Alison
movie	is	volcanoes
partner	has been	footprint
statue	is	success
mountains	were	orchid

PREDICATE ADJECTIVES

13f A *predicate adjective* is an adjective that follows a linking verb and describes the subject of the sentence.

EXAMPLE   I felt **tired** after the bus ride. [*Tired* follows the linking verb *felt* and describes the subject *I*.]

Like the predicate nominative, a predicate adjective may be compound.

EXAMPLE   The grapes were **cold** and **crisp**. [Both *cold* and *crisp*, following the linking verb *were*, describe the subject *grapes*.]

EXERCISE 11   Identifying Predicate Adjectives and Linking Verbs

In each of the following sentences, underline the linking verb once and the predicate adjective twice. [Remember: Predicate adjectives may be compound.]

EX.   1. That towel is still damp.

1. By the end of the marathon, I was tired.

2. The music sounded loud and unusual.

3. "That meal was wonderful," Josiah exclaimed.

4. My friend Lim Sing looked satisfied with her grade.

5. The warm cranberry bread smelled delicious.

6. Does that picture seem crooked to you?

7. Vanya became bored with that long speech.

8. The rain today was cold and steady.

9. Over the weekend, the stores were busy.

10. Everyone appeared happy with the results of the contest.

11. The museum remains open throughout the holidays.

12. That jazz clarinet player is popular and talented.

13. The sunflowers grow taller each day.

14. My father's lentil soup tastes marvelous.

15. My little brother felt proud because of his perfect attendance award.

16. Michi was nervous before his solo.

17. Because of the wood-burning stove, we stay warm in the winter.

18. You look thrilled!

19. Estelle was unforgettable in that play.

20. That street is long and bumpy.

EXERCISE 12   Prewriting for a Book Review

You've been asked to write a book review for a local newspaper. Think about a book you've recently read. Then do your prewriting on the lines below. Remember that a review tells why you think people should or should not read the book. In your prewriting, include at least five sentences that contain predicate adjectives. Underline each predicate adjective.

EX.   1. Title: Harriet Tubman: Conductor on the Underground Railroad
         Author: Ann Petry
         The book is well written. It shows that Harriet Tubman's life was remarkable.

Title: _____

Author: _____

_____

_____

_____

_____

_____

_____

_____

_____

_____

CHAPTER REVIEW

A. Classifying Complements

In the sentences below, identify each italicized complement. On the line before each sentence, write *d.o.* for *direct object*, *i.o.* for *indirect object*, *p.n.* for *predicate nominative*, or *p.a.* for *predicate adjective*. [Remember: Complements may be compound.]

EX. __i.o.; d.o.__ 1. Jordan told *me* a good *story*.

_____ 1. Uncle Ernesto was a *teacher* for eleven years.

_____ 2. I felt *scared* on that roller coaster because the ride was so *fast*.

_____ 3. On Arbor Day, my class planted a maple *tree* on the school's front lawn.

_____ 4. "That gives *me* an *idea*," Marshall said excitedly.

_____ 5. My sister is a *chef*, so she made the *refreshments*.

_____ 6. The seas remained *choppy* and *rough*.

_____ 7. Robert Redford is an *actor* and a *director*.

_____ 8. The principal showed the *class* his old roll-top *desk*.

_____ 9. The artist needs some *paint* and a *brush* for his work.

_____ 10. The sky became *cloudy* and *dark*.

_____ 11. That brick building was an old train *station*.

_____ 12. Will you show *me* your mountain *bike*?

_____ 13. The squirrel appeared *delighted* to find sunflower seeds on the ground.

_____ 14. In the newspaper, Martha reads her *aunt* the *editorials* and the cartoons.

_____ 15. Ruth gave her *husband* the *message*.

B. Identifying and Classifying Complements

Underline all of the complements in each of the following sentences. On the line before each sentence, identify each complement by writing *d.o.* for *direct object*, *i.o.* for *indirect object*, *p.n.* for *predicate nominative*, or *p.a.* for *predicate adjective*. [Remember: Complements may be compound.]

EX. ___*p.n.*___ 1. Ms. Amos is the <u>principal</u> of Franklin High School.

_____ 1. Our friend Addie Sue was late.

_____ 2. Was Grandmother Burney a poet and an actress?

_____ 3. Last year that company developed a new computer.

_____ 4. The boss gave his employees a raise.

_____ 5. My friend Simba wrote me a song.

_____ 6. That old building was a museum.

_____ 7. Rodrigo built that birdhouse.

_____ 8. Who gave Myra the carnation yesterday?

_____ 9. My Mexican blanket is warm and colorful.

_____ 10. I gave my mother that chair for her birthday.

C. Writing Sentences with Complements

Write a sentence for each of the kinds of complements below. Underline the complement or complements in each sentence. Use a variety of subjects and verbs in your sentences.

EX.   1. a predicate nominative
         The blue whale is a <u>mammal</u>.

1. a predicate adjective

_____

2. an indirect object

_____

3. a direct object

_____

4. a predicate nominative

_____

5. a compound predicate adjective

_____

NUMBER

Number is the form of a word that indicates whether the word is singular or plural.

14a When a word refers to one person, place, or thing, it is *singular* in number. When a word refers to more than one person, place, or thing, it is *plural* in number.

Singular	tree	I	pony	goose	deer
Plural	trees	we	ponies	geese	deer

 REFERENCE NOTE: Most nouns ending in *–s* are plural (*igloos, sisters*). However, most verbs that end in *–s* are singular (*sings, tries*). For more about spelling the plural forms of nouns, see pages 279–281.

EXERCISE 1   Identifying Singular and Plural Nouns

On the line before each word below, write *sing.* if the word is singular, or *pl.* if it is plural.

EX.   1. _pl._ books

_____ 1. them

_____ 2. sweater

_____ 3. airplanes

_____ 4. Colorado

_____ 5. castles

_____ 6. raccoon

_____ 7. teeth

_____ 8. Fords

_____ 9. sunlight

_____ 10. mountains

_____ 11. they

_____ 12. amoebae

_____ 13. elk

_____ 14. haircut

_____ 15. socks

_____ 16. fish

_____ 17. ours

_____ 18. injuries

_____ 19. she

_____ 20. edge

EXERCISE 2   Classifying Singular and Plural Nouns in Sentences

In the sentences below, identify each italicized noun as singular or plural. Above the word write *sing.* for *singular* or *pl.* for *plural*.

EX.   1. I saw the *fish* jump three *feet* out of the *water.*
                  sing.   pl.   sing.

1. The *ships* returned to the *harbor* during the *storm.*

2. *Soldiers* in the *cavalry* ride *horses.*

3. *Laurindo* made the *tortillas* with special *cornmeal.*

4. *Jason* found a *computer* and three *discs* in the *box.*

5. The *Pilgrims* arrived in *Massachusetts* over three *centuries* ago.

6. The two *inventors* discussed their *project.*

7. *Mice* like *cheese.*

8. Wild *foxes* are easier to spot in the *winter.*

9. In *1847*, the *United States* issued its first postage *stamps.*

10. The *scores* from other *games* were shown on the *scoreboard.*

11. It took several *days* for the *men* to sell the *encyclopedias.*

12. *Luke* and his *father* carved a soapstone *walrus.*

13. *Jared* always likes to read the *papers* on *Sunday.*

14. The wheat *fields* seemed to stretch out for *miles.*

15. More *people* live in *Scotland* than in *Maine.*

16. Yesterday we went to visit *Maria,* and she showed us her new *drawings.*

17. The *doctors* made some important *decisions* later in the *afternoon.*

18. Julio's *family* moved west so he could work as a computer *technician* in *California.*

19. Just follow the *signs* to the *exit* for *Peoria.*

20. *Otto* thanked *Al* for explaining the *directions.*

SUBJECT-VERB AGREEMENT

14b A verb agrees with its subject in number.

A subject and verb *agree* when they have the same number.

(1) Singular subjects take singular verbs.

EXAMPLES   The **fire flickers** in the soft breeze. [The singular verb *flickers* agrees with the singular subject *fire*.]

Tina has a role in the play. [The singular verb *has* agrees with the singular subject *Tina*.]

(2) Plural subjects take plural verbs.

EXAMPLES   **Fireflies glow** at night. [The plural verb *glow* agrees with the plural subject *Fireflies*.]

The **bricks make** a sturdy path. [The plural verb *make* agrees with the plural subject *bricks*.]

 NOTE   The singular pronouns *I* and *you* take plural verbs.

EXAMPLE   **I start** with the baton, and **you begin** with the flag.

When a sentence has a verb phrase, the first helping verb in the phrase agrees with the subject.

EXAMPLES   The **runner is** tired.
The **runners are** tired.
Was Helen running in the race?
Were they running in the race?

EXERCISE 3   Identifying the Number of Subjects and Verbs

On the line before the following sentences, identify each subject and verb as either singular or plural. Write *sing.* for *singular* or *pl.* for *plural*. [Note: All verbs agree with their subjects in number.]

EX.   __pl.__ 1. Our student officers have formed a committee.

_____ 1. Henry runs the Jamaican restaurant on the corner.

_____ 2. The post office closes at 5:00 P.M.

_____ 3. My neighbors take a walk around the block in the afternoon.

_____ 4. Agnes has invited ten people to her birthday party.

_____ 5. The paintings were hung in the upstairs sitting room.

_____ 6. That actor is speaking French.

_____ 7. Renaldo's sisters are putting together their new train set.

_____ 8. Anita has a new hat.

_____ 9. Circus performers lead colorful lives.

_____10. Marita's best qualities were enthusiasm and courage.

EXERCISE 4 Choosing Verbs That Agree in Number with Their Subjects

For each sentence below, underline the subject and the form of the verb in parentheses that agrees with the subject.

EX.   1. My <u>cat</u> always (<u>*jumps*</u>, *jump*) into my lap.

1. Five candidates (*was running*, *were running*) for president.

2. On May 27, Delia (*has*, *have*) her twelfth birthday.

3. Hank (*does*, *do*) such a good job helping out at the store.

4. The piñatas (*is*, *are*) ready for *Las Posadas*.

5. Marta (*was*, *were*) tired after work.

EXERCISE 5 Changing the Number of Subjects and Verbs

On your own paper, rewrite the sentences below. If the subject and verb are singular, change both to plural. If they are plural, change both to singular.

EX.   1. The mechanic has fixed Dad's car.
　　　 1. Two mechanics have fixed Dad's car.

1. Three brown bears were climbing the hill.
2. Before baseball practice, the player works out for half an hour.
3. The doctor prescribes a warm bath and a good night's sleep.
4. My cousins sit in the back yard eating grapes.
5. My math teachers always grade papers during exams.
6. The cooks use the freshest ingredients in their recipes.
7. I like photography.
8. Often kind words soothe hurt feelings.
9. Two priests at my church are active in Amnesty International.
10. Does she know how to use the pottery wheel?

PHRASES BETWEEN SUBJECT AND VERB

14c **The number of a subject is not changed by a phrase following the subject.**

EXAMPLES   The **girl** in the red shoes **rides** on my bus. [singular subject and verb]

The **caves** by the river **hold** all our supplies. [plural subject and verb]

The **poster** blown off the wall during the storm **was** replaced. [singular subject and verb]

Those **boys** having their hair cut **are** going to camp. [plural subject and verb]

 REFERENCE NOTE: For more information about phrases, see pages 133–137.

EXERCISE 6   Choosing Verbs That Agree in Number with Their Subjects

For each sentence below, underline the subject and the form of the verb in parentheses that agrees with the subject.

EX.   1. The <u>window</u> under the stairs (*is*, *are*) difficult to open.

1. Those cattle grazing in the pasture (*comes, come*) from Illinois.

2. The sack of meal for the corn pone (*was, were*) heavy.

3. In this parade, the float with the cute animals (*is winning, are winning*) all the prizes.

4. The cheerleaders in our school all (*wears, wear*) the same brand of sneakers.

5. Both doors to that building (*is, are*) locked.

6. Eleanor, waiting to go onstage, (*was getting, were getting*) nervous.

7. The senators from California (*has called, have called*) a press conference.

8. The monks at our temple still (*remembers, remember*) how to speak Thai perfectly.

9. The results of the drawing (*has been announced, have been announced*).

10. Echoes from the explosion still (*shakes, shake*) the room.

EXERCISE 7   Proofreading Sentences for Subject-Verb Agreement

In the sentences below, if the verb does not agree with the subject, write the correct form of the verb on the line before the sentence. Write C if a sentence is correct.

EX. _____*leads*_____ 1. That path between the trees lead to a river.

_____ 1. Each year, a million tons of honey is produced throughout the world.

_____ 2. Those three boys in my Hebrew class likes to study together.

_____ 3. The officers of the association meets on Friday morning.

_____ 4. Women singing a Christmas carol was walking down the street.

_____ 5. A dinosaur bone discovered by archeologists rest in a case in the museum.

_____ 6. Employees in that office gets an extra day of vacation.

_____ 7. The states voting for the amendment to the Constitution were in the majority.

_____ 8. Those girls wearing orange saris are my sisters.

_____ 9. A postcard from the Canary Islands have arrived for you today.

_____ 10. Forty soldiers known for their bravery was chosen.

_____ 11. My uncle's words of wisdom is something I'll always remember.

_____ 12. In Arthurian legends, the Knights of the Round Table sets out on many quests.

_____ 13. The eggs in the pan is done.

_____ 14. Only one number out of a hundred were called.

_____ 15. Birds from a nearby forest often flies past my window.

_____ 16. The winner of the first four events get to choose the fifth event.

_____ 17. Films with a happy ending is my favorite.

_____ 18. The island of Cuba were my family's home for six hundred years.

_____ 19. That tall firefighter standing next to the truck was given a medal by the mayor.

_____ 20. Students wishing to sign up for the class trip is lining up outside the principal's door.

AGREEMENT WITH INDEFINITE PRONOUNS

Personal pronouns refer to specific people, places, things, or ideas. A pronoun that does not refer to a definite person, place, thing, or idea is known as an *indefinite pronoun*.

14d **The following indefinite pronouns are singular:** *anybody, anyone, each, either, everybody, everyone, neither, no one, nobody, one, somebody, someone.*

EXAMPLES   **Each** of the students **gets** a copy of the poem.
Everyone thinks the decision was unfair.
Has either of the classes **been** to St. Louis?

14e **The following indefinite pronouns are plural:** *both, few, many, several.*

EXAMPLES   **Several** of the fish **had** bright spots.
Both of your hands **need** mittens.

14f **The indefinite pronouns** *all, any, most, none,* **and** *some* **may be either singular or plural.**

The number of the pronouns *all, any, most, none,* and *some* is determined by the number of the object in the prepositional phrase following the subject. If the pronoun refers to a singular object, the pronoun is singular. If the pronoun refers to a plural object, the pronoun is plural.

EXAMPLES   **Most** of the laundry **is** washed. [*Most* is singular because it refers to one thing—*laundry*. The helping verb *is* is singular to agree with *laundry*.]
Most of the clothes **are** washed. [*Most* is plural because it refers to more than one thing—*clothes*. The helping verb *are* is plural to agree with *clothes*.]
None of the crew **has** started to paint yet. [*None* is singular because it refers to one thing—*crew*. The helping verb *has* is singular to agree with *crew*.]
None of the painters **have** started to paint yet. [*None* is plural because it refers to more than one thing—*painters*. The helping verb *have* is plural to agree with *painters*.]

EXERCISE 8   Choosing Verbs That Agree in Number with Their Subjects

In each of the sentences below, underline the form of the verb in parentheses that agrees with the subject. Remember that the subject is never part of a prepositional phrase.

EX.   1. All of the flowers (*was planted, were planted*).
                                    —————————

1. During Rosh Hashana, everybody (*stay, stays*) at our house.

2. Many of the best scenes (*doesn't, don't*) occur until later in the play.

3. Neither of the guards ever (*smiles, smile*) at the tourists.

4. Every one of my friends (*has, have*) a tape by Natalie Cole.

5. Most of the barber's customers (*visits, visit*) him about twice a month.

6. Some of this speech (*was, were*) written by Sheila.

7. After running, no one (*feels, feel*) much like talking.

8. (*Have, Has*) either of your parents ever been back home to Ecuador?

9. Few of my friends (*takes, take*) what she says very seriously.

10. Practically everyone (*appreciates, appreciate*) good weather.

11. Somebody on that block (*is singing, are singing*) songs from Broadway shows.

12. All of Mom's peach pie (*is, are*) still left.

13. Several of the workmen (*has, have*) done this kind of job before.

14. Nobody (*makes, make*) a sound during one of Mr. Conrad's lectures.

15. One of the nicest things about the winter (*is, are*) the fresh air right after a snowfall.

16. This year some of my classes (*was, were*) very interesting.

17. Each of the members of the orchestra (*has memorized, have memorized*) the music.

18. Both of those computers (*performs, perform*) well.

19. None of my brother's friends (*plays, play*) basketball.

20. On Tuesday, several of the gardeners (*is replanting, are replanting*) the trees near the lake.

OTHER PROBLEMS IN AGREEMENT

A *compound subject* is made up of two or more subjects that are connected by *and, or,* or *nor.* These connected subjects share the same verb.

14g **Subjects joined by *and* take a plural verb.**

EXAMPLES **Rain** and **hail were rattling** on the window.
Frogs and **newts have** moist skins.
Prabha, Indira, and **Mr. Singh come** from India.

14h **When compound subjects are joined by *or* or *nor,* the verb agrees with the subject nearer the verb.**

EXAMPLES A **swim** or a **game** of tennis **is** on the schedule this afternoon.
Either a green **salad** or fruit **slices are** the first course.
Neither **ice cubes** nor a **heating pad seems** to help.

14i **When the subject follows the verb, find the subject. Then make sure that the verb agrees with it.**

EXAMPLES Here **are** the **petitions** we collected.
Have the **Itohs become** citizens of the United States?

The contractions *there's* and *here's* contain the verb *is.* These contractions are singular and should be used only with singular subjects.

EXAMPLE There**'s** no **answer** to that puzzle.

EXERCISE 9 **Choosing Verbs That Agree in Number with Their Subjects**

For each of the following sentences, underline the correct form of the verb in parentheses. If you choose a singular verb with any of these compound subjects, be prepared to explain why.

EX. 1. Tapes and compact discs (*is sold, are sold*) in that store.

1. Your address and telephone number (*goes, go*) under your name.

2. Either his sister or his cousins (*is waiting, are waiting*) for him at the station.

3. (*Wasn't, Weren't*) Norwegians among the first European settlers in Minnesota?

4. Here (*is, are*) the package you requested.

5. Nayati and Jenna (*is organizing, are organizing*) the dance.

6. Neither tomatoes nor lettuce (*was included, were included*) in that salad.

7. The pitcher, the second baseman, and the center fielder often (*sits, sit*) in the dugout after the game.

8. There (*is, are*) three applicants for that job.

9. My family and our neighbors (*fasts, fast*) during Ramadan.

10. (*Has, Have*) Naomi telephoned yet?

EXERCISE 10   Proofreading for Errors in Subject-Verb Agreement

In each sentence below, if the verb does not agree with its subject, write the correct form of the verb on the line provided. Write *C* if a sentence is correct.

EX. _____*are*_____ 1. St. Louis and Chicago is both midwestern cities.

_____ 1. Weren't the plumber supposed to have been here by now?

_____ 2. Mercury and Venus is nearer to the Sun than Earth is.

_____ 3. As for losing games, neither the team nor its fans likes it.

_____ 4. Rosalinda, Harry, and Florence is going to see the movie.

_____ 5. Patience and organization often leads to a good project.

_____ 6. There is fifteen counties in that state.

_____ 7. Here's the pen I borrowed.

_____ 8. Either a squirrel or some pigeons always comes over to the bench to eat the popcorn.

_____ 9. Was the O'Connells the last ones to leave?

_____ 10. Hasn't I told you about this before?

_____ 11. Last night either the stereo or the radio were playing until 11:00 P.M.

_____ 12. Pens, rulers, and paper was all on sale.

_____ 13. This weekend there are a picnic and soccer game at the park near the school.

_____ 14. My friend and I likes to sled whenever we can.

_____ 15. Either Miriam or the twins knows the combination to that lock.

AGREEMENT WITH DON'T AND DOESN'T

14j The word *don't* is a contraction of *do not*. Use *don't* with all plural subjects and with the pronouns *I* and *you*.

EXAMPLES   **I don't** eat meat.   The **kittens don't** have mittens.
          We don't litter.   **You don't** need a jacket today.

14k The word *doesn't* is a contraction of *does not*. Use *doesn't* with all singular subjects except the pronouns *I* and *you*.

EXAMPLES   **He doesn't** understand.   **Greta doesn't** talk much.
          It doesn't fly.   That **toaster doesn't** work.

EXERCISE 11   Using *Don't* and *Doesn't* Correctly

For each sentence below, underline the correct contraction in parentheses.

EX.   1.   The Quinns (*doesn't*, *don't*) live there anymore.

1. Lian usually (*doesn't*, *don't*) work in the garden at noon.

2. I (*doesn't*, *don't*) know much about geometry yet.

3. My aunt's two dogs (*doesn't*, *don't*) like to get wet.

4. Karen's five-year-old brother (*doesn't*, *don't*) read too well.

5. (*Doesn't*, *Don't*) you ever do that again!

6. That tall boy (*doesn't*, *don't*) say much.

7. (*Doesn't*, *Don't*) anybody here have an extra notebook?

8. The sun (*doesn't*, *don't*) set for another hour.

9. Will and Ted (*doesn't*, *don't*) let a day go by without saying hello.

10. Alma (*doesn't*, *don't*) understand why she can't solve the problem.

11. (*Doesn't*, *Don't*) he have another plan for tomorrow?

12. (*Doesn't*, *Don't*) several of the players have two or three years experience?

13. Actually, I (*doesn't*, *don't*) want to go downtown yet.

14. (*Doesn't*, *Don't*) those shoes match her hat well?

15. The rug (*doesn't*, *don't*) entirely cover the floor.

EXERCISE 12   Writing *Don't* and *Doesn't* Correctly

Identify the subject in each of the sentences below. Then on the line provided, write either *don't* or *doesn't* to complete the sentence correctly.

EX.   1. Those people _____*don't*_____ worry about it.

1. _____ Hector's new car look great!

2. I _____ work on the yearbook anymore.

3. _____ use the new cards yet, Tao.

4. This area _____ receive much snow.

5. The landlord _____ take very good care of that building.

6. We _____ want to go home yet.

7. Suke _____ live in Honolulu anymore.

8. Sally _____ want twelve candles on her cake.

9. The supervisor _____ know where we should put this lumber, either.

10. If you _____ want to go with us, you can stay with your aunt.

11. Even this terrible weather _____ put Rosalie in a bad mood.

12. Mary says she _____ recognize any of the trees or shrubs.

13. I wonder why that company _____ advertise?

14. I _____ want to go to a different school.

15. Do you know anyone who _____ listen to music?

16. We _____ have much homework because our exams are next week.

17. Thelma _____ play the trumpet as well as Latisha.

18. Todd's parents _____ let him play with video games.

19. It _____ look as if you've cleaned your room yet.

20. I like to practice, but I_____ like to sing in public.

CHAPTER REVIEW

A. Choosing Verbs That Agree in Number with Their Subjects

For each sentence below, underline the subject of the sentence and the form of the verb in parentheses that agrees with the subject.

EX. 1. (*Has*, *Have*) you ever been in a canoe?

1. Canoeing (*is*, *are*) a lot of fun when done properly.

2. My older brothers (*owns*, *own*) a canoe.

3. The canoe paddles in their closet (*was made*, *were made*) by expert craftsmen.

4. Either Rick or Fernando (*steers*, *steer*) from the back, or stern, of the boat.

5. The other one (*paddles*, *paddle*) in the front, or bow.

6. Near our house, there (*is*, *are*) a river good for canoeing.

7. All of their friends (*wants*, *want*) my brothers to take them for a ride.

8. Anyone with a life preserver (*is allowed*, *are allowed*) to go.

9. I (*doesn't want*, *don't want*) to miss this chance to learn how to canoe.

10. The joys of canoeing (*seems*, *seem*) clear to me.

11. Neither Emilio nor Rivka (*has*, *have*) a key.

12. The boy in the galoshes (*seems*, *seem*) to enjoy the rain.

13. No one I know (*likes*, *like*) beets very much.

14. Several of them (*has*, *have*) been damaged.

15. How many of you (*wants*, *want*) orange juice?

16. Both of the squirrels (*was*, *were*) red squirrels.

17. Each statue in front of the museum (*is*, *are*) from Greece.

18. Either René or Catherine (*is*, *are*) repairing the torn pages.

19. That horse wearing the fancy saddle (*belongs*, *belong*) to Lucy.

20. Some of you (*has been*, *have been*) waiting very patiently.

B. Proofreading a Paragraph for Subject-Verb Agreement

In the following paragraph, draw a line through each verb that does not agree with its subject. Write the correct form above the error.

EX.   [1] Many fish ~~has~~ amazing shapes.
               have

[1] There are an almost endless variety of fish. [2] Knifefishes' bodies is shaped just like carving knives. [3] Rabbitfish and elephant-trunk fish is named for the shapes of their noses. [4] The extended jaw of the longnose gars look quite strange. [5] This streamlined fish dart from its grassy hideaway to capture its prey. [6] Its long jaw and sharp teeth makes it a terrible enemy. [7] A cowfish have big eyes and protective spines that look just like little horns. [8] A crescent shape and large, softly waving fins give the angelfish its name. [9] Perhaps most amazing, though, are the Harriott's longnose chimaera. [10] Its winglike fins and its long, skinny snout makes it look a lot like a rocket ship.

C. Writing Sentences for a Presentation

You are making a presentation on dreams to your class. Use the following prewriting notes to write at least ten sentences for your presentation. Be sure to make your subjects and verbs agree.

    product of the brain's activity
    most occur toward morning
    four cycles of sleep
    REM—stands for rapid eye movement
    usually stories
    most in color
    most adults—3 to 5 dream periods a night
    REMs usually occur when people dream
    physician Sigmund Freud—studied meanings of dreams
    can seem real
    some pleasant, some frightening
    connected to electrical activity in the brain
    may be related to day's real experiences

EX.   1. Dreams are a product of the brain's activity.

PRINCIPAL PARTS OF VERBS

The four basic forms of a verb are called the *principal parts*.

15a The four principal parts of a verb are the *base form***, the** *present participle***, the** *past***, and the** *past participle***.**

Base Form	Present Participle	Past	Past Participle
sing	(is) singing	sang	(have) sung
use	(is) using	used	(have) used

Notice that the present participle and the past participle require helping verbs (forms of *be* and *have*).

As you can see from their names, the principal parts of a verb are used to express time.

PRESENT TIME   Every morning we **sing** a wake-up song.
                        Larry **is singing** it right now.
PAST TIME   Isabel **sang** her first song out of tune.
                        She **had sung** it better during her lesson.
FUTURE TIME   Sudi **will sing** a traditional Swahili song during the assembly.
                        He **will have sung** at three assemblies this year.

Because *use* forms its past and past participle by adding *–d*, it is called a *regular verb*. *Sing* forms its past and past participle differently, so it is called an *irregular verb*.

EXERCISE 1   Identifying the Principal Parts of Verbs

Identify the principal part of the italicized verb in each of the following sentences. Write your answers on the lines provided.

EX. _____past_____ 1. We *did* our homework after lunch.

_____ 1. Mr. Tran *explained* the formula to the class.

_____ 2. *Has* Mom *washed* your uniform?

_____ 3. *Toss* me the towel, Julian.

_____ 4. The teacher *is forming* a softball team.

_____ 5. Diego Rivera, a famous painter, *painted* many murals.

_____ 6. I *am sewing* my own mariachi costume for the festival.

_____ 7. The girl *pointed* toward the exit.

_____ 8. In the story, who *kidnapped* the pirate?

_____ 9. Nan and Alan *have* never *looked* through a telescope.

_____ 10. Who *is reporting* on the World Series?

_____ 11. The book *had listed* the author's name in the front.

_____ 12. *Is* Bethany *scraping* the mud off her boots?

_____ 13. Eli and I *entered* through the side doors.

_____ 14. The art fair *is continuing* through Saturday.

_____ 15. After the morning assembly, *call* Mr. Turner.

EXERCISE 2 Writing Sentences with the Principal Parts of Verbs

On the lines below, create a sentence for each of the following directions.

EX.   1.   a sentence with the past tense of *whisper*
          Salvador whispered a secret to his friend.
          _____

1. a sentence with the base form of *travel* (Use *to*.) _____

   _____

2. a sentence with the past form of *jump* _____

   _____

3. a sentence with the present participle of *look* _____

   _____

4. a sentence with the past participle of *paint* _____

   _____

5. a sentence with the past form of *push* _____

   _____

REGULAR VERBS

15b A *regular verb* forms its past and past participle by adding *–ed* or *–d* to the base form.

Base Form	Present Participle	Past	Past Participle
help	(is) helping	helped	(have) helped
like	(is) liking	liked	(have) liked
start	(is) starting	started	(have) started
nap	(is) napping	napped	(have) napped

NOTE Most regular verbs that end in *–e* drop the *e* before adding *–ing*. Some regular verbs double the final consonant before adding *–ing* or *–ed*. For a discussion of these spelling rules, see pages 275–277.

One common error in forming the past or past participle of a regular verb is to leave off the *–d* or *–ed* ending.

NONSTANDARD Gert and her brother use to argue about the chores.
STANDARD Gert and her brother **used** to argue about the chores.

 REFERENCE NOTE: For more about standard English, see page 217.

EXERCISE 3 Forming the Principal Parts of Regular Verbs

The base form is given for each of the following verbs. Fill in the chart with the present participle, past, and past participle forms of each verb.

Base Form	Present Participle	Past	Past Participle
EX. 1. play	(is) playing	played	(have) played
1. carve	(is)		(have)
2. carry	(is)		(have)
3. join	(is)		(have)

Base Form	Present Participle		Past	Past Participle	
4. grab	(is)			(have)	
5. pull	(is)			(have)	
6. watch	(is)			(have)	
7. study	(is)			(have)	
8. wish	(is)			(have)	
9. cook	(is)			(have)	
10. climb	(is)			(have)	
11. bury	(is)			(have)	
12. cover	(is)			(have)	
13. push	(is)			(have)	
14. want	(is)			(have)	
15. live	(is)			(have)	

EXERCISE 4   Using the Principal Parts of Regular Verbs

On the line in each of the sentences below, write the correct form (past or past participle) of the verb shown in italics.

EX.   1. *move*   In 1893, Irving Berlin ____moved____ from Russia to the United States.

1. *compose*   Throughout his life, he _____ many popular songs.

2. *perform*   Before his fame, Irving Berlin _____ in New York as a singing waiter.

3. *learn*   You probably have _____ some of his songs in music class.

4. *create*   He _____ both the words and the music for the song "God Bless America."

5. *enjoy*   People have _____ the music of Irving Berlin for many years.

IRREGULAR VERBS

15c An *irregular verb* forms its past and past participle in some other way than by adding *–d* or *–ed* to the base form.

 If you are not sure about the principal parts of a verb, look in a dictionary. Entries for irregular verbs list the principal parts of the verb. If the principal parts are not listed, the verb is a regular verb.

COMMON IRREGULAR VERBS			
Base Form	**Present Participle**	**Past**	**Past Participle**
begin	(is) beginning	began	(have) begun
blow	(is) blowing	blew	(have) blown
break	(is) breaking	broke	(have) broken
bring	(is) bringing	brought	(have) brought
burst	(is) bursting	burst	(have) burst
catch	(is) catching	caught	(have) caught
choose	(is) choosing	chose	(have) chosen
come	(is) coming	came	(have) come
cut	(is) cutting	cut	(have) cut
do	(is) doing	did	(have) done
draw	(is) drawing	drew	(have) drawn
drink	(is) drinking	drank	(have) drunk
drive	(is) driving	drove	(have) driven
eat	(is) eating	ate	(have) eaten
fall	(is) falling	fell	(have) fallen
freeze	(is) freezing	froze	(have) frozen
give	(is) giving	gave	(have) given
go	(is) going	went	(have) gone
hurt	(is) hurting	hurt	(have) hurt
know	(is) knowing	knew	(have) known

COMMON IRREGULAR VERBS			
Base Form	**Present Participle**	**Past**	**Past Participle**
lead	(is) leading	led	(have) led
lend	(is) lending	lent	(have) lent
make	(is) making	made	(have) made
ride	(is) riding	rode	(have) ridden
ring	(is) ringing	rang	(have) rung
run	(is) running	ran	(have) run
see	(is) seeing	saw	(have) seen
shrink	(is) shrinking	shrank	(have) shrunk
sing	(is) singing	sang	(have) sung
sink	(is) sinking	sank *or* sunk	(have) sunk *or* sunken
speak	(is) speaking	spoke	(have) spoken
steal	(is) stealing	stole	(have) stolen
swim	(is) swimming	swam	(have) swum
take	(is) taking	took	(have) taken
tear	(is) tearing	tore	(have) torn
throw	(is) throwing	threw	(have) thrown
wear	(is) wearing	wore	(have) worn
win	(is) winning	won	(have) won
write	(is) writing	wrote	(have) written

Frank & Ernest reprinted by permission of NEA, Inc.

EXERCISE 5   Identifying the Correct Forms of Irregular Verbs

For each of the sentences below, underline the correct verb form in parentheses.

EX.   1. All the leaves have (*fallen, fell*) from the trees.

1. In 1844, Horace Greeley (*made, maked*) Margaret Fuller the first female journalist for a major newspaper.

2. Have you (*took, taken*) the time to check the spelling on your papers?

3. The magician (*chose, choosed*) Kay to help him with his next trick.

4. Mr. Caputo (*drew, drawed*) four names out of a hat.

5. We have (*went, gone*) to the shore for several days every fall.

6. The final bell has (*rang, rung*), and it's time to go home.

7. I have (*knew, known*) my friend Billy for six years.

8. Absalom Jones, an African American religious leader, (*began, begun*) his life as a slave in Delaware.

9. I have always (*wore, worn*) a special outfit on the first day of school.

10. May has (*sang, sung*) her solo, and everyone is clapping.

11. All our friends had (*came, come*) to the play.

12. During the big storm, Will and I (*saw, seen*) an amazing lightning show.

13. Jack (*tore, torn*) the article about the Amazon rain forest out of today's paper.

14. Linh's parents (*brought, brung*) her to the United States from Vietnam when she was two.

15. By the time of the party, Kelly and Don had (*blowed, blown*) up hundreds of balloons.

16. Last summer, Clara and her parents (*rode, rided*) their bikes through Holland.

17. Every Thursday, Mrs. Freeman (*drove, driven*) Leon and me to basketball practice.

18. Maura has (*did, done*) the laundry for her mother.

19. I was four years old the first time I (*swam, swum*) underwater.

20. I had never (*catched, caught*) a fish before today.

EXERCISE 6   Proofreading for Errors in Irregular Verbs

In the sentences below, draw a line through the incorrect verb form. Write the correct form above the error. If a sentence is correct, write C on the line before the sentence.

EX. _____ 1.   Cora and I ~~seen~~ *saw* an in-line skating show.

_____ 1.   On Saturday afternoon, Cora's dad drived us to the show.

_____ 2.   Before we left home, we had ate lunch.

_____ 3.   When we got to the auditorium, we goed right to our seats.

_____ 4.   An usher led us to our row and pointed out where we should sit.

_____ 5.   Cora had brung binoculars to the show.

_____ 6.   Her older brother had lend the binoculars to her for the afternoon.

_____ 7.   Soon, all the people in the audience had took their seats.

_____ 8.   The lights in the building went down.

_____ 9.   Loud, lively music rung out.

_____ 10.   Skaters bursted out onto the floor, speeding around on their skates.

_____ 11.   They all worn bright, shiny costumes.

_____ 12.   The show begun with a dance routine.

_____ 13.   I had never knowed that people could dance like that on in-line skates.

_____ 14.   One girl done a flip and a split.

_____ 15.   I would have fell on my face, but she landed on her feet.

_____ 16.   One skater spun his partner above his head and throwed her in the air.

_____ 17.   The audience applauded and cheered when he catched her.

_____ 18.   Then the stunt skaters come out.

_____ 19.   They really gave the audience a thrill as they performed on a halfpipe, a huge pipe cut in half.

_____ 20.   These professional in-line skaters maked their jumps, flips, and spins look easy.

15d The *tense* of a verb indicates the time of the action or the state of being expressed by the verb.

Every verb has six tenses.

Tenses	Examples
Present	I speak, you speak, she speaks
Past	I spoke, we spoke, they spoke
Future	I will (shall) speak, you will speak, they will speak
Present Perfect	I have spoken, you have spoken, she has spoken
Past Perfect	I had spoken, you had spoken, he had spoken
Future Perfect	I will (shall) have spoken, you will have spoken, they will have spoken

This time line shows the relationship between tenses.

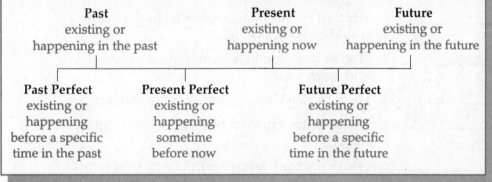

EXERCISE 7 Writing Correct Tenses of Verbs

For each of the following sentences, change the italicized verb to the tense identified in parentheses. Write your answer on the line provided.

EX. __has learned__ 1. Pete *learn* a new song. (*present perfect*)

_____ 1. The train *leave* five minutes early. (*past perfect*)

_____ 2. Tammy *choose* a book from the top shelf. (*past*)

_____ 3. Hot water *shrink* that woolen sweater. (*future*)

_____ 4. Josh *swim* for an hour before school every day. (*present*)

_____ 5. The movie *start* by now. (*future perfect*)

_____ 6. I *broke* the zipper on my jacket. (*present perfect*)

_____ 7. The African state of Sierra Leone *gain* its independence from Great Britain in 1961. (*past*)

_____ 8. On Sunday afternoon, we *hike* to the top of Mt. Monadnock. (*future*)

_____ 9. Hector *see* his grandparents every Sunday for three months. (*present perfect*)

_____ 10. We *decorate* our basement for the party. (*past*)

_____ 11. The lake *freeze* over by January. (*future perfect*)

_____ 12. The chorus never *sing* more beautifully. (*past perfect*)

_____ 13. Marika *ride* horses her whole life. (*past perfect*)

_____ 14. Tony and I *solve* the puzzle. (*present perfect*)

_____ 15. Rosie *write* her book report on Nicholasa Mohr's novel *Nilda*. (*future*)

_____ 16. Stanford *call* his mother when he found out he would be home late. (*past*)

_____ 17. "Father *want* you to help me with the leaves," I said. (*present*)

_____ 18. We *go* to visit Grandpa on Saturday. (*future*)

_____ 19. You *be* to this museum how many times ? (*present perfect*)

_____ 20. I *finish* my math homework already. (*past perfect*)

EXERCISE 8 Writing Sentences with Different Tenses

Do you ever make up stories about people you see in paintings and pictures? Think about an interesting painting or picture that you've seen recently. It may have been in a museum or in a newspaper, magazine, or book. What is the story behind the scene? On your own paper, write five sentences telling what you think is happening, has happened, and will happen in the picture. Use a different tense in each sentence. After each sentence, write the tense that you used in the sentence.

EX. 1. A girl leans over a fence and looks toward the dark woods. (present)

REVIEW EXERCISE

A. Proofreading for Correct Use of Regular Verbs

In the sentences below, draw a line through the incorrect verb form. Write the correct form above the error. Some sentences may be correct.

EX. 1. Some people with visual impairments have use guide dogs to get around more easily.

1. The Guide Dog Foundation for the Blind has train guide dogs since 1946.

2. The trainers are always look for smart, gentle, friendly puppies to be guide dogs.

3. Golden and Labrador retrievers are suppose to be dependable dogs.

4. When a guide dog is a year old, it learns how to guide.

5. A guide dog can helped its owner move more quickly than he or she could move with a cane.

6. Guide dogs have provide companionship to their owners.

7. The owner lived and trains with the guide dog at the school.

8. By the time a student and a dog go home, they have work together for almost a month.

9. The two of them have form a great friendship.

10. The foundation depending on donations to support its program.

B. Proofreading for Correct Use of Irregular Verbs

In the following sentences, draw a line through the incorrect verb form. Write the correct form above the error. Some sentences may be correct.

EX. 1. A thief has ~~stole~~ *stolen* my wallet.

1. A Spanish ship sinked near the island of Hispaniola, which is now Haiti and the Dominican Republic.

2. He rided around in his car for an hour before going home.

3. I must have catched a cold at the New Year's Day parade.

4. Hurricane winds blowed down the oak tree in our yard.

5. In the book *Alice in Wonderland*, Alice's adventures begun after she fell down a hole.

6. During the 1400s, Italian merchants bought silk and other goods in China and brung them to Europe on their ships.

7. Who won the essay contest?

8. Ninita may have hurted her toe when she dropped the box on her foot.

9. Our teacher's dog teared our test papers into pieces before our teacher had a chance to grade them.

10. The artist has drawed a picture of the children playing on the beach.

C. Identifying Tenses in Sentences

For each of the sentences below, change the italicized verb to the tense identified in parentheses. Write your answer on the line provided.

EX.   _____celebrate_____ 1. Jewish people *celebrated* Purim in late winter. (*present*)

_____ 1. Jewish children always *enjoy* this happy holiday. (*present perfect*)

_____ 2. Purim *honor* the story of Queen Esther. (*present*)

_____ 3. Queen Esther *defeat* the evil ruler Haman. (*past*)

_____ 4. Haman *plan* the destruction of the Jewish people in Persia. (*past perfect*)

_____ 5. Because of Esther, the king *punish* Haman instead. (*past*)

_____ 6. Children always *love* this story. (*present perfect*)

_____ 7. They *meet* at home or in a synagogue for the Purim celebration and storytelling. (*future*)

_____ 8. Children often *wear* costumes of the characters in the Purim story. (*present perfect*)

_____ 9. At every mention of Haman's name, each child *hiss*. (*present*)

_____ 10. By the end of the story, they *make* lots of noise. (*future perfect*)

SIT *AND* SET

15e The verb *sit* means "to be seated" or "to rest." *Sit* seldom takes an object. The verb *set* means "to place (something)" or "to put (something)." *Set* usually takes an object. Notice that *set* has the same form for the base form, past, and past participle.

Base Form	Present Participle	Past	Past Participle
sit	(is) sitting	sat	(have) sat
set	(is) setting	set	(have) set

EXAMPLES   You **will sit** on the chair next to Yori. [no object]
You **will set** the iron on a potholder. [You will set what? *Iron* is the object.]
The three hikers **have sat** on the old stone wall. [no object]
Ms. Sullivan **has set** my books on a special shelf. [Ms. Sullivan has set what? *Books* is the object.]

NOTE   If you don't know whether to use *sit* or *set* in a sentence, try substituting *put*. If the sentence makes sense with *put*, use *set*.

EXERCISE 9   Choosing the Correct Forms of *Sit* and *Set*

For each of the following sentences, underline the correct form of *sit* or *set* in parentheses.

EX.   1.   Jill (*sat, set*) in her seat and waited for Miss Newman.

1.   He (*sat, set*) his lunch bag down on the table.

2.   The field trip leaders were (*sitting, setting*) in the back of the bus.

3.   Nobody was (*sitting, setting*) when the dragon went by on Chinese New Year's.

4.   Sophia and I (*sat, set*) next to each other at the movies.

5.   I will (*sit, set*) these three packages by the mailbox for our letter carrier to pick up.

6.   Can that huge elephant really (*sit, set*) on that tiny stool?

7. I was (*sitting, setting*) on the bench when a clown rode by backwards on a giant unicycle.

8. A juggler (*sat, set*) beach balls on his head and balanced them.

9. Nick had never (*set, sat*) still for so long in his whole life.

10. He was (*sitting, setting*) the box of china on the floor when he tripped and fell.

11. I accidentally (*sat, set*) my foot on her eyeglasses.

12. While Hamako waits for her father in the park, a squirrel comes and (*sits, sets*) by her feet.

13. I couldn't see, so the man in front of me took his hat off and (*sat, set*) it in his lap.

14. Corey (*sat, set*) on the floor for the tea ceremony.

15. Those dirty pots have (*sat, set*) in the sink all afternoon.

EXERCISE 10   Writing the Forms of *Sit* and *Set*

On the line in each sentence below, write the correct form of *sit* or *set*.

EX.   1. Let's _____*sit*_____ at a table by the window so we can watch the boats.

1. Yesterday, I _____ in my bedroom and read a book.

2. Our puppy can only _____ still for a few minutes each day.

3. Please _____ your pencils down now.

4. Where do you _____ your glasses before you go to sleep?

5. Jeff is _____ the dishes on the table and putting out the napkins.

6. My bike has _____ in the garage all winter.

7. Our coach will _____ our medals in the school trophy case.

8. The director is _____ on his stool and telling the actors where to stand.

9. Dad _____ out the map of Tibet and showed us the parts he had visited when he was younger.

10. Bert had _____ and waited for the bus for three hours before it finally came.

RISE *AND* RAISE

15f The verb *rise* means "to go upward" or "to get up." *Rise* never takes an object. The verb *raise* means "to lift (something) up." *Raise* usually takes an object.

Base Form	Present Participle	Past	Past Participle
rise	(is) rising	rose	(have) risen
raise	(is) raising	raised	(have) raised

EXAMPLES   The bunch of balloons **is rising**. [no object]

The students **are raising** their hands. [The students are raising what? *Hands* is the object.]

The plane **rose** through the thick fog. [no object]

Before school we **raised** the flag. [We raised what? *Flag* is the object.]

EXERCISE 11   Choosing the Correct Forms of *Rise* and *Raise*

For each of the following sentences, underline the correct form of *rise* or *raise* in parentheses.

EX.   1. Mom and Dad always (<u>rise</u>, raise) early on Sunday mornings.

1. A delicious smell (*rose, raised*) from the hot platter of chicken fajitas.

2. Strange sounds are (*rising, raising*) from the dark basement.

3. The strong winds had (*risen, raised*) the kites high into the air.

4. We watched the rescue helicopter (*rise, raise*) from the riverbank.

5. By noon in Boston, the sun has not yet (*risen, raised*) in the Philippines.

6. Nancy turned the handle and (*rose, raised*) the bucket of water from the well.

7. The tall pine (*rose, raised*) nearly thirty feet into the sky.

8. We tried to peek at the new ballpark, but the town had (*risen, raised*) a high fence to keep it a secret.

9. Please (*rise, raise*) when it is your turn to speak.

10. The concert hall was silent as the violinist (*rose, raised*) to his feet.

11. Can you (*rise, raise*) your voice so we can hear you at the back of the room?

12. The fans are (*rising, raising*) a giant banner to honor the winning team.

13. When the plane had (*risen, raised*) high enough, the seat belt sign turned off.

14. To keep cool, an elephant (*rises, raises*) his trunk and sprays himself with cool water.

15. After everyone had (*rose, risen*) from the table, Meg and I cleaned up.

EXERCISE 12   Writing the Forms of *Rise* and *Raise*

On the line in each of the sentences below, write the correct form of *rise* or *raise*.

EX. 1. If the temperature keeps _____*rising*_____ , we'll have to open the windows.

1. It seemed as if the giant oak was _____ its branches to the sky.

2. I _____ from my seat on the bus so that my brother could sit down.

3. The man _____ the little girl above the crowd so that she could see the parade.

4. Some Mayan sculptures, which were carved from stone, _____ to more than 30 feet high.

5. Hugo _____ his eyebrows to show that he didn't believe our story.

6. Those good smells _____ from the kitchen have made me hungry.

7. Why did Theresa _____ the volume on her radio so loud?

8. The conductor is _____ his hands and will soon begin directing the orchestra.

9. We have _____ to the sounds of the birds every morning since Dad put up that new bird feeder.

10. It's been two years since Mr. Davis has _____ the price of his tomatoes.

LIE *AND* LAY

15g The verb *lie* means "to recline," "to be in a place," or "to remain lying down." *Lie* never takes an object. The verb *lay* means "to put (something) down" or "to place (something)." *Lay* usually takes an object.

Base Form	Present Participle	Past	Past Participle
lie	(is) lying	lay	(have) lain
lay	(is) laying	laid	(have) laid

EXAMPLES   That rug **lies** crooked on the floor. [no object]
The cat **lays** its toys on the doormat. [The cat lays what? *Toys* is the object.]
The logs **have lain** under the leaves for a long time. [no object]
Arturo **has laid** the bricks on the path. [Arturo has laid what? *Bricks* is the object.]

EXERCISE 13   Choosing the Correct Forms of *Lie* and *Lay*

For each of the following sentences, underline the correct form of *lie* or *lay* in parentheses.

EX.   1. I neatly (*lay, laid*) my clothes in the suitcase.

1. How long has Ned been (*lying, laying*) out in the sun?

2. Wendall (*lay, laid*) on his back and watched the snow until he got cold.

3. The sweater (*lay, laid*) in the lost-and-found box until someone claimed it.

4. Wait until Uncle Joe has (*lain, laid*) his bag down and taken off his coat.

5. Every time it rains, our cat (*lies, lays*) down under my bed and chews on a sock.

6. (*Lie, Lay*) your napkin in your lap before you start eating.

7. I have no idea how long that salad has (*lain, laid*) on the counter.

8. Ken is (*lying, laying*) down to take a nap before leaving on his trip to Denmark.

9. Lili has (*lain, laid*) that rope on the ground to mark the edges of the volleyball court.

10. That package (*lay, laid*) on the doorstep for two days before anyone noticed it.

11. My dog was (*lying, laying*) by the back door, waiting for me to take him for a walk.

12. Dad is (*lying, laying*) our old toys in a box to take to the flea market.

13. On rainy days I will (*lie, lay*) on the couch and do crossword puzzles.

14. That old book had (*lain, laid*) on the shelf for years.

15. Does Turkey (*lie, lay*) to the north or the south of Romania?

EXERCISE   Proofreading for the Correct Forms of *Lie* and *Lay*

If the sentence contains the wrong form of *lie* or *lay*, write the correct form on the line before the sentence. If a sentence is correct, write *C*.

EX. _____ lain _____ 1. There was fur all over the couch after the cat had laid on it.

_____ 1. Rafi thought he had lain his boots at the back of the closet.

_____ 2. When I can't sleep, I lay in bed and count the flowers on my wallpaper.

_____ 3. Have you ever lay outside at night and looked at the stars?

_____ 4. We laid a fork and a knife next to each plate.

_____ 5. The crew is lying a tarp over the baseball field to protect the field from the rain.

_____ 6. Mrs. Stein's strudel had laid on the table for only a minute before we ate it all.

_____ 7. My lucky penny always lies on my desk when I study for a test.

_____ 8. I threw away the empty boxes that were laying on the floor in the basement.

_____ 9. Argentina lays at the southern tip of South America.

_____ 10. Marta washed the dishes, Lee dried them, and I lay them on the shelf.

CHAPTER REVIEW

A. Proofreading Paragraphs for Correct Verb Forms

If a sentence in the paragraphs below contains an incorrect verb form, draw a line through the error. Write the correct form above the verb. Some sentences may be correct.

> EX. [1] Some children in Wenatchee, Washington, have ~~join~~ *joined* a circus just for kids.

[1] The Wenatchee Youth Circus begun in 1952. [2] Paul Pugh had start a tumbling group with youngsters at the YMCA in Wenatchee. [3] Soon, Paul's tumbling team become a circus of over fifty young performers. [4] After practicing their routines all winter, the performers are took on the road. [5] By the end of the season, the circus will have went to two or three different towns a week to perform. [6] By then, the kids in the circus have maked close friends with each other.

[7] Any young person can apply to join the circus, and many kids in the Wenatchee area have applied. [8] If there is space, the circus will accepted any child who applies. [9] The circus has gived college scholarships to performers staying with the circus for five years. [10] These young performers have did many exciting and thrilling acts. [11] They have rode bicycles on a high wire. [12] They have throwed flaming objects in the air. [13] Some kids, though, have decide to be funny instead of daring. [14] They have choosed to be the circus clowns. [15] As in all circuses, the clowns often draw the biggest smiles from the audience.

B.   Identifying the Correct Forms of *Sit* and *Set*, *Rise* and *Raise*, and *Lie* and *Lay*

For each of the sentences below, underline the correct form of the verb in parentheses.

EX.   1. I (*rose*, *raised*) my hand to ask the teacher a question.

1. I (*set*, *sat*) in my seat and read aloud the poem by Langston Hughes.

2. Eve's mother had (*lain*, *laid*) out a platter of fruit for dessert.

3. The rabbit is (*rising*, *raising*) his ears to listen for noises.

4. We had (*sat*, *set*) and waited for the bus for two hours.

5. Do you know which country (*lies*, *lays*) directly north of England?

6. The wave (*rose*, *raised*) higher and higher and then finally crashed onto the beach.

7. Don't (*sit*, *set*) your new jacket on that dirty bench.

8. The little boy (*rose*, *raised*) his head from the pillow and yawned.

9. I (*sat*, *set*) next to Shana at lunch, and she told me about her trip to India.

10. Every day, Mr. Lee (*lies*, *lays*) a button on someone's desk, and that person gets to feed the classroom fish.

C.   Working Cooperatively to Write a News Story

You and a classmate are reporters for the school newspaper. You covered the championship playoff game in basketball. Use the following prewriting questions to gather information about the game. Then write a short news story about it. Create a headline for your story. Be sure to use the correct verb forms.

Who?	Who was playing? Who won?
What?	What happened? What was the score?
Where?	Where was the game played?
When?	When was the game?
Why?	Why did your team win?
How?	How did each team play?

EX.   Eagles Win a Close One
Last night the Eagles played an exciting playoff game against their old rivals, the Rockets.

THE FORMS OF PERSONAL PRONOUNS

16a **The form of a personal pronoun shows its use in a sentence.**

(1) **Pronouns used as subjects and predicate nominatives are in the** *subject form.*

EXAMPLES   **She** and **I** brought the package. [subject]
The announcers for the play are Lekeshia and **he.** [predicate nominative]

(2) **Pronouns used as direct objects and indirect objects of verbs and as objects of prepositions are in the** *object form.*

EXAMPLES   Ms. Tran saw **us** at the mall. [direct object]
Mom gave **them** tickets to the game. [indirect object]
Are you going with Ted and **me?** [object of the preposition]

(3) **The** *possessive form (my, mine, your, yours, his, her, hers, its, their, theirs, our, ours)* **is used to show ownership or relationship.**

PERSONAL PRONOUNS			
Subject Form		**Object Form**	
Singular	**Plural**	**Singular**	**Plural**
I	we	me	us
you	you	you	you
he, she, it	they	him, her, it	them

Notice that the pronouns *you* and *it* are the same in the subject form and the object form.

EXERCISE 1   Classifying Pronouns

Classify each of the following pronouns. On the line before each pronoun, write *poss.* for *possessive form, subj.* for *subject form, obj.* for *object form,* or *either* if the pronoun can be subject form or object form.

EX. _____either_____ 1.   you

_____ 1.   me   _____ 3.   their

_____ 2.   she   _____ 4.   I

_____ 5. it   _____ 8. them

_____ 6. us   _____ 9. we

_____ 7. his   _____ 10. you

EXERCISE 2   Writing Complete Sentences with Personal Pronouns

Complete each sentence below by writing an appropriate pronoun on the line in the sentence. Use a variety of pronouns.

EX.   1. Ms. Olivier sent _____me_____ a letter.

1. _____ finished the decorations for the party.

2. At the end of the play, _____ clapped for the actors.

3. The captain of the team is _____ .

4. We asked _____ several questions.

5. Please give this note to _____ .

6. Jesse made a birthday card for _____ .

7. Katya thanked _____ for the gift.

8. Giorgio will sit beside _____ on the bus.

9. Yesterday _____ went to a basketball game.

10. The people next door to _____ are from Portugal.

11. Our coach last season was _____ .

12. Can you call _____ sometime this afternoon?

13. Tell _____ about your trip to the beach.

14. Please explain the directions to _____ .

15. Let's invite _____ to our club meeting.

16. Is that serape _____ or _____ ?

17. Those uniforms are just like _____ .

18. My dad said _____ new apartment will be larger.

19. My cousins' new dog is bigger than _____ old one.

20. Oops! I forgot _____ lunch box on the bus.

THE SUBJECT FORM

16b   Use the subject form for a pronoun that is the subject of a verb.

EXAMPLES   **I** carried the groceries home. [*I* is the subject of the verb *carried*.]
We and **they** have been rivals in baseball. [*We* and *they* are the compound subject of the verb phrase *have been*.]

16c   Use the subject form for a pronoun that is a predicate nominative.

A *predicate nominative* follows a linking verb and explains or identifies the subject of the sentence. A pronoun used as a predicate nominative usually follows a form of the verb *be* (such as *am, are, is, was, were, be, been,* or *being*).

EXAMPLES   Is the girl on the right **she?** [*She* follows the linking verb *is* and identifies the subject *girl*.]
The first ones in line were **he** and **I.** [*He* and *I* follow the linking verb *were* and identify the subject *ones*.]

To test if a pronoun is used correctly in a compound subject or compound predicate nominative, try each form of the pronoun separately.

EXAMPLE   Doreen and (*he, him*) finished their projects.
He finished. [correct]
Him finished. [incorrect]
ANSWER   **Doreen** and **he** finished their projects.

EXAMPLE   The winners of the race were Felicia and (*him, he*).
The winner was him. [incorrect]
The winner was he. [correct]
ANSWER   The winners of the race were **Felicia** and **he.**

 NOTE   Expressions such as *It's me* or *That's him* are acceptable in everyday speaking. In writing, however, you should avoid using such expressions.

 REFERENCE NOTE: For more information about predicate nominatives, see page 149.

EXERCISE 3   Identifying the Correct Use of Pronouns

In each of the following sentences, underline the pronoun that completes the sentence correctly.

EX.   1. Moira and (<u>she</u>, her) are my best friends.

1. The boy in the center of the picture is (him, he).

2. My sister and (I, me) collect stamps.

3. Hank and (us, we) are studying the Koran after school.

4. The best spellers in the class are Pierre and (she, her).

5. While on vacation, Dad and (I, me) visited the Alamo.

6. It was (she, her) who left this note for you.

7. The new members of the team are Jake and (me, I).

8. The students selling the most tickets were Elena and (he, him).

9. Are (them, they) waiting in line?

10. Can (he, him) help me paint the kachinas?

EXERCISE 4   Writing Sentences with Pronouns Used as Subjects and Predicate Nominatives

Complete each sentence below by writing an appropriate pronoun on the line in the sentence. Use a variety of pronouns, but do not use *you* or *it*.

EX.   1. The winners were Flora and ____I____.

1. _____ is my favorite author.

2. Quickly, _____ ran to the bus stop.

3. The owner of the store is _____.

4. Where did _____ buy that funny costume?

5. While the dinner cooked, _____ played a game.

6. Gloria and _____ really enjoyed the concert.

7. This story's main characters are Rafael and _____.

8. When did _____ call?

9. Each holiday, the volunteers have been Sheila and _____.

10. The stars of the show were _____.

THE OBJECT FORM

16d Use the object form for a pronoun that is the direct object of a verb.

A *direct object* follows an action verb and tells *whom* or *what* receives the action of the verb.

EXAMPLES   James thanked **us** for our help. [James, the subject of the verb, thanked *whom*? The direct object is *us*.]

Tia made **them** out of clay. [Tia, the subject of the verb, made *what*? The direct object is *them*.]

Mari picked **her** and **me** for the team. [Mari, the subject of the verb, picked *whom*? The direct objects are *her* and *me*.]

To help you choose the correct pronoun in a compound object, try each pronoun separately in the sentence.

EXAMPLE   Mr. Goldberg thanked Eli and (*he, him*) for the gift.

Mr. Goldberg thanked *he* for the gift. [incorrect]

Mr. Goldberg thanked *him* for the gift. [correct]

ANSWER   Mr. Goldberg thanked Eli and **him** for the gift.

16e Use the object form for a pronoun that is the indirect object of a verb.

An *indirect object* comes between an action verb and its direct object. It tells *to whom* or *to what* or *for whom* or *for what* something is done.

EXAMPLES   Sue's brother made **her** some spaghetti. [Sue's brother made *what*? *Spaghetti* is the direct object. *For whom* did Sue's brother make spaghetti? The indirect object is *her*.]

Robinson gave **it** a new title. [Robinson gave *what*? *Title* is the direct object. *To what* did Robinson give a title? The indirect object is *it*.]

Kim's neighbor offered **him** and **me** a job. [The neighbor offered *what*? *Job* is the direct object. *To whom* did the neighbor offer a job? The indirect objects are *him* and *me*.]

16f   Use the object form for a pronoun that is the object of a preposition.

A *prepositional phrase* begins with a preposition and ends with a noun or a pronoun, called the *object of the preposition.*

EXAMPLES   about **her**   against **us**   before **me** and **you**
            from **them**   toward **you**   without **him** or **her**

When a preposition is followed by two or more pronouns, try each pronoun alone to be sure that you have used the correct form.

EXAMPLE   Michael played basketball with Damion and (*I, me*).
           Michael played basketball with *I.* [incorrect]
           Michael played basketball with *me.* [correct]
ANSWER   Michael played basketball with Damion and **me.**

EXAMPLE   Patrick divided the grapes between (*they, them*) and (*we, us*).
           Patrick divided the grapes between *they.* [incorrect]
           Patrick divided the grapes between *them.* [correct]
           Patrick divided the grapes between *we.* [incorrect]
           Patrick divided the grapes between *us.* [correct]
ANSWER   Patrick divided the grapes between **them** and **us.**

 REFERENCE NOTE: For a list of prepositions, see page 121.

EXERCISE 5   Identifying Pronouns Used as Direct Objects and Indirect Objects

In each of the following sentences, underline the pronoun that completes the sentence correctly.

EX.   1. Carrie gave Ethel and (*I, me*) her new address.

1. Did you tell (*he, him*) that the projects are due tomorrow?

2. The waiter brought (*us, we*) a plate of egg rolls.

3. Gloria invited Jemma and (*I, me*) to her party.

4. Send (*them, they*) postcards when you arrive in Puerto Rico.

5. At the skating rink, I met (*she, her*) and her cousin.

6. The usher gave (*they, them*) seats in the front row.

7. If you have any questions, just ask (I, me).

8. The teacher taught (*we, us*) about the Inuit carvers from Alaska.

9. Dr. Valdez gave Henry and (*me, I*) the medicine for our dog.

10. Pass Mr. Kyoto and (*she, her*) these bowls of soup.

11. Did you make (*he, him*) a birthday present this year?

12. Will you show Joni and (*us, we*) how to program the VCR?

13. Dad brought (*they, them*) from Mexico last April.

14. In the Earth Day program, their class sang (*we, us*) a song.

15. The police officer warned (*him, he*) about the flooded highway.

EXERCISE 6   Identifying Pronouns Used as Objects of Prepositions

In each of the sentences below, underline the pronoun that completes the sentence correctly.

EX.   1. I made these ties for Grandfather and (*he, him*).

1. Miguel and Oscar ran against (*me, I*) in the race.

2. I loaned my book about Geronimo to (*she, her*).

3. Emma Mae sat next to Grandma and (*me, I*) at the concert.

4. Just between you and (*I, me*), I don't really like this dessert.

5. We learned about (*they, them*) in science class.

6. He threw the ball toward Bertie and (*she, her*), but neither of (*them, they*) caught it.

7. I don't want to go to the movies without Kim and (*him, he*).

8. That's the boy who lives above (*we, us*) in our apartment building.

9. You can get in front of Roberto and (*me, I*).

10. Curtis and Veronica were interviewed by (*she, her*) for the school paper.

11. For (*they, them*), the best part of the story was the surprise ending.

12. These presents are for Geraldo and (*we, us*).

13. The poems that we read were by Nikki Giovanni and (*he, him*).

14. I read an article about (*them, they*) in *American Girl* magazine.

15. Did you get a letter from (*her, she*) yet?

EXERCISE 7   Proofreading Sentences for Correct Use of Pronouns

If a sentence below contains an incorrect pronoun, draw a line through the incorrect pronoun. Then write the correct pronoun on the line before the sentence. If the sentence contains no pronoun errors, write *C* on the line.

EX. ___*me*___ 1. The principal gave Jamie and I our prizes.

_____ 1. I'm ready to play against Gordon and he.

_____ 2. Mom planned a party for Clara and I.

_____ 3. Give Sal and I your ideas about the party decorations.

_____ 4. Tell Aunt Lois and she about your dancing class.

_____ 5. I missed Jeremy and they after I moved to Austin.

_____ 6. Did you make these biscuits for Mary and me?

_____ 7. Please pass the papers to David and we.

_____ 8. The neighborhood party was planned by they.

_____ 9. Did you help Mrs. Tomas and she with the raking?

_____ 10. Where did you meet Miguel and he?

_____ 11. For Chris and I, the game was really exciting.

_____ 12. Fred divided the free tickets among his neighbors and us.

_____ 13. Please bring enough guanabana custard for Jake and she, too.

_____ 14. Tell Molly and they about your report on Hawaii.

_____ 15. Where did the stage manager take Margie and he?

_____ 16. Kareem brought his prayer rug with him.

_____ 17. Please give Maurice and I directions to your house.

_____ 18. At the corner, we saw Barbara and he.

_____ 19. Invite the captain and they to share our refreshments.

_____ 20. He thanked Josie and we for washing the fava beans.

SPECIAL PRONOUN PROBLEMS

Who and Whom

16g The pronoun *who* has two different forms. *Who* is the subject form. *Whom* is the object form.

When you are choosing between *who* or *whom* in a question, follow these steps.

Step 1: Rephrase the question as a statement.

Step 2: Identify how the pronoun is used in the statement—as subject, predicate nominative, direct object, indirect object, or object of a preposition.

Step 3: Determine whether the subject form or the object form is correct according to the rules of standard English.

Step 4: Select the correct form—*who* or *whom.*

EXAMPLE To (*who, whom*) did you give the house keys?

Step 1: The statement is *You did give the house keys to (who, whom).*

Step 2: *You* is the subject, the verb is *did give*, and the pronoun is the object of the preposition *to.*

Step 3: As the object of a preposition, the pronoun should be in object form.

Step 4: The object form is *whom.*

ANSWER To **whom** did you give the house keys?

NOTE The use of *whom* is becoming less common in spoken English. When you are speaking, you may correctly begin any question with *who*. In written English, however, you should distinguish between *who* and *whom*. *Who* is used as a subject or a predicate nominative, and *whom* is used as an object.

Pronouns with Appositives

16h Sometimes a pronoun is followed directly by a noun that identifies the pronoun. Such a noun is called an *appositive.*

To help you choose which pronoun to use before an appositive, omit the appositive and try each form of the pronoun separately.

EXAMPLE (*Us, We*) players cheered for the other team. **[*Players* is the appositive identifying the pronoun.]**

Us cheered for the other team. **[incorrect]**

We cheered for the other team. **[correct]**

ANSWER **We** players cheered for the other team.

EXERCISE 8   Identifying the Correct Forms of Pronouns in Sentences

In each sentence below, underline the pronoun in parentheses that completes the sentence correctly.

EX.   1. (Who, *Whom*) did you meet at the game?

1. (Who, Whom) won the prize?

2. (We, Us) club members made posters to tell people about our magic show.

3. The winners of the talent show were (we, us) dancers.

4. (Who, Whom) is the lead singer in that band?

5. Please give (we, us) actors more time to practice our lines.

6. (Who, Whom) did you vote for?

7. Yesterday (we, us) class members went on a field trip.

8. (Who, Whom) has the correct answer?

9. (Who, Whom) has Marissa invited?

10. The store owner asked (we, us) workers to come in early on Saturday.

11. That job was easy for (we, us) sixth graders.

12. (Who, Whom) needs a ride home?

13. Tell (we, us) volunteers what needs to be done.

14. (Who, Whom) is the author of the book *Old Yeller?*

15. (We, Us) children always enjoyed *Carnaval* back home in Veracruz.

16. (Who, Whom) are you sitting with at lunch today?

17. For (we, us) hikers, the Mountain Club has planned a great trip.

18. For (who, whom) did you make these huaraches?

19. Of course, (we, us) players want to win!

20. Against (who, whom) are we playing in the basketball game?

21. The World Series is an important event for (we, us) baseball fans.

22. (Who, Whom) said you sing like Mahalia Jackson?

23. (We, Us) Eagles may have a hard time against the Giants.

24. (Who, Whom) was the inventor of the telephone?

25. Uncle Harold gave (we, us) children a ride in his new boat.

CHAPTER REVIEW

A. Choosing Correct Pronoun Forms

In each sentence below, underline the correct pronoun in parentheses.

EX. 1. Ms. Gillmore gave the awards to Jody and (*I, me*).

1. Barbara Beckman asked David Hu and (*he, him*) many questions.

2. The leading roles were played by Denzel Washington and (*she, her*).

3. Diana Ross and (*they, them*) were once in a group called "The Supremes."

4. Shari bought the new CD by Ella Fitzgerald and (*he, him*).

5. (*Who, Whom*) wrote the play *Our Town*?

6. We people of Philadelphia are proud of (*our, us*) city.

7. The best runners in the race were Don Cornett and (*he, him*).

8. Can you tell (*we, us*) swimmers the schedule of today's events?

9. To (*who, whom*) did you send the package?

10. (*Who, Whom*) have we invited to the picnic?

B. Proofreading Sentences for Incorrect Pronoun Forms

In each of the following sentences, look for errors in pronoun use. Draw a line through the incorrect pronoun, and write the correct pronoun in the space above it. A sentence may be correct.

EX. 1. ~~Us~~ We students read an article about Isaac Bashevis Singer.

1. Him was a writer of Yiddish and Hebrew folk tales.

2. Many of they have been translated into other languages.

3. To Jerry and I, Singer's best folk tale is "Zlateh the Goat."

4. When Singer was a boy, his family and him lived in Poland.

5. He and his sister and brothers studied Hebrew and Yiddish in school.

6. Their father, a rabbi, taught they respect for their religion.

7. Singer's stories give we readers a picture of Jewish culture.

8. Many of the characters teach we lessons about life.

9. Between you and I, one of the funniest characters is Shlemiel.

10. Singer chose that name for he because it means "fool."

11. Whom is Shlemiel in the folk tale?

12. He is a farmer with a family, and them live in Chelm, Poland.

13. Shlemiel tells them about his dreams.

14. Us readers are also told about Shlemiel's dreams of going to Warsaw, a big city.

15. Shlemiel says goodbye to him family and starts out for Warsaw.

16. Along the way, him gets tired and falls asleep.

17. Before lying down to sleep, he points his boots toward Warsaw.

18. Then a man comes along and points the tips of they back toward Chelm.

19. Shlemiel walks back to Chelm, but him thinks that it is a different village.

20. Him wife and children cannot make foolish Shlemiel understand the truth.

C. Writing a Memo Using Pronouns

You are a writer for a television network. You have been asked to come up with an idea for a new cartoon show for Saturday morning. After seeing the road sign below, you come up with an idea. On your own paper, write a memo to your boss to explain your ideas. You might talk about the title of the show, the characters, and the story line. Include at least five subject forms and five object forms of pronouns. Underline the pronouns you use.

EX.   An idea came to <u>me</u> about a new cartoon called "DinoMite Days." The story will be about three young people <u>who</u> live in prehistoric times.

REGULAR COMPARISON OF ADJECTIVES AND ADVERBS

A *modifier* is a word or a phrase that describes or limits the meaning of another word. The two kinds of modifiers—adjectives and adverbs—may be used to make comparisons. In making comparisons, adjectives and adverbs take special forms. The form that is used depends on how many things are being compared.

17a   The three degrees of comparison of modifiers are the *positive*, the *comparative*, and the *superlative*.

(1) The *positive degree* is used when only one thing is being described.

EXAMPLES   Alma is a **good** player.   The last class goes **slowly**.

(2) The *comparative degree* is used when two things are being compared.

EXAMPLES   Perhaps Ruth is a **better** player than Alma.
No other hour passes **more slowly** than that class.

(3) The *superlative degree* is used when three or more things are being compared.

EXAMPLES   The **best** player on the team is Teresa.
Which hour of the day goes **most slowly** for you?

 NOTE   In conversation you may hear such expressions as *Put your best foot forward*. This use of the superlative is acceptable in spoken English. In your writing, however, you should follow rule (3).

 REFERENCE NOTE: For a discussion of standard English, see page 217.

17b   Most one-syllable modifiers form the comparative degree by adding *–er* and the superlative degree by adding *–est*.

Positive	Comparative	Superlative
cold	colder	coldest
mad	madder	maddest
near	nearer	nearest
pure	purer	purest
small	smaller	smallest
quick	quicker	quickest

17c   Some two-syllable modifiers form the comparative degree by adding *–er* and the superlative degree by adding *–est*. Other two-syllable modifiers form the comparative degree by using *more* and the superlative degree by using *most*.

Positive	Comparative	Superlative
happy	happier	happiest
early	earlier	earliest
funny	funnier	funniest
briefly	more briefly	most briefly
honest	more honest	most honest
peaceful	more peaceful	most peaceful

☞   **REFERENCE NOTE:** For guidelines on how to spell words when adding *–er* or *–est*, see pages 275–277.

17d   Modifiers that have three or more syllables form their comparative and superlative degrees by using *more* and *most*.

Positive	Comparative	Superlative
carefully	more carefully	most carefully
different	more different	most different
easily	more easily	most easily
intelligent	more intelligent	most intelligent
generous	more generous	most generous
educational	more educational	most educational

Whenever you are unsure about which way a modifier forms its degrees of comparison, look in a dictionary.

EXERCISE 1   Writing Comparative and Superlative Forms

On the lines provided, write the forms for the comparative and superlative degrees of each of the following modifiers. Use a dictionary as necessary.

EX. 1. strong _____*stronger*_____ _____*strongest*_____

1. clean _____ _____

2. ready _____ _____

3. thoughtful _____ _____

4. exciting _____ _____

5. old _____ _____

6. funny _____ _____

7. difficult _____ _____

8. confused _____ _____

9. modern _____ _____

10. fair _____ _____

11. surprised _____ _____

12. cleverly _____ _____

13. challenging _____ _____

14. late _____ _____

15. clear _____ _____

16. impressive _____ _____

17. blue _____ _____

18. generous _____ _____

19. daring _____ _____

20. sad _____ _____

EXERCISE 2   Proofreading Sentences for Comparative and Superlative Forms

On the line before each of the following sentences, write the correct form of the modifier in italics. Write C if a sentence is correct. Use a dictionary as necessary.

EX. _____*nearest*_____ 1. Of all the planets, Mercury is *near* to the sun.

_____ 1. I think dogs are *more faithful* pets than cats.

_____ 2. Which of these two sweaters is *warm*?

_____ 3. Of all the sprinters, Peter runs *most fast*.

_____ 4. The air feels *cold* than it did this morning.

_____ 5. "Flying would be *quickest* than driving," the travel agent recommended.

_____ 6. The crowd is *impatient* for the game to begin.

_____ 7. That chili pepper was *hot* than I expected!

_____ 8. The first question on the ten-question test was the *simpler*.

_____ 9. This building is the *newer* one in the city.

_____ 10. No other star shines *more bright*.

_____ 11. Francie is *most prepared* than Lydia.

_____ 12. This year's carnival was the *more successful* ever!

_____ 13. Gordon is the *friendliest* person I know.

_____ 14. No type of music is *most popular* than rock-and-roll.

_____ 15. Kenji is the *most outgoing* of the twins.

_____ 16. Steel is *more sturdy* than cardboard.

_____ 17. Rock climbing can be a *more dangerous* sport.

_____ 18. The sidewalk is *iciest,* so be careful.

_____ 19. Is San Francisco or Seattle *foggiest*?

_____ 20. The witness answered the questions *more honestly*.

EXERCISE 3   Writing a Letter

The students in your school are tired of looking at the basketball court. The court has been run-down for years. Now you and your fellow students would like to restore the court so that it will be safe and usable. Write a letter to the president of the student council, explaining why the council should sponsor such a project. In your letter, use at least five comparative and five superlative forms of modifiers. Underline each comparative and superlative form that you use.

EX.   1.   We, the students of Filmore Middle School, are writing to ask that the student council sponsor a project to have the basketball court restored. We believe that this court could be a tool to encourage students to be <u>more physically</u> fit.

IRREGULAR COMPARISON OF ADJECTIVES AND ADVERBS

17e Some modifiers do not form their comparative and superlative degrees by using the regular methods.

Positive	Comparative	Superlative
bad	worse	worst
far	farther	farthest
good	better	best
many	more	most
much	more	most

NOTE You do not need to add anything to an irregular comparison. For example, *worse*, all by itself, is the comparative form of *bad*. *Worser* and *more worse* are nonstandard forms.

EXERCISE 4 Proofreading Sentences for Irregular Comparative and Superlative Forms

On the line before each of the following sentences, write the correct form of the modifier in italics. If a sentence is correct, write *C*.

EX. __worse__ 1. My cold is getting *worst*.

_____ 1. Jack's Diner serves the *good* chili in town.

_____ 2. Elena hit the ball *farthest* than any of the other players.

_____ 3. California has *many* people than any other state in the United States.

_____ 4. These skis are *best* for cross-country skiing than for downhill racing.

_____ 5. Tanya performed *better* at her recital.

_____ 6. It rains *much* in April than in May.

_____ 7. That was the *baddest* song I've ever heard!

_____ 8. Which of the two towns is *farthest* away?

_____ 9. Kay woke up ill, but she felt *best* after she ate breakfast.

_____ 10. *Most* people came to the crafts fair than to the bake sale.

_____ 11. The author's new book is *better* than her last one.

_____ 12. When I was six years old, I had a *bad* case of measles.

_____ 13. Which of those stores is *more far* from the house?

_____ 14. Uncle Ruben tells the *better* jokes of anyone in our family.

_____ 15. We raised *much* money this year than last year.

EXERCISE 5   Proofreading for Correct Use of Irregular Comparative and Superlative Forms

In the paragraph below, draw a line through modifiers that are incorrect. Write the correct form above the error. Some sentences may be correct.

EX. [1] Being an archaeologist would be the ~~goodest~~ *best* job.

[1] I think nothing could be more well than digging for clues from the past. [2] The books I've read make archaeology sound like the most good adventure. [3] I just read a book I liked very much about the huge stone statues on Easter Island in the Pacific. [4] When I found Easter Island on a map, I realized it's more far away from here than I thought. [5] Many archaeologists travel more far than I can imagine. [6] Archaeologists traveled there to get most understanding of how the statues were made. [7] Although a few of them are taller, many statues are between 10 and 20 feet tall. [8] What worked wellest for moving the statues was rolling them on wooden logs. [9] Moving those heavy statues so farther was a great accomplishment. [10] I think reading about these discoveries is gooder than reading mystery novels. [11] The only bad part is that more of what I know about archaeology comes from books. [12] I think it would be more good to do some real digging, rather than just to read about it. [13] But reading isn't the most bad thing I could do. [14] I still have a better time reading about how archaeologists piece together mysteries from the past. [15] Maybe someday I'll be an archaeologist who solves more mysteries.

USING GOOD *AND* WELL

17f The modifiers *good* and *well* have different uses.

(1) Use *good* to modify a noun or a pronoun.

EXAMPLES Ask the librarian for a **good** story. [The adjective *good* modifies the noun *story*.]
This calculator is **better** than that one. [The adjective *better* modifies the noun *calculator*.]
Aladdin was the **best** movie I saw last year. [The adjective *best* modifies the noun *movie*.]

Good should not be used to modify a verb.

NONSTANDARD   Uncle Harry drives good.
STANDARD   Uncle Harry drives **well**.

(2) Use *well* to modify a verb.

EXAMPLE Ulani spoke her lines **well**. [The adverb *well* modifies the verb *spoke*.]
The children played together **better** after lunch. [The adverb *better* modifies the verb *played*.]
The team batted **best** in the final inning. [The adverb *best* modifies the verb *batted*.]

NOTE *Well* can also mean "in good health." When *well* has this meaning, it acts as an adjective with a linking verb.

EXAMPLE   I did not feel **well** on Sunday. [The adjective *well* modifies the pronoun *I*.]

EXERCISE 6   Choosing the Correct Modifier

In the following sentences, underline the correct modifier in parentheses.

EX.   1. The morning got off to a (*good*, *well*) start.

1. Keith's skateboard is working (*good*, *well*) since he oiled the wheels.

2. "Are you feeling (*good*, *well*) today?" Dr. Franklin asked.

3. Everyone agrees that Nanci is a (*good*, *well*) singer.

4. The children behaved (*good, well*) for their baby sitter.

5. That's a (*good, well*) suggestion.

6. Fresh tomatoes make the sauce taste (*well, good*).

7. Scott does (*good, well*) in his social studies class.

8. Rebecca understands German as (*well, good*) as she speaks it.

9. Our soccer team plays (*good, well*) defense.

10. The painter shows her (*well, good*) work at the gallery.

11. Amy didn't feel (*good, well*) after the roller coaster ride.

12. This cactus grows (*good, well*) in dry climates.

13. (*Good, Well*) manners are very important.

14. My grandfather cooks (*well, good*).

15. "I'm feeling very (*good, well*)," answered Hiroshi.

16. That jacket fits you (*good, well*).

17. Wyatt plays the trumpet as (*good, well*) as anyone else in the school band.

18. Have a (*good, well*) time!

19. Your pen works as (*well, good*) as mine.

20. Did you make a (*good, well*) impression?

EXERCISE 7 Using the Correct Forms of *Good* and *Well* in a Review

You are a writer for a children's consumer magazine. You review new products and make recommendations to your readers. This week you're reviewing a new brand of in-line skates. Write five sentences that you might use in your review. In your sentences, use a correct form of either *good* or *well*. Underline the modifier in your sentences.

EX.   1.   Zippy In-Line Skates are a <u>good</u> choice if you're concerned about your safety and your budget.

MODIFIERS AFTER LINKING VERBS

17g   Use adjectives, not adverbs, after linking verbs.

Linking verbs, such as *look, feel,* and *become,* are often followed by predicate adjectives. These adjectives describe, or modify, the subject.

EXAMPLES   The crowd became **restless** waiting for the band. [*Restless* modifies the subject *crowd.*]
Lee looks **hungry.** [*Hungry* modifies the subject *Lee.*]

NOTE   Some linking verbs can also be used as action verbs. As action verbs, they may be modified by adverbs.

EXAMPLE   Lee looked **hungrily** at the Thanksgiving turkey. [*Hungrily* modifies the action verb *looked.*]

 REFERENCE NOTE: For a list of linking verbs, see page 115.

EXERCISE 8   Choosing the Correct Modifier

In the following sentences, underline the correct modifier in parentheses.

EX.   1. Marina looks (<u>*tired*</u>, *tiredly*).

1. The teacher seems (*proud, proudly*) of his class.

2. The sapling grew (*steady, steadily*) throughout the spring.

3. Does the trout smell (*fresh, freshly*)?

4. The house looks (*empty, emptily*).

5. Our cat is always (*restless, restlessly*) at night.

6. My younger sister becomes (*shy, shyly*) around strangers.

7. The clouds appeared (*sudden, suddenly*).

8. Jonah felt (*sorry, sorrily*) after the argument.

9. The snow is (*silent, silently*) falling.

10. This peach tastes too (*sweet, sweetly*).

11. Maggie stays (*busy, busily*) throughout the long day.

12. That name sounds (*familiar, familiarly*) to me.

13. All of the windows are locked (*tight, tightly*).

14. Your idea sounds (*wonderful, wonderfully*)!

15. Jerome felt (*bad, badly*) about what he said to Kenny.

16. The storyteller looked (*warm, warmly*) at the children.

17. The float turned (*slow, slowly*) to the right.

18. Paula's sunburn became (*painful, painfully*).

19. The grease stain (*stubborn, stubbornly*) remained in the tablecloth.

20. "The experiment seems (*successful, successfully*)," declared the scientist.

21. Do you feel (*hungry, hungrily*) yet?

22. As the day went on it became (*warm, warmly*).

23. Tova touched the duckling (*gentle, gently*).

24. We looked (*happy, happily*) at the proud child.

25. Marc seemed (*content, contentedly*) when he heard the plans.

EXERCISE 9   **Proofreading for Correct Modifiers in a Paragraph**

In the paragraph below, there are ten misused modifiers. Draw a line through each error, and write the correct form above it.

EX.   [1] I walked to the front of the class nervous.

                                              nervously

[1] I might have appeared calmly, but I didn't feel that way. [2] My mouth felt dryly. [3] My hands felt coldly as I clutched my poem tightly. [4] I looked quick around the room. [5] My classmates looked at me expectant. [6] I coughed loud a few times and began reading. [7] I was afraid I would read too quick. [8] I was also afraid my voice would sound strangely. [9] But once I started reading, I felt relieved. [10] After I finished reading, it seemed impossibly that I had ever been nervous.

REVIEW EXERCISE

A. Writing Comparative and Superlative Forms in Sentences

On the line before each of the sentences below, write the correct form of the modifier in italics.

EX. _noisier_ 1. The crowd tonight is _noisy_ than the crowd last night.

_____ 1. August 16 was the _hot_ day of the whole summer.

_____ 2. The water jug is _wide_ at the base than at the mouth.

_____ 3. At today's track meet, Brenda ran her _good_ time so far.

_____ 4. Tanya is _excited_ about the science fair than Sam is.

_____ 5. "The bag filled with canned goods is the _heavy_ of all the bags," warned Raymond.

_____ 6. The old rocking chair is the _comfortable_ chair in the room.

_____ 7. The storm hit _hard_ than expected.

_____ 8. That's the _incredible_ story I've ever heard!

_____ 9. No one else is _concerned_ than the parents.

_____ 10. Of all the students in the class, Kichi lives _far_ from the school.

B. Proofreading for Correct Forms of Modifiers

In the paragraph below, there are twenty misused modifiers. Draw a line through each error, and write the correct form above it. Some sentences may have no errors.

EX. [1] The Andes Mountains are the ~~most long~~ longest mountain chain in the world.

[1] The 4,500 miles of the Andes Mountains cut jagged down the length of South America. [2] Many changes take place along those miles than you can imagine. [3] The wider part of the mountains is over 370 miles across. [4] They become most narrow at Tierra del

Fuego. [5] Tierra del Fuego is the southernmost part of the chain.
[6] Many active volcanoes lie along the Andes, and much of them are
in the northern Andes. [7] In Ecuador you'll find Cotopaxi, the
world's most high active volcano. [8] The eastern slopes facing the
Amazon River get more rain than any other area. [9] Tropical rain
forests grow good in these areas. [10] The western slopes are more
dry. [11] If you're looking for rain, the western coasts of Peru and
Chile are the baddest places to be. [12] Fewest inches of rain fall there
than at any other point along the chain. [13] You'll also find some of
the most cold temperatures there. [14] In these high elevations, the
oxygen supply is more bad because the air is thinner. [15] These areas
of the Andes aren't very well for growing plants and trees.

C.   Writing a Treasurer's Report

As treasurer for your class, you are responsible for the report to the class
sponsor about the sales at the class concession stand. Using the graph below
for information, create ten sentences to explain the sales for different items.
Use and underline five comparative and five superlative forms of modifiers.

EX.   1.   I'm happy to report that sales last month were the <u>best</u> so far this
           year.

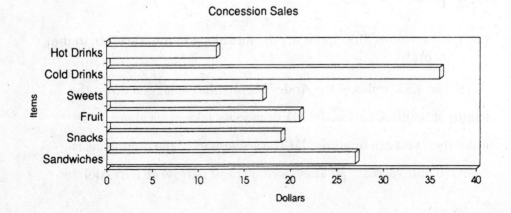

Concession Sales

DOUBLE COMPARISONS AND DOUBLE NEGATIVES

17h   Avoid double comparisons.

A *double comparison* is the use of both *-er* and *more* or *-est* and *most* to form a single comparison. When you make a comparison, use only one of these forms, not both.

NONSTANDARD   The starling is one of the most noisiest birds here.
STANDARD   The starling is one of the **noisiest** birds here.

NONSTANDARD   The puppy is growing more faster than the kitten.
STANDARD   The puppy is growing **faster** than the kitten.

17i   Avoid the use of double negatives.

A *double negative* is the use of two negative words to express one negative idea. Some common negative words are *barely, hardly, neither, never, no, nobody, none, no one, not (–n't), nothing, nowhere,* and *scarcely.*

NONSTANDARD   We couldn't find none of the berries.
STANDARD   We **could find none** of the berries.
STANDARD   We **couldn't find any** of the berries.

NONSTANDARD   Ms. Garfield didn't see nobody for three days.
STANDARD   Ms. Garfield **didn't see anybody** for three days.
STANDARD   Ms. Garfield **saw nobody** for three days.

EXERCISE 10 · Eliminating Double Comparisons and Double Negatives

On your own paper, revise the following sentences to eliminate the double comparisons and double negatives.

EX.   1. Josh doesn't want none of the popcorn.
　　　1. Josh doesn't want any of the popcorn.

1. These apples are the most sourest I've ever tasted.

2. As we got closer to the crowded auditorium, the music sounded more louder.

3. There weren't barely enough seats for everyone.

4. The sunshine makes it seem more warmer outdoors.

5. The spy didn't reveal his true identity to no one.

6. Camilla never misses none of her violin lessons.

7. The giraffes are more taller than I thought they'd be.

8. Why wasn't none of the mail delivered?

9. "There isn't no line in the express lane," the grocery manager announced.

10. The new public library is more closer to the school than the old library was.

11. Put the photographs in the most smallest box.

12. We had hardly no problems following the directions.

13. Alex doesn't remember nothing about his dream.

14. The children were more sleepier after dinner.

15. I can't find my keys nowhere.

16. Karen ran the most fastest of all.

17. We couldn't hardly hear because of the crying baby.

18. Paul says he is more stronger than Raoul, but I'm not sure.

19. I never said that to nobody!

20. Dad hadn't scarcely walked in when the dog jumped on him.

CHAPTER REVIEW

A. Choosing the Correct Modifier

In the sentences below, underline the correct modifier in parentheses.

EX. 1. Farmers are predicting a (<u>good</u>, well) harvest.

1. I think the (worse, worst) part of the storm has passed.

2. Howard looked (worried, worriedly) at his watch.

3. "Doesn't (anyone, no one) have a question?" Ms. Huang asked the class.

4. February is the (shortest, most shortest) month.

5. Andrea took the news (good, well).

6. The puzzle was (more difficult, most difficult) than it looked.

7. Elliot seems (happy, happily) with his performance.

8. If you're not feeling (good, well), then perhaps you should go home.

9. The living room looks (brighter, brightest) with the curtains open.

10. Austria is the (farther, farthest) I've traveled.

11. There (was, wasn't) scarcely time to eat lunch.

12. Ryan is the (more reliable, most reliable) person I know.

13. Everyone wrote a (good, well) report.

14. There aren't (any, no) penguins at the North Pole.

15. The pottery is the (older, oldest) that has ever been found.

B. Revising Sentences by Correcting Errors in the Use of Modifiers

For the following sentences, draw a line through the incorrect modifiers. Write the correct form above the error.

EX. 1. I'm feeling ~~more well~~ today.
   better

1. The train is moving slow.

2. Not none of the leaves have been raked.

3. Larry plays the guitar good.

4. Many people thought that movie was the better one of the year.

5. Chicago's O'Hare International Airport is the most busiest airport in the world.

6. This restaurant serves the goodest Thai noodles in town.

7. I can't hardly wait for summer.

8. Alice seems patiently with the kindergartners.

9. Most of the pictures I took are quite well.

10. We're getting more closer to the campground.

11. Jane was angrier that she did not get the part in the play.

12. The music was even surprisinger than the way the musicians dressed.

13. A warm, crackling bonfire was the enjoyablest ending to the day.

14. Which game do you like most, soccer or football?

15. Of all his subjects, Fong Chung did more better in history.

16. Juana's carpentry skills were very well.

17. "You look thoughtfully, Helen," Jee said.

18. We didn't go nowhere all day.

19. Egrets are some of the most biggest birds.

20. Is this the farther you've been from home?

C.   Writing Copy for an Amusement Park Advertisement

You work for an advertising company that has the new Atlantis Undersea Amusement Park as its client. You have been told to write the words that will be used in the advertisement for this new park. Create at least ten sentences that will make people want to go see the park. Use at least three comparative forms and two superlative forms of adjectives and adverbs in your writing. Underline the comparative and superlative forms you use. Use your imagination to describe what the new rides look like, where the park is, and how much tickets cost.

EX.   1.   Get ready for the most exciting adventure of your life at the Atlantis Undersea Amusement Park!

This chapter contains a **glossary,** or alphabetical list, of common problems in English usage. You will notice throughout the chapter that some examples are labeled *standard* or *nonstandard*. **Standard English** is the most widely accepted form of English. It is used in *formal* situations, such as speeches and compositions for school. It is also used in *informal* situations, such as conversations and everyday writing. **Nonstandard English** is language that does not follow the rules and guidelines of standard English.

a, an   Use *a* before words beginning with a consonant sound. Use *an* before words beginning with a vowel sound.

EXAMPLES   **a** lizard   **an** iguana   **an** hour

accept, except   *Accept* is a verb. It means "to receive." *Except* may be either a verb or a preposition. As a verb, it means "to leave out." As a preposition, *except* means "excluding" or "but."

EXAMPLES   Betty happily **accepted** her friend's ticket to the concert. **[verb]**
Roscoe was **excepted** from football practice because he already knew all the plays. **[verb]**
I visited every New England state **except** Maine. **[preposition]**

ain't   Avoid this word in speaking and writing. It is nonstandard English.

NONSTANDARD   I ain't finished with this book.
STANDARD   I **am not** finished with this book.

all right   *All right* can be used as an adjective that means "satisfactory" or "unhurt." As an adverb, *all right* means "well enough." *All right* should always be written as two words.

EXAMPLES   Joshua thought he'd sprained his ankle, but he was **all right** a few minutes later. **[adjective]**
My aunt's old car still runs **all right**. **[adverb]**

a lot   *A lot* should always be written as two words.

EXAMPLES   Sissy likes asparagus **a lot**.
We saw **a lot** of elephants at the circus.

already, all ready   *Already* means "previously." *All ready* means "completely prepared" or "in readiness."

EXAMPLES   Hoshi had **already** finished speaking when the bell rang.
Is everyone **all ready** for the exam?

---

among   See **between, among.**

anywheres, everywheres, nowheres, somewheres   Use these words without the final -s.

EXAMPLES   My dog Biff would follow me **anywhere.**
The tomatoes are located **somewhere** along the third aisle.

at   Do not use *at* after *where.*

EXAMPLE   Where is my baseball? [not *baseball at*]

EXERCISE 1   Identifying Correct Usage

Underline the correct word or words in parentheses in each of the sentences below.

EX.   1. At the end of that story, everything turns out (*all right, allright*).

1. Benji stood up to (*accept, except*) the award.

2. Lita planted a small garden (*somewhere, somewheres*) in the trees.

3. Our science class built (*a, an*) interesting project.

4. Dad asked if we were (*already, all ready*) to go to the beach.

5. Owen drove the car to the mall and then forgot (*where he had parked it, where he had parked it at*).

6. Put the tray down (*anywhere, anywheres*) on the table.

7. Clarence thinks he's the best field-goal kicker in the school, but he (*ain't, isn't*).

8. History tells us that George Washington was (*a, an*) honest man.

9. Every Saturday, Phil practiced (*a lot, alot*) on the piano.

10. I rang the bell, but my cousin had (*already, all ready*) opened the door.

11. After the accident, a doctor said Dad would be (*all right, allright*).

12. I think I left the sweater (*somewhere, somewheres*) in this room.

13. Everyone was happy (*accept, except*) Mamie.

14. Did the three children know where the crayons (*were at, were*)?

15. You (*ain't, are not*) going without me!

BETWEEN, AMONG / HOW COME

between, among   Use *between* when you are referring to two things at a time. The two things may be part of a group consisting of more than two. Use *among* when you are referring to a group rather than to separate individuals.

EXAMPLES   The judges finally had to decide **between** Alicia and Rene.
There were only a few feet **between** each of the three fence posts. [Each post is compared with the others separately.]
Lon, Roger, and Harold sat in the lunchroom arguing **among** themselves. [The three boys are thought of as a group.]

bring, take   *Bring* shows action directed *toward* the speaker or writer. *Take* shows action directed *away from* the speaker or writer. Think of *bring* as related to *come*. Think of *take* as related to *go*.

EXAMPLES   Please **bring** that chair over here.
Did you **take** the message to Flora?

could of   Do not write *of* with the helping verb *could*. Write *could have*. Also avoid *ought to of, should of, would of, had of, might of,* and *must of*.

EXAMPLES   Her smile **could have** melted ice. [not *could of*]
It **must have** been Sancho. [not *must of*]

everywheres   See **anywheres,** etc.

except, accept   See **accept, except.**

fewer, less   *Fewer* is used with plural words. *Less* is used with singular words. *Fewer* tells "how many." *Less* tells "how much."

EXAMPLES   The **fewer** complaints we get, the better.
There seemed to be **less** noise on the beach today.

had of   See **could of.**

had ought, hadn't ought   The verb *ought* should not be used with *had*.

EXAMPLES   He **ought** to know that by now. [not *had ought*]
They **ought not** to wait too long. [not *hadn't ought*]

hisself, theirself, theirselves   These words are nonstandard English. Use *himself* and *themselves*.

EXAMPLES   Brandon said that he would do it **himself**. [not *hisself*]
The team earned **themselves** a day off from practice. [not *theirselves*]

> **how come**   In informal English, *How come?* is often used instead of *Why?* In formal English, *Why?* is always preferred.
>
> INFORMAL   "**How come** you always wear blue on Monday?" Janet asked.
>   FORMAL   Our teacher explained **why** we had been given the assignment.

EXERCISE 2   Identifying Correct Usage

Underline the correct word or words in parentheses in each of the following sentences.

EX.   1.   Darryl had never thought of (*hisself, himself*) as a mountain climber.

1.   The place where he lived had (*fewer, less*) mountains than my town.

2.   While on vacation one summer, his older brother Bert told Darryl that he (*ought, had ought*) to try an easy climb.

3.   The hill behind their cabin (*must have, must of*) looked too big.

4.   Darryl wondered (*how come, why*) they should try to climb it.

5.   Bert said encouragingly, "We can make it with (*fewer, less*) difficulties if we are well prepared for the climb."

6.   Each boy dressed (*hisself, himself*) in a long-sleeved shirt and long pants.

7.   Bert also reminded Darryl to (*bring, take*) a canteen with him.

8.   They (*would have, would of*) forgotten to pack something to eat, but their mother made them some sandwiches.

9.   They knew they (*had ought, ought*) to watch out for bears.

10.   At the last minute, Darryl complained again, "(*How come, Why do*) we have to go?"

11.   "(*Among, Between*) you and me, I was scared, too, when I was your age," said Bert.

12.   The two boys started out, but Darryl still wished that he (*could have, could of*) gone fishing with his parents.

13.   But halfway up, he discovered that he was enjoying (*hisself, himself*), particularly when they found the patch of wild blueberries.

14.   Just around lunchtime, they found (*theirselves, themselves*) at the top.

15.   The view from the top was wonderful, and Darryl wished he had (*brought, taken*) his camera.

ITS, IT'S / THAN, THEN

its, it's *Its* is the possessive form of the personal pronoun *it*. *Its* is used to show ownership. *It's* is a contraction of *it is, it was,* or *it has.*

EXAMPLES   We heard the robin singing **its** first song of the spring.
It's been years since I saw that film.

kind of, sort of In informal English, *kind of* and *sort of* are often used to mean "somewhat" or "rather." In formal English, however, it is better to use *somewhat* or *rather.*

INFORMAL   Muriel laughed and said, "That joke was kind of funny."
FORMAL   Muriel laughed and said, "That joke was **rather** funny."

learn, teach *Learn* means "to gain knowledge." *Teach* means "to instruct" or "to show how."

EXAMPLES   I **learned** to play chess last year.
Life **teaches** us new lessons all the time.

less See **fewer, less.**

might of, must of See **could of.**

nowheres See **anywheres,** etc.

of Do not use *of* with prepositions such as *inside, off,* and *outside. Of* is also unnecessary with helping verbs like *could* or *had.*

EXAMPLES   Hong put his hands **inside** his pockets. [not *inside of*]
Outside the stadium, there's a big parking lot. [not *outside of*]

ought to of See **could of.**

somewheres See **anywheres,** etc.

sort of See **kind of, sort of.**

take See **bring, take.**

than, then Do not confuse these words. *Than* is a conjunction. *Then* is an adverb.

EXAMPLES   Nobody rows a boat faster **than** my brother does. [conjunction]
Sandy waved goodbye, **then** boarded the airplane. [adverb]

EXERCISE 3   Identifying Correct Usage

Underline the correct word or words in parentheses in each of the following sentences.

EX. 1. (*Its*, *It's*) fine with me if you want to take a walk.

1. Every time we go to visit Rudy at the garage, he (*learns*, *teaches*) us something new about fixing cars.

2. Lenora showed her sisters a (*kind of*, *rather*) difficult layup shot.

3. First the storm blew all the leaves off the maple tree; (*then*, *than*) the strong winds knocked over the telephone pole.

4. Shivering at the bus stop (*learned*, *taught*) me to wear a warmer coat the next time.

5. Felipe was sure that there must be life (*outside*, *outside of*) our solar system.

6. Sometimes (*its*, *it's*) a good idea to stop and ask for directions.

7. "That's (*sort of*, *rather*) interesting," Tommy told Fred, peering over his shoulder at the newspaper article.

8. Nobody enjoys playing chess more (*then*, *than*) Eva.

9. Eddie thought his new skateboard was (*inside*, *inside of*) the garage.

10. The watchmaker spent more than a week taking the old clock apart and examining (*its*, *it's*) parts.

11. Our neighbors (*might have*, *might of*) arrived home late last night, but we didn't see them.

12. The aide warned the president that the senator's speech would be (*sort of*, *rather*) long.

13. Abbie (*learned*, *taught*) Jack that poem for their skit.

14. I told Winifred that it wasn't Bryan Adams she saw at the restaurant, but she said it (*must have*, *must of*) been.

15. Rhonda slipped (*off*, *off of*) the icy sidewalk.

THAT THERE / YOUR, YOU'RE

that there   See **this here, that there.**

their, there, they're   *Their* is the possessive form of *they*. It is used to show ownership. *There* is used to mean "at that place" or to begin a sentence. *They're* is a contraction of *they are.*

EXAMPLES   The ranch hands all treat **their** horses well.
She left the papers over **there**.
Matt said **they're** arriving on the afternoon train.

theirself, theirselves   See **hisself,** etc.

them   *Them* should not be used as an adjective. Use *these* or *those.*

EXAMPLE   Just look at **these** flowers! [not *them* flowers]

this here, that there   The *here* and *there* are not necessary after *this* and *that.*

EXAMPLES   The colors in **this** painting are wonderful. [not *this here* painting]
That party was so much fun. [not *That there* party]

try and   In informal English, *try and* is often used for *try to*. In formal English, *try to* is preferred.

EXAMPLE·   **Try to** speak a little more quietly. [not *Try and*]

use to, used to   Be sure to add the *−d* to *use. Used to* is in the past tense.

EXAMPLE   That woman **used to** be my hockey coach.

way, ways   Use *way*, not *ways*, when referring to a distance.

EXAMPLE   It's a long **way** from here to the moon.

when, where   Do not use *when* or *where* incorrectly in writing a definition. Do not use *where* for *that.*

EXAMPLES   A pun **is** a humorous play on a word's sound or meaning.
[not *is when you use*]
Most people like **that** you're on time. [not *when*]
The instant replay showed **that** the referee had been right.
[not *where*]

whose, who's   *Whose* is the possessive form of *who*. It shows ownership. *Who's* is a contraction of *who is* or *who has.*

EXAMPLES   **Whose** jacket is that?
Let's find out **who's** going to the game tomorrow.

> **would of**   See **could of.**
>
> **your, you're**   *Your* is the possessive form of *you.* *You're* is the contraction of *you are.*
>
> EXAMPLES   Do you sew **your** own clothes?
> Tell Annie that **you're** home.

EXERCISE 4   Identifying Correct Usage

Underline the correct word or words in parentheses in each of the following sentences.

EX.   1.   Do you know (*who's*, *whose*) going to be the first one to sign up for the track team?

1.   Julia will (*try and, try to*) qualify for the high jump.

2.   She (*use to, used to*) practice every summer in her back yard.

3.   Harry, our best distance runner last year, moved to another school, and now he's on (*their, there, they're*) team.

4.   No other team member has as much experience running such a long (*way, ways*).

5.   It's too bad, but sometimes (*them, those*) things happen.

6.   As for the broad jump, last year Robin did better in (*that, that there*) event than almost anybody else in the league.

7.   Al and his sister Loretta, (*who's whose*) only a sophomore, are both fast sprinters.

8.   The coach told us (*where, that*) the best track teams are the ones that keep improving.

9.   Without a doubt, if (*your, you're*) on a track team, you should stay in good physical shape.

10.   You should also (*try and, try to*) get plenty of rest.

11.   Some team members wonder (*who's, whose*) record will be the best.

12.   "Improve (*your, you're*) own abilities," the coach said, "and you'll come out winners no matter what."

13.   All the team members work hard at (*their, there, they're*) events.

14.   We have found that these efforts go a long (*way, ways*) toward helping us get ready for our track meets.

15.   To be a winner (*is when you, means to*) do your best every day.

CHAPTER REVIEW

A. Identifying Correct Usage

Underline the correct word or words in parentheses in each of the sentences below.

EX. 1. (*Bring*, <u>*Take*</u>) these flowers home with you when you go.

1. After we got to the beach, we discovered that Alani (*all ready*, *already*) knew how to surf.

2. My grandmother was certain that (*somewhere*, *somewheres*) in the attic was the trunk containing the old photographs.

3. No one (*would have*, *would of*) thrown the football to Floyd, because he had his hands in his pockets.

4. The hidden gate lay in the valley (*between*, *among*) the ancient ruins and the pine forest.

5. You (*had ought*, *ought*) to see how wonderful the trees look when the leaves return after a long winter.

6. Ronnie thought that the old house on the corner was (*sort of*, *rather*) mysterious.

7. Luanne has a stronger crosscourt shot (*then*, *than*) I have.

8. The jury couldn't understand (*how come*, *why*) that man had committed the crime.

9. If someone you didn't know offered you a million dollars for no reason at all, would you (*accept*, *except*) it?

10. (*Fewer*, *Less*) people came to the play on Sunday afternoon than on Saturday night.

11. Those beavers get so busy whenever they (*try and*, *try to*) build a dam.

12. When the Kwan family went for a boat ride down the Amazon, they didn't forget to (*bring*, *take*) along a big bottle of insect repellent.

13. Oscar pointed to the newspaper story (*where it*, *that*) explained how the Blue Jays had won the game.

14. If I get rid of my cold, I'll be (*all right*, *allright*).

15. Running red lights just (*ain't*, *isn't*) right.

16. Columbus and his crew had to sail a long (*way*, *ways*) before they reached land.

17. Nobody mentioned the incident that happened yesterday because it had already been discussed (*a lot, alot*).

18. Frannie and I looked at the map to find out (*where the shortcut was, where the shortcut was at*).

19. Mrs. Canares always (*learns, teaches*) her piano students the basics before she gets into the more difficult lessons.

20. Please (*bring, take*) me that game so that I may read the directions.

B. Proofreading a Paragraph for Correct Usage

The paragraph below contains usage errors. Draw a line through each incorrect word. Then write the correct word on your own paper.

EX.   [1] Giant pandas can't be found just ~~anywheres.~~
　　　1. anywhere

　　[1] These pandas are certainly not you're ordinary bear. [2] There native habitat is the wooded mountains of western China. [3] Until quite recently, this 355-pound black-and-white animal use to be considered a myth by most people outside China. [4] The panda can eat meat, but it's diet consists mainly of bamboo shoots and roots. [5] A adult panda usually lives alone. [6] Giant pandas can spend ten to twelve hours a day stuffing themselves with bamboo. [7] Their paws have a thumb that they use to strip the leaves off of the bamboo. [8] This here thumb is the sixth "finger" they have on their paws. [9] A giant panda whose having cubs may take shelter in a cave or a hollow tree. [10] Giant pandas don't live in trees, but they can climb up them quite a ways when they need to escape from hunters.

C. Writing a Flyer

Your class is putting on a winter carnival as a money-making project. As a class officer, you have been asked to create a one-page flyer that describes the event. Include the time, date, and activities offered. Use at least ten examples of the standard usage guidelines covered in this chapter, and underline each example.

EX.   The sixth grade at Bradford Township School is proud to announce that on January 15, 1995, <u>it's</u> sponsoring <u>a</u> winter carnival. We hope that you and <u>your</u> family and friends will all attend. <u>There</u> will be <u>a</u> <u>lot</u> of rides and games. We even plan to have <u>an</u> ice-sculpture contest. Everyone <u>ought to</u> have a good time.

THE PRONOUN I, PROPER NOUNS, AND ABBREVIATIONS

19a   Capitalize the pronoun *I*.

EXAMPLES   Yesterday **I** came home early.
I know you; **I** mowed your lawn.

19b   Capitalize proper nouns.

A *proper noun* names a particular person, place, thing, or idea. Such a word is always capitalized. A *common noun* names a type of person, place, thing, or idea. A common noun is not capitalized unless it begins a sentence or is part of a title.

Common Nouns	Proper Nouns
day	Saturday
state	Oregon
mountain	Mount Everest
singer	Stevie Wonder
street	Cedar Avenue

19c   Capitalize certain abbreviations.

Many abbreviations are capitalized.

EXAMPLES   **M.D., Mr., Ms., Mrs., FBI, CIA, TV, UN, U.S.A., NCAA, VA, NY, TX, VT**

However, some abbreviations, especially those for measurements, are not capitalized.

EXAMPLES   **in., yd, cu., ft, lb, etc., cc, ml, mm**

☞ **REFERENCE NOTE:**   For information about punctuating abbreviations with capital letters, see page 241.

Some proper nouns consist of more than one word. In these names, short prepositions (those of fewer than five letters) and articles (*a, an,* and *the*) are not capitalized.

EXAMPLES   Richard **the** Lionhearted   Stratford-**on**-Avon
Bill **of** Rights   Anne **of** Cleves

☞ **REFERENCE NOTE:**   For more information about proper nouns, see page 101.

EXERCISE 1   Identifying Correct Capitalization

On the line before each of the pairs below, write the letter of the phrase or sentence that is capitalized correctly.

EX. _*b*_ 1. a. the atlantic ocean
            b. the Atlantic Ocean

_____ 1. a. our teacher, Ms. Jiménez
           b. our teacher, ms. Jiménez

_____ 2. a. If i can, i will.
           b. If I can, I will.

_____ 3. a. a pioneer named daniel boone
           b. a well-known pioneer

_____ 4. a. the Painted Desert
           b. a Desert in Arizona

_____ 5. a. sam the cat
           b. Sam the cat

_____ 6. a. Tufts University
           b. University Of Texas

_____ 7. a. my best friend
           b. Lee, the Grocery Clerk

_____ 8. a. Lake Michigan
           b. a Lake in Michigan

_____ 9. a. a Jazz musician
           b. John Coltrane

_____ 10. a. my Street
           b. Highland Road

_____ 11. a. dr. Trent Tucker
           b. Trent Tucker, M.D.

_____ 12. a. 15 CC
           b. 15 cc

_____ 13. a. The State of Ohio
           b. the United States

_____ 14. a. today
           b. monday

_____ 15. a. River Rafting
           b. Delaware River

_____ 16. a. Mrs. T. I. Brown
           b. Mrs. t. i. Brown

_____ 17. a. 3 yds
           b. 3 Yds

_____ 18. a. Ivan The Terrible
           b. Ivan the Terrible

_____ 19. a. John Jones, jr.
           b. John Jones, Jr.

_____ 20. a. Bay of Bengal
           b. Bay Of Bengal

EXERCISE 2   Using Capitalization in Proper Nouns

For each common noun given below, write two proper nouns on your own paper. You may use a dictionary and an atlas. Be sure to use capital letters correctly.

EX. 1. state capital
     1. Nashville; Honolulu

1. building
2. city
3. country
4. relative
5. holiday
6. park
7. musician
8. company
9. river
10. president
11. baseball team
12. friend
13. character
14. teacher
15. planet
16. singer
17. explorer
18. king
19. store
20. writer

PLACES AND PEOPLE

19d Capitalize geographical names.

Type of Name	Examples
continents	Europe, Africa, Australia, Asia
countries	India, Mexico, Switzerland, Japan
cities, towns	Los Angeles, Chatham, Wilkes-Barre
states	Arizona, Kentucky, Pennsylvania
bodies of water	Lake Huron, Red Sea, Gulf of Guinea
streets, highways	Lexington Avenue, Route 91, Highway 1
parks and forests	Everglades National Park, Black Forest
mountains	Green Mountains, Andes Mountains
sections of a country	the Northwest, the South, the Congo

 NOTE In a hyphenated street number, the second part of the number is not capitalized.

EXAMPLE West Seventy-third Street

 NOTE Words such as *east*, *west*, *north*, or *south* are not capitalized when the words indicate directions.

EXAMPLES The ship sailed east, [direction]
The dogs pulled the sleds across the frozen North. [section of the country]

19e Capitalize the names of planets, stars, and other heavenly bodies.

EXAMPLES Saturn, Betelgeuse, Milky Way

 NOTE The words *earth*, *sun*, and *moon* are not capitalized unless they are used along with the capitalized names of other heavenly bodies.

EXAMPLES The number of trees on the earth is decreasing rapidly.
Mars is farther away from the Sun than Earth is.

19f Capitalize the names of persons.

EXAMPLES Abraham Lincoln, Napoleon Bonaparte, Christopher Columbus

EXERCISE 3   Recognizing the Correct Use of Capital Letters

If a sentence below contains an error in capitalization, write correctly the word or words that should be capitalized. If the sentence is correct, write C. Separate your answers with a semicolon.

EX.   1. Marjorie lives on Pine street.
            Street
_____

1. My family traveled from our house in new haven, connecticut, to washington, D.C., on our vacation.

_____

2. Scientists know more about the planet mars than they do about the planet neptune.

_____

3. The man in the drugstore told us we could find a shopping mall on thirty-third street, just west of the railroad station.

_____

4. Have you ever heard of mohandas gandhi, the Indian leader?

_____

5. Rebecca's sister is in the back yard, filling the flower boxes with earth.

_____

6. John candy was morris's favorite comedian.

_____

7. I read that Australia is the smallest continent.

_____

8. In 1541, the Spanish explorer hernando de Soto reached the Mississippi river.

_____

9. Did you know that ireland is an island?

_____

10. Perhaps the most famous African queen was named cleopatra.

_____

GROUPS, ORGANIZATIONS, AND RELIGIONS

19g **Capitalize the names of organizations, teams, businesses, institutions, and government bodies.**

Type of Name	Examples
organization	National Audubon Society
team	Toronto Maple Leafs
business	Johnson & Johnson
institution	Centre City Hospital
government body	Department of State

 NOTE Do not capitalize words such as *hotel, theater,* and *middle school* unless they are part of the name of a particular building or institution.

EXAMPLES   the **Rialto Theater**   the theater on the corner

19h **Capitalize the names of nationalities, races, and peoples.**

EXAMPLES   **Micronesian, Caucasian, Aleut, Hispanic, Chinese**

 NOTE The words *Black* and *White* may or may not be capitalized when they refer to people.

EXAMPLE   Most of the people in my neighborhood are **b**lack [*or* **B**lack], but there are some **w**hite [*or* **W**hite] people as well.

19i **Capitalize the names of religions and their followers, holy days, sacred writings, and specific deities.**

Type of Name	Examples
religions	Judaism, Christianity
religious followers	Mormons, Muslims
holy days	Ramadan, Good Friday
sacred writings	Bible, Torah, Upanishads
specific deities	God, Odin, Allah, Kali

 NOTE The word *god* is not capitalized when it refers to a god of ancient mythology. The names of specific gods are capitalized.

EXAMPLE   Egyptian pharoahs worshiped **R**a, the sun **g**od.

EXERCISE 4   Identifying Correct Capitalization

On the line before each of the pairs of phrases below, write the letter of the phrase that is capitalized correctly.

EX. __b__ 1. a. the Greek Goddess, Hera
              b. the Greek goddess, Hera

_____ 1. a. worldwatch institute   _____ 6. a. Delta Air Lines
             b. Worldwatch Institute   b. Delta air lines

_____ 2. a. Glendale middle school   _____ 7. a. Carnegie Hall
             b. Glendale Middle School   b. Carnegie hall

_____ 3. a. the New York knicks   _____ 8. a. the Cherokee people
             b. the New Orleans Saints   b. the cherokee people

_____ 4. a. Judaism   _____ 9. a. buddhists
             b. a hindu teaching   b. Buddhists

_____ 5. a. those russian singers   _____ 10. a. easter Sunday
             b. an Italian opera singer   b. Easter Sunday

EXERCISE 5   Proofreading Sentences for Correct Capitalization

For each sentence below, correct the errors in capitalization. Either change capital letters to lowercase letters or change lowercase letters to capital letters. Write your corrections on the line after each sentence. Separate your answers with a semicolon. A sentence may be correct.

EX. 1. Dad worked for the national science foundation and mayfair company.
         National Science Foundation; Mayfair Company

1. The Hewlett-packard company makes printers for computers.

_____

2. My friends, the Haskells, observe rosh hashana every year.

_____

3. Have you seen the big new hotel near the beach?

_____

4. The greek god pan roamed the woods and fields, playing a pipe.

_____

5. In 1967, the green bay packers won the first Super Bowl.

_____

OBJECTS, EVENTS, STRUCTURES, AND AWARDS

19j   Capitalize the brand names of business products.

EXAMPLES   Macintosh computer, General Mills cereals [Notice that the names of the types of products are not capitalized.]

19k   Capitalize the names of historical events and periods, special events, and calendar items.

Type of Name	Examples
historical event	Industrial Revolution
historical period	Reconstruction
special event	Mardi Gras
holiday	Saint Patrick's Day
calendar item	Columbus Day

NOTE   Do not capitalize the name of a season unless it is part of a proper name.

EXAMPLES   summer vacation   the **B**ridgeport **S**ummer Festival

19l   Capitalize the names of ships, trains, aircraft, buildings and other structures, and awards.

Type of Name	Examples
ships	**SS** *United States*, *Queen Mary*
trains	*Orient Express*, *Broadway Limited*
aircraft	*Voyager*, *Blackbird*, *Spruce Goose*
buildings and other structures	John Hancock Tower, Statue of Liberty
awards	Most Valuable Player, Pulitzer Prize

EXERCISE 6   Proofreading Sentences for Correct Capitalization

For each sentence below, correct the errors in capitalization. Draw a line through each incorrect letter. Write your revision in the space above the error. Some sentences may be correct.

EX.   1. We crossed the golden gate bridge during our trip to California.
(Corrections shown above: golden→G, gate→G, bridge→B)

1. The persian gulf conflict was fought in the Middle East.

2. Many states celebrate lincoln's birthday as an official holiday.

3. Cousin Harry rode the *concorde* back from France.

4. Jessica Tandy won the academy award for Best Actress in 1989.

5. The *silver bullet* is the smallest jet plane ever built.

6. Leonardo da Vinci was an artist and inventor who lived during the renaissance.

7. Do you believe that if a groundhog sees its shadow on groundhog day, winter will continue for six more weeks?

8. In Sweden, nobel prizes are awarded every year for outstanding achievements in several categories.

9. My father has one braun clock and one seiko clock.

10. Last october we toured Vermont to see the Fall colors.

11. We bought some Campbell's soup and Prego spaghetti sauce.

12. New York City's chrysler building is a terrific example of a design style that was popular in the 1920s and the 1930s.

13. The *merrimack* and the *monitor* were armored ships that fought in the Civil war.

14. Thea drove the john deere tractor in for some exxon gas.

15. Can your dad take us to the Newport jazz festival next summer?

TITLES

19m Capitalize titles.

(1) Capitalize the title of a person when the title comes before the name.

EXAMPLES   **G**eneral Ulysses S. Grant, **D**r. Luís Calderón

(2) Capitalize the title used alone or following a person's name only when the title refers to someone holding a high office.

EXAMPLES   Was it really the **G**overnor who spoke at your luncheon?
That woman, the new governor of South Carolina, will be
speaking today.

A title used by itself in direct address is usually capitalized.

EXAMPLE   Please explain, **C**aptain.

(3) Capitalize a word showing a family relationship when the word is used before or in place of a person's name.

EXAMPLES   Roland said that **M**om would help us build the bookshelf.
I wrote a note to **C**ousin Rachael.
Could you take us to the beach, **U**ncle?

Do not capitalize a word showing a family relationship when a possessive comes before the word.

EXAMPLE   Can Steven's **b**rother and your **n**ephew Jason play together?

(4) Capitalize the first and last words and all important words in titles of books, magazines, newspapers, poems, short stories, movies, television programs, works of art, and musical compositions.

Unimportant words in titles include articles (*a, an, the*), coordinating conjunctions (*and, but, for, nor, or, so, yet*), and prepositions of fewer than five letters (*by, for, on, with*).

EXAMPLES   *Horton Hears a Who*   *Beauty and the Beast*
"America the **B**eautiful"   *The New York Times*

   REFERENCE NOTE: For more about using underlining (italics) and quotation marks with titles, see pages 259 and 263.

EXERCISE 7   Proofreading Sentences for Correct Capitalization

For each of the sentences below, write correctly the word or words that should be capitalized. If the sentence is correct, write C. Use your own paper. [Note: Use underlining and quotation marks where needed.]

EX.   1.   My brother is a big fan of *star trek: deep space nine.*

    1.   <u>Star Trek: Deep Space Nine</u>

1.   Mick and Julie are playing "chopsticks" on the piano in the den.

2.   My teacher said that *the Music Man* and *south pacific* are two of the best musicals ever made.

3.   Please tell Uncle Charlie and my father that we'll be a little late.

4.   Have you read the article on fishing in the *sun-times*?

5.   I heard mayor Sanford is running for reelection.

6.   Otis asked me if I knew what the lady in Leonardo's painting *mona lisa* is smiling about.

7.   You don't really mean that you saw the president himself?

8.   The captain asked lieutenant Flowers to send the message.

9.   Did mom place the ad in the *pinetree gazette*?

10.   Toshi was made secretary-treasurer of our new committee.

EXERCISE 8   Writing Titles for Imaginary Works

Create a title for each item described below. Be sure each title is capitalized correctly. Use underlining and quotation marks where needed.

EX.   1.   a magazine for stamp collectors

    1.   the <u>Stamp Collectors Monthly</u>

1.   a newspaper about water sports

2.   a song about a favorite animal

3.   a painting of a building in your home town

4.   a short story about an ocean adventure

5.   a movie about the old West

6.   a book about dinosaurs

7.   a magazine for model-train hobbyists

8.   a movie about bicycle racing

9.   a story about getting a stepparent

10.   a book about baseball skills

FIRST WORDS, PROPER ADJECTIVES, SCHOOL SUBJECTS

19n   Capitalize the first word in every sentence.

EXAMPLES   You can see the sunset from here every morning.
            Bill, close the door.

The first word of a direct quotation should begin with a capital letter, whether or not the quotation starts the sentence.

EXAMPLE   Hannah asked, "Are we going to the movies tonight?"

Traditionally, the first word of every line of poetry begins with a capital letter.

EXAMPLE   The ship arrived one April day
            And left upon the first of May.

Some modern poets do not follow this style. If you are quoting lines from a poem, be sure to follow the capitalization that the poet uses.

19o   Capitalize proper adjectives.

A *proper adjective* is formed from a proper noun and is always capitalized.

Proper Noun	Proper Adjective
Japan	Japanese garden
Shakespeare	Shakespearean theater
Baptist	Baptist minister

19p   Do not capitalize the names of school subjects, except languages and course names followed by a number.

EXAMPLES   art, mathematics, Typing II, Latin, Spanish, Science 201

EXERCISE 9   Proofreading for the Correct Use of Capital Letters

Proofread the following passage, and correct all errors in the use of capital letters. Draw a line through each incorrect letter, and write your correction in the space above the error. Some sentences may contain no errors.

EX. [1] ~~y~~esterday my sister Samantha and I were discussing what we've been doing in school.

[1] I said, "we've been studying american poetry."

[2] "Oh, yeah?" she said. "i didn't know you were taking literature."

[3] I replied, "yes, every seventh-grader has to take it."

[4] "I guess I forgot," she said. "Do you have Ms. Jewel?"

[5] "no," I said, "I have Mr. Carbonetti. [6] we're studying american literature first. [7] then we'll study latin american, asian, and european literature."

[8] "Wow!" she said. "that sounds like a lot."

[9] "I guess so," I said. "but it will be fun. [10] the first thing we're doing is writing our own poems."

[11] "Will these poems be called the famous literature of our town?" she asked.

[12] "Cut it out!" I said. [13] "listen to the poem I'm writing.

> [14] My sister, friend and counselor,
>
> hid behind the kitchen door,
>
> hoping that when I came in,
>
> surprising me, she'd jump and . . .

[15] could you help me? I can't think of the next word."

CHAPTER REVIEW

A. Correcting Sentences by Capitalizing Words

For each sentence below, correct the errors in capitalization. Draw a line through each incorrect letter. Write your correction in the space above the error. Some sentences may contain no errors.

EX. 1. Three members of my family have birthdays in ~~s~~eptember.

1. To see the distant planet pluto, you must use a very powerful telescope.

2. On father's day I gave dad a book by a new author.

3. The houston rockets were matched against the phoenix suns in the playoffs.

4. Have you seen glenn close in *sarah, plain and tall*?

5. Our english teacher read us a poem called "the blossom," by John Donne.

6. The tower of london is located along the river thames.

7. Lana exclaimed, "we've been looking all over idaho for you!"

8. Bianca showed us the mexican Hat Dance.

9. The valley of the Connecticut river is quite beautiful in the spring.

10. Last year, I attended oxford junior high.

11. We have been studying buddhism and hinduism in our unit on southeast asia.

12. Jamesville high school has bought some digital equipment corporation computers.

13. In december we always go to the Allen High winter concert.

14. My aunt Jessie reads the *Wall Street Journal*.

15. What do you know about ishtar, the babylonian goddess of love and war?

B. Using Correct Capitalization in a Paragraph

In the paragraph below, all capital letters have been omitted. On your own paper, rewrite the paragraph, and add the necessary capital letters.

EX.   [1] my classmates and i entered the talent contest sponsored by the oakwood parents' council last february.

      1. My classmates and I entered the talent contest sponsored by the Oakwood Parents' Council last February.

[1] the contest was held at the former cattleman's bank and trust building on twenty-second street, which is now the elm street theater. [2] to start the show, ethel sang a song entitled "when summer comes." [3] Steve's dad, who trains cadets at the u.s. air force academy, presented a multimedia exhibit on the customs of the far east. [4] i recited my poem called "traveling in the west," which describes the platte river and the rocky mountains. [5] the contest ended in a three-way tie, and it was written up in our school paper, the *oakwood courier*.

C. Writing Answers on a Questionnaire

The year is 2050. As the first person to have walked on Mars, you have been asked to appear on several talk shows. One program director has asked that, before the show, you fill out the questionnaire below. On your own paper, answer every question. You may use real or made-up answers. Be sure you capitalize correctly.

1. Where and when were you born?
2. What are your parents' names?
3. What are the names of your brothers and sisters?
4. What schools did you attend?
5. Where did you receive your astronaut training?
6. What is your rank in the Astronaut Corps?
7. What are some of your hobbies and interests?
8. What clubs and organizations do you belong to?
9. What was the name of your ship that traveled to Mars?
10. What other planets have you traveled to?

EX.   1. Peoria, Illinois, August 18, 2000
      2. Frederick and Katherine O'Neill

END MARKS AND ABBREVIATIONS

An **end mark** is a punctuation mark placed at the end of a sentence. *Periods, question marks,* and *exclamation points* are end marks.

20a   Use a period at the end of a statement.

EXAMPLE   Tofu is made from soybeans.

20b   Use a question mark at the end of a question.

EXAMPLE   Does tofu contain lots of protein?

20c   Use an exclamation point at the end of an exclamation.

EXAMPLE   This vegetable-and-tofu dish is delicious!

20d   Use either a period or an exclamation point at the end of a request or a command.

EXAMPLES   Please pick up some tofu at the store. [a request]
Don't drop the package! [a command]

20e   Use periods after certain abbreviations.

Abbreviations with Periods	
Personal Names	E. M. James, Carrie C. L. Catt
Titles Used with Names	Mrs., Ms., Mr., Dr., Jr., Sr.
Organizations and Companies	Assn., Co., Corp., Inc.
Addresses	St., Blvd., Ave., P.O. Box
Times	A.M., B.C., Sept., Mon.
Units of Measure	in.
Abbreviations Without Periods	
Government Agencies	IRS, WPA, FBI
State Abbreviations Followed by ZIP Code	FL 32922 PA 17405
Units of Measure	m, kg, ml, gal, lb, mi
Certain Widely Used Abbreviations	CD, NAACP, SOS, TV

NOTE   If you are not sure whether to use periods with an abbreviation, look in a dictionary, an encyclopedia, or another reliable reference source.

> When an abbreviation that has a period ends a sentence, another period is not needed. However, a question mark or an exclamation point is used in such situations, if needed.
>
> EXAMPLES   I stayed at the game until 6:30 P.M.
>   Did you leave the game at 6:30 P.M.?

EXERCISE 1   Using End Marks Correctly

Write the end mark that should appear at the end of each sentence, as well as any periods that are needed for abbreviations.

EX.   1.   How happy we are to see you !

1.   Did you see a chickadee at the bird feeder

2.   Derek's sixth-grade teacher was Ms Watson

3.   Send your change of address to P O Box 4302, Hightstown, N J

4.   Please help me fix the flat tire

5.   On weekends at Jim's Landscaping Co, Josh works part-time

6.   Dr and Mrs Peter A Brackett said they cannot come to the party

7.   The package weighed 5 lbs 6 oz

8.   Stop the printer quickly

9.   May we visit the FBI when we go to Washington, D C

10.   What a breathtaking sunset

11.   Alani and his family live at 453 Western Ave, Pearl City, HI 96782

12.   Every morning at 7:00 A M we see Mr Robinson at the bus stop

13.   The pyramids in Egypt were built from 3,000 to 1,800 B C

14.   Animal Crackers Inc carries pet and aquarium supplies

15.   We watched a TV program about Mount Everest

EXERCISE 2   Writing Sentences Using End Marks Correctly

Write ten sentences on your own paper, using each end mark at least twice. Then label which type of sentence you used.

EX.   1.   My father took us bird-watching near our house. (statement)

COMMAS IN A SERIES

End marks separate complete thoughts. *Commas* separate words or groups of words within a complete thought.

20f   Use commas to separate items in a series.

A *series* is three or more items written one after another. The items in a series may be words, phrases, or clauses.

Words in a Series
We saw pottery, fabrics, and blankets at the Arizona State Museum. [nouns]   Then I turned, stumbled, and fell. [verbs]   The dog was black, tan, and white. [adjectives]
Groups of Words in a Series
In Kyoto, Percy ate noodles, shopped for bamboo baskets, and slept at an old inn. [predicates]   The hamster ran through the kitchen, into the den, and up the curtain. [prepositional phrases]

NOTE   Some writers do not use a comma before *and* in a series. It is a good idea always to use that comma, however. Sometimes you need the comma to make your meaning clear. Notice how using a comma before *and* changes the meanings of the examples.

EXAMPLES   Maridel, Bo, and Mamie are going to see a movie.
[Three people are going to the movie.]
Maridel, Bo and Mamie are going to see a movie.
[Maridel is being told who is going to the movie.]

20g   Use commas to separate two or more adjectives before a noun.

Do not place a comma between an adjective and the noun immediately following it.

EXAMPLES   Chim climbed up the narrow, dark staircase.
Everyone wants that pretty, spinning whirligig.

EXERCISE 3   Proofreading Sentences for the Correct Use of Commas

Add commas where they belong in the sentences below. On the line before the sentence, write C if the sentence is correct.

EX.   _____ 1. Ingrid skis, skates, and jogs.

_____ 1. In winter, birds eat suet grain and sunflower seeds.

_____ 2. We made a fruit salad of apples oranges and grapefruit.

_____ 3. Please bring your camera and some film.

_____ 4. In the sunlight, the waves seemed to be green blue and gray.

_____ 5. Three of the nine planets are Mars, Mercury, and Venus.

_____ 6. Ginny gazed up at the clear starlit sky.

_____ 7. Nora collects stamps plays the cello and sings in the choir.

_____ 8. The geography class made wall maps of North America, South America and Europe.

_____ 9. The plane stops in Norway in Denmark and in Sweden.

_____ 10. At night the puppy jumps out of its box, into my bed and under the covers.

_____ 11. Where can I buy books about hiking camping and backpacking?

_____ 12. The cactus has one stem, sharp thorns, and a few branches.

_____ 13. Onni chops the wood stacks it and covers it with a waterproof cloth.

_____ 14. Eric Julian and Isaac are all planning to go camping.

_____ 15. Do you like classical music country music or rock music?

_____ 16. Naomi's ring had purple blue white and silver beads.

_____ 17. Soup a salad and juice was his usual lunch.

_____ 18. My parrot's favorite toy is an old plastic bell.

_____ 19. Sara wants to know where she can buy the bike how much it costs and when she can pick it up.

_____ 20. Tony's van started stalled and did not start again.

COMMAS WITH COMPOUND SENTENCES

> **20h** Use a comma before *and, but, for, nor, or, so,* and *yet* when they join independent clauses in a compound sentence.
>
> EXAMPLES We walked along the street, and Botan spotted the temple.
> Bruce got to the theater early, for he wanted a good seat.
>
> **REFERENCE NOTE:** For more about compound sentences, see pages 95 and 253.
>
> In many cases, a very short compound sentence does not need a comma before *and, but,* or *or.*
>
> EXAMPLE She washed and he dried.
>
> Don't confuse a compound sentence with a simple sentence containing a compound verb. No comma is needed between parts of a compound verb.
>
> COMPOUND SENTENCE Mr. Mabry wanted a yo-yo, and he found one at the drugstore.
> COMPOUND VERB Mr. Mabry wanted a yo-yo and found one at the drugstore.
>
> **REFERENCE NOTE:** For more about compound verbs, see pages 93 .

EXERCISE 4   Correcting Compound Sentences by Adding Commas

For each of the following sentences add any needed commas. On the line before the sentence, write *C* if the sentence is correct.

EX. _____ 1. The book was about lizards and the poster had pictures of turtles.

_____ 1. Steven wanted to throw darts but his sister wanted to throw horseshoes.

_____ 2. Karen needed four quarters for the bus but she only had three.

_____ 3. Liza was hungry for she had been practicing for three hours.

_____ 4. Dad got the baby ready and I helped Ming with her hat and coat.

_____ 5. Louise chopped the wood and brought it into the house.

_____ 6. Did you give Meredith the keys or did you leave them with Grace?

_____ 7. I don't want to ride on a horse nor do I want to milk a cow.

_____ 8. When playing soccer, don't crowd around the ball but keep your eyes on it.

_____ 9. My uncle and I wanted to build a robot but we couldn't find a kit.

_____ 10. We brought binoculars to the stadium for our seats were far from the field.

_____ 11. I have neither seen nor ridden a llama.

_____ 12. It's time to leave for Grandma's so get your shoes on!

_____ 13. Hector was tired yet he still had one more chapter to read.

_____ 14. Andy rinsed the dishes yet Alex said they smelled like soap.

_____ 15. We can write essays about the Indian Ocean or give oral reports.

EXERCISE 5   Using Commas When Combining Sentences

On your own paper, rewrite each pair of sentences below as a single compound sentence or as a simple sentence with a compound verb.

EX.   1. Bill couldn't carry the box alone. Ronald helped him carry it.
      1. Bill couldn't carry the box alone, so Ronald helped him carry it.

1. Martha took off the bike's tire. Martha replaced the inner tube.

2. Some pilaf is made with rice. This pilaf is made with bulgur wheat.

3. Dave does not have a CD player. His brother does have one.

4. Elaine does not paint her fingernails. Elaine does paint her toenails.

5. French horns are made of brass. English horns are made of wood.

6. Betty may want to play flute in the marching band. She may want to play flute in the orchestra.

7. My pen leaked in my pocket. I had to change my shirt.

8. Mom took the important papers out of the drawer. She put them in a safe-deposit box at the bank.

9. Sondra likes to play cashier. She wants to work as a banker when she gets older.

10. Do you want to go to the mall? Would you rather go downtown?

COMMAS WITH SENTENCE INTERRUPTERS

20i **Use commas to set off an expression that interrupts a sentence.**

Two commas are needed if the expression to be set off comes in the middle of the sentence. One comma is needed if the expression comes first or last.

EXAMPLES Lorna's teacher, Ms. Hill, will help with the planting.
Of course, Salim can't quit until noon.
How do I find your house, Hoshi?

(1) **Use commas to set off appositives and appositive phrases that are not needed to understand the meaning of a sentence.**

An *appositive* is a noun or a pronoun that identifies or explains another noun or pronoun beside it. An *appositive phrase* is an appositive with its modifiers.

EXAMPLES A town in New Mexico, Madrid, used to be owned by a coal company. [The appositive *Madrid* identifies which town.]
In biology class Nora studied leeches, a type of worm. [*A type of worm* is an appositive phrase that explains the word *leeches*.]

Do not use commas when an appositive is needed to understand the meaning of a sentence.

EXAMPLES My cousin Roberto lives in Puerto Rico. [I have more than one cousin and am using his name to identify which cousin I mean.]
My cousin, Roberto, lives in Puerto Rico. [I have only one cousin and am using his name as extra information.]

(2) **Use commas to set off words used in direct address.**

Direct address is using the name of the person to whom you are speaking.

EXAMPLES Mr. Grau, I didn't hear the late bell.
If you like, Mika, we can try again.

(3) **Use a comma after such words as *well, yes, no,* and *why* when they begin a sentence.**

EXAMPLES Well, you could have a six o'clock appointment.
Yes, I did enjoy skating.

EXERCISE 6   Using Commas Correctly

In the sentences below, insert commas where they are needed.

EX.   1.   My dog, the one with the spots, is a Dalmatian.

1.   Lisa will you come here, please.

2.   Why I have never been to Islamabad.

3.   Does Jorge keep his bicycle a twelve-speed in top shape?

4.   Lin bought a CD by Andrés Segovia a Spanish guitarist.

5.   He had planted the flowers his favorite kind last summer.

6.   During the storm, the waves came up onto the road Beach Street.

7.   I would guess Rita that this will work.

8.   Yes I did see your sculpture.

9.   My piano teacher Mr. Jones grew up in Hong Kong.

10.   How much corn would you like Clara?

11.   Luke please hand me the scissors.

12.   No I am planning a trip to Oaxaca.

13.   Maria placed the cups four of them on the table.

14.   Jamie and Moira played HORSE a basketball game.

15.   Todd brought home a souvenir a plastic flamingo.

16.   The leaves maple and oak were piled high on the lawn.

17.   I say Reginald that's quite an accomplishment!

18.   Well you never told me what time you would be finished.

19.   We rode a trolley a red one on a sightseeing tour.

20.   Where are you going Roger?

21.   My mother you might have heard is an excellent metalsmith.

22.   No there's no extra charge for the trip.

23.   An architect I met Sherry Haskins said she might have a summer job for my older sister.

24.   He lives in that big building the Santos Arms.

25.   Lennie please help me with my math homework.

COMMAS IN CONVENTIONAL SITUATIONS

20j Use commas in certain conventional situations.

(1) Use commas to separate items in dates and addresses.

EXAMPLES   On January 1, 1863, Abraham Lincoln issued the Emancipation
Proclamation.
Write to me at 542 Oak Circle, Wilmette, IL 60091.

Notice that a comma separates the last item in a date or in an address from
the words that follow it. However, a comma does not separate a month
and a day (*July 12*) or a house number and street name (*102 Main Street*).

 NOTE   Usethe correct ZIP Code on every envelope you address. No
punctuation is used between the state name or abbreviation and
the ZIP Code.

EXAMPLE   Pungo, NC 27860

**(2) Use a comma after the salutation of a friendly letter and after the
closing of any letter.**

EXAMPLES   Dear Mom and Dad,   Sincerely,

EXERCISE 7   Using Commas Correctly
in Dates, Addresses, and Salutations

In the following sentences and word groups, insert commas where they are
needed. Some sentences contain no errors.

EX.   1.   I plan to live in San Francisco, California

1.   Dear Mr. Pease

2.   On June 10 we are going to Montreal for a graduation party.

3.   Send this package to Aberdeen SD 57401.

4.   I sent a change-of-address notice to Postmaster Pecos TX 79772.

5.   They drove to Hauppauge New York.

6.   Sincerely Dixie

7.   We sent a letter to 5747 West Howard Street Niles IL 60648.

8.   I signed the letter "Your friend Doris."

9. Please send the mail to 15 Sherman Avenue Takoma Park, MD 20912.

10. On January 9 2000 my little brother was born.

11. Rory's family moved to 54 Main Street Rockport Massachusetts.

12. My pen pal lives in Fairfax Virginia.

13. Do you think we can have the reunion on March 15?

14. My dearest Althea

15. Theo set the deadline for April 14 2009.

EXERCISE 8   Proofreading a Letter for the Correct Use of Commas

The letter below contains ten errors in the use of commas. Add or delete commas as needed. Some sentences contain no errors.

EX.   I will see you on May 2, 2008.

> 620 Essex Avenue
> Gloucester MA, 01930
> February 1 2008

Dear Luís

    I hope you are doing well. I really miss you since you moved. I am writing to invite you to my grandparents' anniversary party on May, 4 2008. I know it's a two-hour bus ride, but I think this party will be worth it. We plan to have it here at Cameron's at 206 Main Street. You probably remember the place. We have hired a local band. They played at my cousin's wedding on October 23, and they were great.

    Charlene's family did finally move to California. Her new address is 1739 La Costa Meadows Drive San Marcos CA 92069. She's been there since January 3, and I think she likes it. Don't forget that August, 17 is her birthday.

    Please write to me as soon as possible. If you can make it, I'll call the bus station and make the arrangements.

> Your friend
>
> Wilma

REVIEW EXERCISE

A. Proofreading Sentences for the Correct Use of Punctuation

In the sentences below, insert commas and end marks where they are needed. Some sentences may be correct.

EX. 1. We needed scissors ,paper ,and glue .

1. Joy brought her sled but did Toby bring his toboggan

2. Ben read the *Post* every morning and read the *Times* every evening.

3. Ms Marcos's car a blue sedan had just been washed and waxed

4. Have your heard Chet about the walkathon for the homeless

5. Yes my brother and I will carry your groceries Mr. Simms

6. On June 27 1991 Justice Thurgood Marshall announced his retirement

7. Get information about passports from the U.S. Department of State 2201 C Street NW Washington DC 20520

8. You will need to measure the wood cut it and sand it smooth

9. My how lovely you look

10. Please bring home some pasta tomatoes and zucchini.

11. My cousin works for the International Science Association at 900 East El Monte, San Gabriel, CA 91776.

12. F. W. Woolworth opened his first five-and-ten store on February 22 1879

13. These ice skates need sharpening yet they work quite well

14. Cross only at the corner

15. The shiny speedy train crossed the bridge and scared the pigeons.

16. I enjoy cooking dancing and playing kickball

17. Selma fed the gerbils but did she feed the goldfish

18. Do you know Ms. Chow when the show begins

19. Oh how wonderfully you dance

20. My only brother Ryan was born on January 9 1979

21. The snow will start this evening, so I need to leave early.

22. My father joined the South American Explorers Club at PO Box 18327 Denver CO 80218

23. No Leroy and I are not members Janice

24. Please iron dust and vacuum

25. Sybil sings in a choir and plays softball on a team.

B. Proofreading a Paragraph for the Correct Use of Punctuation

In the following paragraph, insert punctuation where needed. Some sentences may be correct.

EX. [1] My dad took me to visit his friend Seymour, a photographer.

[1] Seymour has been taking pictures since April 4,1998. [2] On that day his tenth birthday his parents gave him a camera. [3] He took pictures of his house the cat and his family. [4] He has been taking pictures black-and-white ones ever since. [5] Well when we visited him, he showed us his darkroom [6] But I was most interested to see his pictures hundreds of them covering every wall and piled high on desks and tables everywhere. [7] "Yes I've got more pictures than I know what to do with," he said. [8] I was amazed fascinated and inspired. [9] "These are terrific Seymour. [10] I wish I could take pictures like these," I said

C. Writing a Letter

You are on a school-sponsored group tour of Mexico. Write a short letter home to your family. Tell them where you have been, some of the sights you have seen, and some of the activities you have been involved in. Use reference books for help with the details. Include compound sentences and sentences with introductory words and phrases. Also use interrupters, appositives, and words of direct address. Be sure to follow the punctuation rules for personal letters.

EX.

June 15, 2008

Dear Ma and Pa,

Well, you were right when you said I'd enjoy Mexico City, Mexico. Our guide, Mr. Sanchez, said we will break open a piñata at a party tomorrow.

SEMICOLONS

A *semicolon* is part period and part comma. Like a period, it separates complete thoughts. Like a comma, it separates items within a sentence.

20k   Use a semicolon between parts of a compound sentence if they are not joined by *and, but, for, nor, or, so,* or *yet.*

EXAMPLES   Twenty Questions is a good game; let's play that next.
Hans read a book about Tokyo; I looked for Japan in an atlas.

NOTE   Don't overuse semicolons. Sometimes it is better to separate a compound sentence into two sentences rather than to use a semicolon.

ACCEPTABLE   We both love pumpkin pie; I find it surprising that some people like eating toasted pumpkin seeds.

BETTER   We both love pumpkin pie. I find it surprising that some people like eating toasted pumpkin seeds.

EXERCISE 9   Proofreading for the Correct Use of Semicolons

In the following sentences add semicolons where they are needed. Some sentences may require no change.

EX.   1.   Tamara will take swimming;Chet will sign up for field hockey.

1.   You can see the meteor shower tonight it begins after dark.

2.   Use popsicle sticks to make a box you will need about thirty.

3.   The candleholder was green ceramic it was made by hand.

4.   Rena wants to be a vet she likes animals of all kinds.

5.   Nick enjoys reading mysteries; Elena reads biographies.

6.   Cape Town is in South Africa so is Pretoria.

7.   The stores in the mall are close together walking between shops is easy and fun.

8.   Our boat rode the waves easily we were safe and dry.

9.   Three students are running for class president they are friends.

10.   Flying fish do not actually fly they glide just above the water.

11.   Do not eat just any mushroom you find some are poisonous.

12. One way to learn about mushrooms is to read a guidebook; the pictures in the book will help you identify different kinds of mushrooms.

13. On Friday, there will be a laser and music show it will have music by twelve rock groups.

14. I have heard about a toy and miniature-train museum; I'm planning to go there soon.

15. From the train, Jovita saw a deer, a pheasant, and a red-tailed hawk she was excited.

16. The team was in a difficult position they had to win all the remaining games of the season.

17. The catfish and monkfish were fresh they were also inexpensive.

18. Bonnie and Erin want to listen to CDs Stan wants to study.

19. My sister has new in-line skates she skates each afternoon.

20. Antoine the Great, a magician, will give his show Saturday; let's go.

EXERCISE 10   Using Semicolons to Combine Sentences

Using semicolons, combine each pair of sentences below into a compound sentence. Write your answers on your own paper.

EX.   1. We talked for a few minutes. Then I understood Paul's problem.
    1. *We talked for a few minutes; then I understood Paul's problem.*

1. That mountain is beautiful. Let's climb it next summer.
2. Keith mashed the potatoes. I made the gravy.
3. I took care of the stray puppy. I love animals.
4. My friend Luther is in a play. I'll be seeing it on Saturday.
5. I want to paint. Jamila wants to read.
6. There are several birds at our bird feeder. Two of them are chickadees.
7. Bruce's car could not climb the hill. The icy road caused the problem.
8. The baby began to feel better. She finally stopped crying.
9. For dessert, we will chop some apples and nuts. Then we will add some raisins.
10. The city of Hong Kong is crowded. The population is more than five million.

COLONS

A colon usually signals that more information follows.

20l Use a colon before a list of items, especially after expressions such as *the following* or *as follows*.

EXAMPLES These colors are available: green, blue, brown, and red.
Put the following ingredients in the bowl: whole-wheat flour, cornmeal, baking powder, and salt.

Never use a colon directly after a verb or a preposition. Instead, either omit the colon or reword the sentence.

INCORRECT The farm stand is selling: peaches, lettuce, radishes, and blueberries.

CORRECT The farm stand is selling the following produce: peaches, lettuce, radishes, and blueberries.

20m Use a colon between the hour and the minute when you write the time.

EXAMPLE We arrived at 7:32 in the evening.

20n Use a colon after the salutation of a business letter.

EXAMPLE Dear Sir or Madam: Dear Ms. Schwartz:

EXERCISE 11   Proofreading Sentences for Correct Use of Colons

In the following sentences and word groups, add or delete colons as needed. Some sentences contain no errors.

EX. 1. At 5 30 each evening, we eat supper.

1. You may have your choice of styles: original, loose, or oversized.

2. Dear Store Manager

3. We checked out the following books from the library *Adam Bede*, *The Mill on the Floss*, and *Silas Marner*.

4. This year our class will be visiting the following places the art museum, the natural history museum, and the science museum.

5. Add the following items to your grocery list fresh fruit, tortillas, eggs, and peppers.

6. The show starts at 8 00. Will you be on time?

7. Dear Rabbi Greenbaum:

8. If we don't leave by 7 21 P.M., we'll miss the bus for sure.

9. To make a bird feeder from these plans, you'll need the following items a hammer, brads, a saw, and a ruler.

10. Seats are still available for the following dates July 7, July 8, July 12, and July 14.

11. Mom was making: grits, stew, turnips, and beets.

12. The orchestra program included these three songs "You're My Everything," "We're in the Money," and "I Only Have Eyes for You."

13. I never go to a restaurant unless it has: red-and-white checked tablecloths, candles, and free bread sticks.

14. I love paintings by the Dutch painters Mondrian, Van Dyck, and Rembrandt.

15. A referee does not need much equipment a whistle, a stopwatch, good shoes, and a black-and-white striped shirt.

16. The program begins at 8 15 P.M., but Mrs. Chandler asked us to be ready by 7 45 P.M.

17. Students will choose from the following shop-class offerings wood shop, cooking, metal shop, print shop, auto shop, and sewing.

18. Dear Members of the School Board

19. Please bring a towel, a swimsuit, sunscreen, and sandals for the beach trip.

20. You may find the following reference books helpful a good dictionary, an atlas, and an encyclopedia.

CHAPTER REVIEW

A. Proofreading Sentences for Correct Use of End Marks, Commas, Semicolons, and Colons

For the sentences and word groups below, add the missing punctuation. Some sentences contain no errors.

EX. 1. I won I won

1. Don't buy new ones instead you can make your own

2. These drinks are available apple juice orange juice milk and water

3. Tommy will do it before school or Joan will finish it after school

4. There will be a fireworks show at 8 00 on July 4 1995.

5. Dear Professor Jameson

6. Meryl have you ever met Ms Chang's son Peter

7. Jason pulled weeds in the garden and took them to the compost heap.

8. Leung's uncle a large man with a big white beard looked great in a Santa suit.

9. No I prefer to leave my hair its original color.

10. I've never been to Maui but I have been to Oahu a few times

11. Sincerely yours Nico

12. Yes, I do like fresh cider.

13. Simon planted several tulip bulbs but the two dogs dug them up.

14. That tennis player deserves his awards he practices every afternoon.

15. Do you understand the question

B. Using End Marks and Colons Correctly in a Paragraph

In the following paragraph, add the missing end marks and colons.

EX. [1] At 4 15 P.M. Maggie went to the library to get books for her essay.

[1] She wanted to write about any of the following subjects marine life, music, and sports [2] Maggie asked the librarian for information

about deep-sea fish [3] The librarian told Maggie to follow him [4] The following types of information were available encyclopedias, films, and books. [5] The essay was for a school contest, and it was due by 2 00 P.M. the following Friday. [6] There was so much information and so little time [7] Maggie went home and sat at her desk [8] These steps helped her to organize her thoughts reading the information, taking notes, and making a short outline. [9] She wrote a draft of her essay, and she asked Darla to read it and her cover letter [10] Her cover letter began, "Dear Judges I am entering my essay about deep-sea fish."

C.   Proofreading a Letter for Correct Punctuation

Some parts of the letter below need end marks, commas, semicolons, or colons. Add the missing punctuation marks.

EX.   I wanted to write sooner, but I've been so busy.

PO Box 8
Urbana IL 61801
November 20 2008

Dear Uncle Pablo

How have you been I hope your job has been going well I just wanted to say hi and I wanted to tell you about my new hobby I joined the Appalachian Mountain Club a trail club This club is in Boston Massachusetts On September 1, my birthday, I got a tent and a compass as presents I want to save my money and buy new hiking boots a backpack and a canteen Dad and I went hiking this past weekend He carried the tent I carried other supplies We had such a great time I try to go out for at least a short walk every day yet it gets dark so early

I hope to see you again soon, maybe over the next holiday Please keep in touch

Your niece

Ariana

UNDERLINING (ITALICS)

Italics are printed letters that lean to the right—*like this*. When you write or type, you show that a word should be *italicized* by underlining it. The examples below show the difference between italics in type and italics in print.

ITALICS IN TYPE   My brother and I rented the movie <u>Kindergarten Cop</u> last Saturday.

ITALICS IN PRINT   My brother and I rented the movie *Kindergarten Cop* last Saturday.

 NOTE   If you use a personal computer, you can probably set words in italics yourself. Most word-processing software and many printers can produce italic type.

21a Use underlining (italics) for titles of books, plays, periodicals, films, television programs, works of art, long musical works, ships, aircraft, and spacecraft.

Type of Name	Examples
Books	*Living with Dinosaurs, Fatherhood*
Plays	*Romeo and Juliet, Lion King*
Periodicals	*National Geographic, Life*
Films	*King Kong, Aladdin*
Television Programs	*CBS News, Star Trek*
Works of Art	*American Gothic, Mona Lisa*
Long Musical Compositions	*West Side Story, Rhapsody in Blue*
Ships	*Mayflower, USS Triton*
Aircraft	*Concorde, Graf Zeppelin*
Spacecraft	*Mars Rover, Discovery*

NOTE   The article *the* before the title of a magazine or newspaper is not italicized or capitalized when it is part of a sentence rather than part of a title.

EXAMPLES   I read an article in **the** *Los Angeles Times.*
Is that the latest issue of ***The*** *Boston Globe?*

REFERENCE NOTE: For examples of titles that use quotation marks instead of italics, see page 263.

EXERCISE 1   Proofreading Sentences for the Correct Use of Underlining (Italics)

Proofread each of the sentences below for correct use of underlining (italics). Some sentences have no errors.

EX.   1. I know someone who saw the movie Beauty and the Beast six times!

1. Did you like the movie Little Man Tate?

2. Our whole family liked the play *Harvey,* which is about an imaginary giant rabbit.

3. Should we stay home and watch the television show Dinosaurs?

4. I'm not sure why John Bernard Flannagan decided to call this sculpture Triumph of the Egg.

5. Some of my information comes from the book The Other America.

6. Our school orchestra is practicing the overture from Mozart's opera *The Magic Flute.*

7. My great-grandparents remember when the steamship Mauretania first crossed the Atlantic in 1924.

8. I was thrilled when I first saw the painting The Snake Charmer.

9. The Wright brothers' plane Flyer I is sometimes called Kittyhawk.

10. My dad says his favorite book is The Education of Henry Adams.

11. In 1976, Viking I landed on Mars.

12. My sister wants to be a dancer in the ballet Swan Lake.

13. Do you prefer to read Car and Driver or Motor Trend?

14. Our teacher read to us from a book about San Juan, Puerto Rico.

15. My brother writes for the Lansing State Journal.

QUOTATION MARKS

21b Use quotation marks to enclose a *direct quotation*—a person's exact words.

EXAMPLES "Let's go outside and play baseball," suggested Sheila.
Dennard said, "Mind if I join you?"

Do not use quotation marks to enclose an *indirect quotation*—a rewording of a person's exact words.

DIRECT QUOTATION Tony said, "The supermarket is closed today."
INDIRECT QUOTATION Tony said that the supermarket was closed.

21c A direct quotation begins with a capital letter.

EXAMPLES Kayla leaned back and said, "This is the most comfortable school desk I have ever sat in."
Larry asked, "When do we eat dinner?"

21d When a quoted sentence is divided into two parts by an expression that identifies the speaker, the second part of the quotation begins with a small letter.

EXAMPLE "The recipe," said Lezcek, "is an old family secret."

When the second part of a divided quotation is a new sentence, it begins with a capital letter.

EXAMPLE "Let's get started early," suggested Uncle Tim. "That way, we will have most of the day free."

21e A direct quotation is set off from the rest of the sentence by a comma, a question mark, or an exclamation point, but not by a period.

EXAMPLES "We will be landing in three hours," the captain said.
"When will we be ready?" Marcie asked.
"Oh, I can't wait to see you!" Anita exclaimed.

21f When a quotation ends with a question mark or an exclamation point, no comma is needed.

EXAMPLES "Did you get a haircut?" Fuyu asked.
"Not on your life!" Wanda exclaimed.

21g A period or a comma should always be placed inside the closing quotation marks.

EXAMPLE   The dentist replied, "Your next checkup is in June**."**

21h A question mark or an exclamation point should be placed *inside* closing quotation marks when the quotation itself is a question or an exclamation. Otherwise, it should be placed outside.

EXAMPLES   "What time does the party start**?"** asked Anthony. [The quotation is a question.]
Who said, "Cats have nine lives"**?** [The sentence itself, not the quotation, is a question.]

EXERCISE 2 Punctuating and Capitalizing Quotations

For each of the sentences below, add capitalization, quotation marks, and other marks of punctuation where needed. Some sentences may contain no errors.

EX.   "D̶do I have to**?"** he asked.

1. When you finish dinner, José asked will you take me to the library?

2. Gabriella asked where did you get those shoes

3. Lorenzo said that he signed up for the cooking club.

4. Grandfather told us an old Ashanti tale, said Lawrence. It was about a farmer.

5. Before you go home, the teacher said, I will return your tests.

6. Who said "All clear"

7. Where are we going tonight Loretta asked

8. My hem is torn said Sue. do you have an extra pin?

9. David yelled whoa

10. Sonya said that she really wants to see *The Nutcracker* next year.

21i   When you write *dialogue* (conversation), begin a new paragraph every time the speaker changes.

EXAMPLE   The salesperson sat down and said, "This new model is our best yet."

"I'm not sure that I need a new vacuum cleaner," replied the customer. "Perhaps I will just get my old one fixed."

"Well, if you decide you need a new one, I strongly recommend our new model. It has many advanced features."

21j   When a quotation consists of several sentences, put quotation marks only at the beginning and the end of the whole quotation.

EXAMPLE   "Guess what happened in school today, Uncle Bill. We chose a director for the spring play. And I was picked!" said Joel.

21k   Use single quotation marks to enclose a quotation within a quotation.

EXAMPLE   Katya explained, "The sign said, 'No food allowed,' so I waited until I finished my sandwich."

21l   Use quotation marks to enclose the titles of short works such as short stories, poems, newspaper or magazine articles, songs, episodes of television programs, and chapters and other parts of books.

Type of Name	Examples
Short Stories	"The Dinner Party" "All Summer in a Day" "Zlateh the Goat"
Poems	"May Day" "Snowflakes" "I'm Nobody"
Articles	"Enchanting Bermuda" "Safer Driving at Any Age" "The Natural Gas Factor"
Songs	"Louisiana 1927" "Yesterday"
Episodes of Television Programs	"The Lip Reader" "The Belarus Fire" "Amelia Earhart"
Chapters and Other Parts of Books	"Birds in Your Garden" "Close Reading of an Essay" "Fishes and How They Live"

EXERCISE 3   Punctuating Quotations

For each sentence below, insert quotation marks where needed.

EX.   1.   Did you like Walter de la Mare's poem "The Listeners"?

1. Annabel Lee is my favorite poem because of its musical sound.

2. The last episode of the show was titled The Tangled Web.

3. The chapter Little Horses of the Sea was in the section called Warmwater Curiosities.

4. I read Dragon, Dragon, a story in our literature book.

5. Monumental Achievement is an article about the new memorial that honors female veterans of the Vietnam War.

6. Kate, did you pick up your coat? asked Mother.
   Yes, and my hat, too, Kate replied.

7. The teacher said, No calculators are allowed, and then I panicked, Harry explained.

8. My favorite fiddle tune is Turkey in the Straw.

9. I enjoyed reading the article Tips, Tricks, and Shortcuts.

10. Did you know that The Pied Piper of Hamelin was written by Robert Browning?

11. My grandfather saw Simon and Garfunkel sing Bridge over Troubled Water during their concert in Central Park.

12. Tonight's episode of *Bill Moyers' Journal* is called Bullish on America.

13. I don't have any more fishing line, Kyle said.
    Neither do I, said Marla.

14. Zane said, I thought I heard you say, He who laughs last.

15. Ira found it in the encyclopedia in the article Mars.

16. The driving instructor said, Slow down at the yield sign. Look both ways. Stop if another car is coming.

17. Have you seen Thinking, the latest episode of that program?

18. I want to learn all of your names. I also want to meet with each of you, the teacher said.

19. Did Mina like the short story The Open Window by Saki?

20. Karl explained, The recipe said, Add spices, so I did.

APOSTROPHES

21m **To form the *possessive case* of a singular noun, add an apostrophe and an *s*.**

The *possessive case* of a noun or a pronoun shows ownership or relationship.

EXAMPLES   the mechanic**'s** hat   Vara**'s** sculpture   **his** skates
                a friend**'s** bicycle   Dave**'s** job   **her** paintings

> A proper noun ending in *s* may take only an apostrophe to form the possessive case if the addition of *'s* would make the name awkward to say.
>
> EXAMPLES   Texas**'** parks   Los Angeles**'** weather

21n **To form the possessive case of a plural noun that does not end in *s*, add an apostrophe and an *s*.**

EXAMPLES   men**'s** shoes   mice**'s** tails
                moose**'s** tracks   teeth**'s** enamel

21o **To form the possessive case of a plural noun ending in *s*, add only the apostrophe.**

EXAMPLES   carpenters**'** union   two weeks**'** salary
                lions**'** habitat   the Garcías**'** apartment

> Do not use an apostrophe to form the plural of a noun. Remember that the apostrophe shows ownership or relationship.
>
> INCORRECT   Luis gave the two girls**'** their folders.
>   CORRECT   Luis gave the two **girls** their folders.

21p **Do not use an apostrophe with possessive personal pronouns.**

EXAMPLES   Is the bicycle **hers**?
              Ours is the best math club in the county.

21q **To form the possessive case of some indefinite pronouns, add an apostrophe and an *s*.**

EXAMPLES   someone**'s** pencil   no one**'s** hat
                everybody**'s** favorite flavor   neither**'s** homework answer

EXERCISE 4   Using Apostrophes Correctly

Rewrite each of the expressions below by using the possessive case. Be sure to insert apostrophes where they are needed.

EX.   1. the records of the singer   *the singer's records*

1. a haircut of Roderick   _____

2. the shoes of Annette   _____

3. the house of the Joneses   _____

4. the mittens of the kittens   _____

5. a ladder of the roofers   _____

6. the lawn of Mr. Ragno   _____

7. a place of anyone   _____

8. the toes of your feet   _____

9. the growth of three months   _____

10. the looks of them   _____

EXERCISE 5   Using Apostrophes Correctly in Sentences

For each of the sentences below, add apostrophes where they are needed. Some sentences may require no change.

EX.   1. Chun's hat is the blue one.

1. Those music stands are ours.

2. Is that the Gomezes house?

3. It's foot is about eight inches long.

4. The womens coveralls were smeared with dirt.

5. Lyles feet were red from the cold.

6. Is that toothbrush mine or your sisters?

7. Nobodys parents were told about the date change.

8. Las Vegas weather can get quite hot.

9. The monkey wrench is hers.

10. Their income taxes were lower this year.

OTHER USES OF APOSTROPHES

21r **Use an apostrophe to show where letters, numerals, or words have been left out in a contraction.**

A *contraction* is a shortened form of a word, a number, or a group of words. The apostrophe in a contraction shows where letters, numerals, or words have been left out.

Common Contractions	
I am ....I'm	they have ....they've
1995................................'95	where is ....where's
let us ....let's	we are ....we're
of the clock ....o'clock	he is............................ he's
she would................she'd	you will....................you'll

The word *not* can be shortened to *n't* and added to a verb, usually without any change in the spelling of the verb.

EXAMPLES	is not...............isn't	has not.................hasn't
	are not..........aren't	should not.....shouldn't
	does not ....doesn't	would not......wouldn't
EXCEPTIONS	will not ....won't	cannot ....can't

Do not confuse contractions with possessive pronouns.

Contractions	Possessive Pronouns
It's time for dinner. **It's** been cold today.	**Its** nest is there.
Who's your teacher? **Who's** been outside?	**Whose** ruler is this?
You're early.	**Your** package has arrived.
They're driving here. **There's** the car.	**Their** cat is two years old. The land is **theirs.**

21s   Use an apostrophe and an *s* to form the plurals of letters, numerals, signs, and words referred to as words.

EXAMPLES   The word *Oregon* has two *o*'s in it.
Some people put dashes through the middle of their 7's.
Why did you use -'s instead of +'s on this test?
Try not to use so many *like*'s when you speak.

EXERCISE 6   Proofreading Sentences for the Correct Use of Apostrophes

For each of the sentences below, underline the word or words requiring an apostrophe, and insert the apostrophe. If the sentence is correct, write *C* on the line before the sentence.

EX.   _____   1. I'm older than my brother Sam.

_____   1. We studied until four o clock, then stopped for a snack.

_____   2. Wheres my red pencil?

_____   3. Your cheeks and ears are turning red.

_____   4. Oh, theres the case for my glasses.

_____   5. Its been a long time since Vincent visited.

_____   6. If youd like, well stop at the rest stop.

_____   7. Tom said, "Its almost half time."

_____   8. "Sally, your friends on the plane," Tru yelled.

_____   9. If she doesnt show up, howll we put on the show?

_____ 10. No, son, you cant go in there without a pass.

_____ 11. Whose car is still running?

_____ 12. Come in, boys and girls. Weve been expecting you.

_____ 13. You're right, Teddy. I did make a mistake.

_____ 14. Your *and*s look like *end*s.

_____ 15. I saw a cardinal feeding it's babies.

CHAPTER REVIEW

A. Proofreading Sentences for the Correct Use of Apostrophes, Quotation Marks, and Underlining (Italics)

On your own paper, rewrite each of the sentences below so that apostrophes, quotation marks, and underlining are used correctly. [Note: Sentences may contain more than one error. Some sentences may be correct.]

EX. 1. Wheres my stopwatch, Chris? Shana asked.

    1. "Where's my stopwatch, Chris?" Shana asked.

1. Lisa asked, Did you like the book The Frog Prince Continued?

2. My moms company is so big that its putting a huge advertisement in the Baltimore Evening Sun.

3. Whose book of poems is under the tree?

4. Its one o clock and time for lunch, he announced.

5. Ravel's long composition *Bolero* is a good introduction to the instruments in an orchestra.

6. Did Ms. Katz really say, There will be no homework tonight?

7. Wasn't there an episode of 7th Heaven called Lost?

8. Im sure youll like this movie I rented; its called Free Willy.

9. Read Kenneth Wapner's article, Into the Woods, in Chriss copy of AMC Outdoors magazine.

10. Jerri asked if Id read everyones poems.

B. Proofreading Paragraphs for Correct Use of Apostrophes, Quotation Marks, and Underlining (Italics)

Proofread the following paragraphs and insert apostrophes, quotation marks, and underlining where needed.

EX. [1] "Hey, it's time to plan for the festival!" Irene said excitedly.

[1] Jesse said, Im impressed that our town has a festival each year.

[2] The festival welcomes spring, and its run by the editor of the

Harperville Gazette. [3] The festival will begin at one o clock sharp a month from Saturday.

[4] "Did you know that Pauls family will be selling food? Irene asked Ms. Wong.

[5] Yes, they own a restaurant and will prepare apple cider and pasta salads Ms. Wong said. [6] "We will also have, Ms. Wong added, "music and dancing groups."

[7] I explained A local cable program, Eye on the Community, will broadcast the event. [8] Since the festival is going to be at the park by the river, people might be able to take short cruises on my father's boat Rippling Water.

[9] "Will your family be at the festival? Jesse asked Irene.

[10] "Of course, they'll be there for the entire day," Irene said.

C. Writing a Dialogue

On your own paper, write a five-sentence dialogue based on the comic strip below. Be sure to use quotation marks and other marks of punctuation correctly. In addition to punctuation marks, you will need to add dialogue tags to identify who is speaking (*asked John, exclaimed Nabil*).

EX.   *"Gee, I love your new necklace, Phil," said Flo.*

THE FAR SIDE   By GARY LARSON

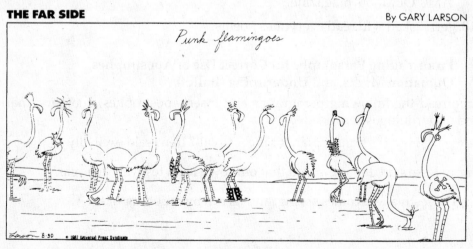

The Far Side copyright 1987 FarWorks, Inc. Distributed by Universal Press Syndicate. Reprinted with permission. All rights reserved.

THE DICTIONARY

A dictionary entry is divided into several parts. Study the parts of the following sample dictionary entry.

a • wake [ə • wāk´] *vt.* a • woke´ or a • waked´,
a • waked´ or a • wok´en, a • wak´ing **1.** to rouse from
sleep; wake [*awake* the crew] **2.** to rouse from rest or
inactivity; activate [*awaken* the senses] **3.** to make
aware [*awoke* the voters] —*vi.* **1.** to come out of sleep;
wake [*awake* at dawn] **2.** to become active [*awaking* to
the truth] —*adj.* **1.** not asleep **2.** active or alert
—a • wak´en • ing, *n.*

SYN. **Stir; revive; activate. ANT. Inactive, asleep,**
unaware.

1. **Entry word.** The entry word is printed in boldface (dark) letters. It shows the way the word should be spelled and how to divide the word into syllables. It may also show if a word should be capitalized or if the word can be spelled in other ways.
2. **Pronunciation.** The pronunciation of an entry word is shown with symbols. These symbols help you pronounce the word correctly. Special letters or markings that are used with letters to show a certain sound are called *phonetic symbols. Accent marks* show which syllables of the word are said more forcefully. Look in the front of your dictionary for an explanation of the symbols and marks your dictionary uses.
3. **Part-of-speech labels.** Some words may be used as more than one part of speech. For each meaning of a word, the dictionary shows the part of speech. In the sample entry, *awake* can be used as an adjective or as a verb, depending on the meaning.

4. **Other forms.** Sometimes your dictionary will show you how to spell other forms of the word. These may include adjective and adverb forms, verb tenses, or the plural form of nouns.
5. **Definitions.** The different meanings of a word are numbered. To help you understand the different meanings, dictionaries often include a sample phrase or sentence after a numbered definition.
6. **Examples.** Examples show how the entry word is used in a sentence. The examples are often in the form of phrases or sentences using the word in context.
7. **Related word forms.** Sometimes the dictionary may show forms of the entry word created by adding suffixes or prefixes. Once you know the meaning of the main word, you can usually understand the meaning of the related word.
8. **Synonyms and antonyms.** Words similar in meaning are *synonyms.* Words opposite in meaning are *antonyms.* Many dictionaries list synonyms and antonyms at the ends of some word entries.

EXERCISE 1   Using a Dictionary

Use a dictionary to answer the questions below.

EX.   1.   How many syllables are in the word *cooperation*? _____five_____

1. How is the word *natural* divided into syllables?_____

2. What are the two spellings for the plural form of *octopus*?_____

   _____

3. What are three different meanings for the word *band*?_____

   _____

4. What is the past tense of *swim*? _____

5. When should the word *native* be capitalized? _____

EXERCISE 2   Writing Words with More Than One Spelling

Write an alternate spelling for each of the words below on the line after the word. Use a dictionary as needed.

EX.   1. color _____*colour*_____

1. likable _____   4. traveled _____

2. cooperate _____   5. tornadoes _____

3. jeweler _____

SPELLING RULES

ie and *ei*

22a Except after *c*, write *ie* when the sound is long *e*.

EXAMPLES   believe, niece, chief, receive, deceit
EXCEPTIONS   weird, leisure, either, seize, neither

22b Write *ei* when the sound is not long *e*, especially when the sound is long *a*.

EXAMPLES   reindeer, veil, weigh, heir
EXCEPTIONS   science, view, friend, pie, tie, diet

–cede, –ceed, and *–sede*

22c The only word ending in *–sede* is *supersede*. The only words ending in *–ceed* are *exceed, proceed,* and *succeed*. All other words with this sound end in *–cede*.

EXAMPLES   secede, accede, precede

EXERCISE 3   Writing Words with *ie, ei, cede, ceed,* and *sede*

On the line in each word below, write the letters *ie, ei, cede, ceed,* or *sede* to spell the word correctly. Use a dictionary as needed.

EX.   1. p _ie_ ce

1. b ____ ge
2. t ____
3. w ____ gh
4. rec ____ pt
5. ex ____
6. bel ____ f
7. p ____ r
8. c ____ ling
9. handkerch ____ f

10. re ____
11. n ____ ther
12. ach ____ ve
13. perc ____ ve
14. th ____ f
15. suc ____
16. n ____ ghbor
17. r ____ gn
18. rel ____ f

19. h ____ ght
20. pro ____
21. sl ____ gh
22. sh ____ ld
23. dec ____ ve
24. bel ____ ve
25. br ____ f

EXERCISE 4   Proofreading a Paragraph to Correct Spelling Errors

The paragraph below contains eight spelling errors. Underline the misspelled words. Write the correct spelling above each misspelled word. If the sentence has no errors, write C above the number before the sentence.

EX.   [1] Yesterday I <u>recieved</u> a letter from my cousin Jocelyn, who
        received
        lives in Australia.

[1] Jocelyn is the only person I know who lives in a foriegn

country. [2] She visited the United States last year, and we proceded to

become pen pals. [3] I enjoy having a friend who lives in a different

country. [4] Her letters are so interesting that they superceed any book

I've ever read about Australia. [5] I especially like her descriptions of

the wierd animals that live in Australia. [6] Sceintists say that in

Australia you can find animals that don't exist anywhere else in the

world. [7] The koala bear, which eats a diet of eucalyptus leaves, is

one strange Australian animal. [8] Jocelyn has sent me photos of

others, such as the dingo, the kookaburra, and an unbeleivably odd

one called the bearded dragon. [9] I'd like a chance to veiw these

animals myself. [10] I hope someday to sucede in visiting Jocelyn in

Australia.

PREFIXES AND SUFFIXES

A *prefix* is a letter or a group of letters added to the beginning of a word to change the meaning of the word. A *suffix* is a letter or a group of letters added to the end of a word to change the meaning of the word.

22d When adding a prefix to a word, do not change the spelling of the word itself.

EXAMPLES   anti + freeze = **anti**freeze   un + noticed = **un**noticed
            dis + like = **dis**like   im + perfect = **im**perfect
            mis + spell = **mis**spell   pre + cook = **pre**cook

22e When adding the suffix –*ness* or –*ly* to a word, do not change the spelling of the word itself.

EXAMPLES   weak + ness = weak**ness**   white + ness = white**ness**
            quick + ly = quick**ly**   real + ly = real**ly**

EXCEPTION   For most words that end in *y*, change the *y* to *i* before –*ly* or –*ness*.

            EXAMPLES   happy + ness = happ**iness**   merry + ly = merr**ily**

22f Drop the final silent *e* before a suffix beginning with a vowel.

Vowels are the letters *a, e, i, o, u,* and sometimes *y*. All other letters of the alphabet are *consonants*.

EXAMPLES   hope + ing = hop**ing**   write + er = writ**er**
            safe + est = saf**est**   move + able = mov**able**

EXCEPTION   Keep the silent *e* in words ending in *ce* and *ge* before a suffix beginning with *a* or *o*.

            EXAMPLES   peace + able = peac**eable**
                       advantage + ous = advantag**eous**

22g Keep the final *e* before a suffix beginning with a consonant.

EXAMPLES   use + ful = use**ful**   care + less = care**less**
            safe + ty = safe**ty**   advertise + ment = advertise**ment**

EXCEPTIONS awe + ful = aw**ful**   nine + th = nin**th**
            whole + ly = whol**ly**   true + ly = tru**ly**

EXERCISE 5   Spelling Words with Prefixes

On the line provided, write the word made by adding the prefix.

EX.   1. im + polite _____ impolite _____

1. un + important _____
2. pre + heat _____
3. dis + charge _____
4. un + happy _____
5. re + do _____
6. over + come _____
7. il + legal _____
8. mis + inform _____
9. un + tie _____
10. dis + regard _____

11. pre +judge _____
12. over + do _____
13. dis + cover _____
14. mis + lead _____
15. re + place _____
16. un + necessary _____
17. im + mature _____
18. il + logical _____
19. dis + appear _____
20. over + coat _____

EXERCISE 6   Spelling Words with Suffixes

On the line provided, write the word made by adding the suffix.

EX.   1. week + ly _____ weekly _____

1. sloppy + ly _____
2. slide + ing _____
3. large + er _____
4. grace + ful _____
5. courage + ous _____
6. soft + ness _____
7. light + ly _____
8. dine + ing _____
9. reck + less _____
10. joyful + ly _____

11. service + able _____
12. sudden + ly _____
13. hike + ing _____
14. manage + ment _____
15. steady + ly _____
16. race + ing _____
17. friendly + est _____
18. use + able _____
19. move + ment _____
20. blame + less _____

22h **For words ending in *y* preceded by a consonant, change the *y* to *i* before any suffix that does not begin with *i*.**

EXAMPLES   easy + est = eas**iest**   pretty + ly = prett**ily**
           funny + er = funn**ier**   bury + ed = bur**ied**

For words ending in *y* preceded by a vowel, do not change the spelling before a suffix.

EXAMPLES   play + ed = pla**yed**   stay + ing = sta**ying**
EXCEPTIONS say + ed = sa**id**   day + ly = dai**ly**

22i **Double the final consonant before adding *–ing*, *–ed*, *–er*, or *–est* to a one-syllable word that ends in a consonant preceded by a single vowel.**

EXAMPLES   sled + ing = sled**ding**   glad + est = glad**dest**
           trip + ed = trip**ped**   bat + er = bat**ter**

Some one-syllable words end in a consonant preceded by two vowels or by a second consonant. For these words, do not double the consonant before adding *–ing*, *–ed*, *–er*, or *–est*.

EXAMPLES   near + est = near**est**   thump + ed = thump**ed**
           feel + ing = feel**ing**   fresh + er = fresh**er**

EXERCISE 7   Spelling Words with Suffixes

On the line provided, write the word made by adding the suffix.

EX.   1. run + er _____ *runner* _____

1. scurry + ed _____   11. carry + ing _____

2. skip + ing _____   12. annoy + ing _____

3. red + er _____   13. big + est _____

4. speak + ing _____   14. cool + er _____

5. happy + ly _____   15. dash + ing _____

6. mad + est _____   16. pray + ed _____

7. pay + ing _____   17. boil + ing _____

8. glory + ous _____   18. cry + ed _____

9. hard + er _____   19. lonely + est _____

10. skid + ed _____   20. stop + ed _____

EXERCISE 8   Proofreading a Paragraph for Correct Spelling

The paragraph below contains several spelling errors. Underline the incorrect words. Then write the correct spellings above the incorrect words. If the sentence has no errors, write *C* above the sentence.

EX.   [1] Adventures often happen when you haven't <u>planed</u> them.
planned

[1] Sonia and Dolores had decided to spend a quiet afternoon ridding their bicycles to the lake. [2] They chose the road, however, that went past the mysteryous, deserted house at the edge of town. [3] Usually, they hurryed past this house because people said it was haunted. [4] On this day they stopped in front of it to rest. [5] Then they noticed that the front door was swingging open. [6] "I suppose it would be all right to take a look inside it," Dolores sayed bravely. [7] Just as they reached the door, they heard a strange, bumpping sound from within the house. [8] Hastyly, they jumped back. [9] They were both running when a small raccoon waddled out the front door. [10] It was hard to say which girl laughed the louder, but certainly the raccoon ran the fasttest when it saw them.

EXERCISE 9   Spelling Words with Prefixes

Create five words by combining the prefixes given below with the words listed beside them. (You may use each prefix and each word more than once.) Check each of your word combinations in a dictionary. Then use each word in a sentence. Write these sentences on your own paper.

Prefixes			Words			
un-	im-	over-	possible	important	cover	just
pre-	re-	mis-	view	print	join	spell

EX.   1. uncover
       Did the detective uncover any information?

PLURALS OF NOUNS

22j   Form the plurals of most nouns by adding –s.

SINGULAR	tree	river	shoe	pizza	duck	convoy
PLURAL	trees	rivers	shoes	pizzas	ducks	convoys

22k   Form the plurals of nouns ending in *s, x, z, ch,* or *sh* by adding –es.

SINGULAR	glass	fox	maze	beach	bush
PLURAL	glass**es**	fox**es**	maz**es**	beach**es**	bush**es**

NOTE   Proper nouns usually follow this rule, too.

EXAMPLES   the Gomez**es**   the Ross**es**   the Burch**es**
the Walsh**es**   the Mannix**es**

EXERCISE 10   Spelling the Plurals of Nouns

On the line after each noun, write its correct plural form.

EX.   1. brush   _brushes_____

1. cat   _____
2. box   _____
3. church   _____
4. waltz   _____
5. Davis   _____
6. mountain   _____
7. Katz   _____
8. dish   _____
9. watch   _____
10. book   _____
11. park   _____
12. dancer   _____
13. march

14. tax   _____
15. wish   _____
16. peach   _____
17. miss   _____
18. topaz   _____
19. house   _____
20. island   _____
21. valley   _____
22. insect   _____
23. branch   _____
24. address   _____
25. street   _____

22l   Form the plurals of nouns ending in _y_ preceded by a consonant by changing the _y_ to _i_ and adding _–es_.

SINGULAR	sky	city	story	party	county
PLURAL	skies	cities	stories	parties	counties

EXCEPTION   With proper nouns, simply add _–s_.

EXAMPLES   the Kellys   the Kandinskys

22m Form the plurals of nouns ending in _y_ preceded by a vowel by adding _–s_.

SINGULAR	boy	monkey	tray	holiday	highway
PLURAL	boys	monkeys	trays	holidays	highways

22n Form the plurals of most nouns ending in _f_ by adding _–s_. The plurals of some nouns ending in _f_ or _fe_ are formed by changing the _f_ to _v_ and adding either _–s_ or _–es_.

SINGULAR	cliff	roof	thief	life	loaf
PLURAL	cliffs	roofs	thieves	lives	loaves

NOTE   When you are not sure how to spell the plural of a noun ending in _f_ or _fe_, look in a dictionary.

22o Form the plural of a compound noun consisting of a noun plus a modifier by making the modified noun plural.

SINGULAR	sister-in-law	lemon tree	basketball
PLURAL	sisters-in-law	lemon trees	basketballs

EXERCISE 11   Spelling the Plurals of Nouns

On the line after each noun, write its correct plural form.

EX.   1. library _libraries_

1. leaf _____
2. cherry _____
3. toy _____
4. turkey _____
5. elf _____
6. calf _____
7. journey _____
8. valley _____
9. brother-in-law _____
10. Tuesday _____

11. reef _____
12. space shuttle _____
13. Hardy _____
14. half _____
15. chief _____
16. gulf _____
17. bay _____
18. runway _____
19. daisy _____
20. wolf _____

22p Form the plurals of nouns ending in *o* preceded by a vowel by adding –*s*. The plurals of many nouns ending in *o* preceded by a consonant are formed by adding –*es*.

SINGULAR	stereo	patio	hero	tomato
PLURAL	stereos	patios	heroes	tomatoes

EXCEPTIONS burritos   hellos   photos   silos

Form the plurals of most musical terms ending in *o* by adding –*s*.

SINGULAR	alto	cello	concerto	soprano
PLURAL	altos	cellos	concertos	sopranos

NOTE To form the plurals of some nouns ending in *o* preceded by a consonant, you may add either –*s* or –*es*.

SINGULAR	mosquito	tornado	volcano
PLURAL	mosquitos	tornados	volcanos
	or	*or*	*or*
	mosquitoes	tornadoes	volcanoes

22q The plurals of a few nouns are formed in irregular ways.

SINGULAR	man	goose	child	mouse	foot	deer
PLURAL	men	geese	children	mice	feet	deer

EXERCISE 12   Spelling the Plurals of Nouns

On the line after each noun, write its correct plural form.

EX. 1. echo _____echoes_____

1. torpedo _____
2. tooth _____
3. radio _____
4. solo _____
5. rodeo _____
6. potato _____
7. grotto _____
8. piccolo _____
9. salmon _____
10. cello _____
11. trio _____
12. video _____
13. trio _____
14. woman _____
15. area _____
16. motto _____
17. moose _____
18. banjo _____
19. larva _____
20. cargo _____

EXERCISE 13   Proofreading a Paragraph for Correct Spelling

The paragraph below contains several errors in spelling. Underline the incorrect words. Write the correct spelling above each misspelled word. If the sentence has no errors, write C above the sentence. [Hint: One sentence contains two errors.]

EX.   [1] The building next to the restaurant that sells the best *tacos* ~~tacoes~~ in town was empty for a long time.

[1] Then two womans decided to turn it into a studio for artists and musicians. [2] It's one of the most unusual studioes you have ever seen. [3] Artists work and musicians practice in the back rooms, but in the front room, the directors have created a gallery where artists can show their work. [4] Right now at the gallery is an exhibit of photoes. [5] It's amazeing how the simplest subject can become a beautiful photo. [6] Most of these pictures are of childs, but the show includes other subjects, too. [7] For example, one photo is just an arrangement of potatos, tomatos, and green peppers. [8] Another is a funny picture just of people's foots. [9] The studio is always full of mans and women. [10] When you sit next door at the restaurant, you can hear the music of pianos and other instruments.

CHAPTER REVIEW

A. Correcting Spelling Errors in Sentences

Underline the misspelled word in each sentence below. Then write the misspelled word correctly on the line before the sentence.

EX. _____sailing_____ 1. On my vacation, I had a chance to try both sailing and snorkeling.

_____ 1. We went to the ocean with our friends, the Sanchezs.

_____ 2. Every day we carried our lunches down to the shore.

_____ 3. On the beachs we found many seashells.

_____ 4. Two people brought radioes so we could listen to music.

_____ 5. I couldn't beleive how clear and blue the water was!

_____ 6. One day the childrens went out fishing.

_____ 7. On the sunnyest days, we spent most of our time in the water.

_____ 8. I loved swiming in the warm ocean water.

_____ 9. We saw beautiful fish in the coral reeves.

_____ 10. Fortunatly, we didn't see any sharks.

B. Proofreading a Paragraph to Correct Spelling Errors

The following paragraph contains twenty spelling errors. Underline the misspelled word or words. Write the correct spelling above each misspelled word. Some sentences have two errors. If the sentence has no errors, write C above the number of the sentence.

galaxies

EX. [1] Astronomy is the study of stars, planets, and galaxys.

[1] This is a subject that realy interests me. [2] Last summer I had a

chance to visit two astronomy observatorys. [3] One observatory had

radio telescopes. [4] These telescopes recieve radio waves from

objects like planets or stars. [5] Scientists use this information to try to

understand what is happenning in space. [6] I likked talking to the
astronomers. [7] I can't imagine what it would be like to work with
telescopes dayly. [8] It must be interesting to try to unrravel the
mysterys of the universe. [9] Astronomers also spend a lot of time
writeing about what they see with thier telescopes. [10] They can't
easly explain everything they see, and they have to be very carful
when they make guesses. [11] Often the astronomers succede by
working with scientists from other countrys. [12] After my visit, I
startted reading everything I could about stares. [13] Now I have
bookshelfs full of information about stars. [14] I think I would like to
be iether an astronomer or an astronaut. [15] I know I will have to
work hard to sucede in either feild.

C.   Writing Sentences That Use the Spelling Rules

Your neighbor, who has just arrived in this country from Russia, is working
hard to learn English. She has asked you to help her understand the
spelling rules of English. On your own paper, write ten of the rules that
were discussed in this chapter. For each rule, write a sentence that uses the
rule. Underline the word or words that show the rule.

EX.   1. Rule: When adding a prefix to a word, do not change the spelling of the
          word itself.

          The children were <u>unhappy</u> that a storm had delayed their picnic.